RPG TnT

101 DYNAMITE
Tips 'n Techniques with RPG IV

Bob Cozzi

MC Press Online, LLC
Ketchum, ID 83340

RPG TnT: 101 Dynamite Tips 'n Techniques with RPG IV
Bob Cozzi

First MC Press Printing—February 2011

MC Press offers excellent discounts on this book when ordered in quantity for bulk purchases or special sales, which may include custom covers and content particular to your business, training goals, marketing focus, and branding interest.

MC Press Online, LLC
    Corporate Offices
    P.O. Box 4886
    Ketchum, ID 83340-4886 USA
For information regarding sales and/or customer service, please contact:
    MC Press
    P.O. Box 4300
    Big Sandy, TX 75755-4300 USA
    Toll Free: (877) 226-5394
For information regarding permissions or special orders, please contact:
    mcbooks@mcpressonline.com

ISBN: 978-1-58347-364-1

For
Yelena...

Acknowledgments

I'd like to extend a warm thank you to my love, Yelena Khenkina, for her assistance in creating this book, reading the examples, and pushing me to finish it.

Thanks also to my longtime friends and cohorts R. Bruce Hoffman for reviewing the Java techniques and most of the RPG IV tips and Greg Veal for letting me know he is still The Master when it comes to OS/400 and i5/OS message handling.

Finally, I'd like to thank the regulars on the RPG IV forum (*www.rpgiv.com/forum*), a group of individuals who volunteered their time to review sections of this book for accuracy and clarity. They did a great job, and I give them each a big thank you:

- SSG Bret Myrick
- Cody Schilke
- Doug Eckersley
- Ed Kirgan
- John Dowling

A Note About the Code

This edition of the book contains references to several Web sites whose content has now been replaced by the site *www.rpgworld.com*. Visit *www.rpgworld.com* to get the latest RPG IV news, information, tools, and updates.

Table of Contents

Conventions Used in this Book xv

1. **Prototype Everything** **1**
   Simple Prototype for the QCMDEXC API 2

2. **Prototyping a Call to a Program** **3**
   Use EXTPGM to Prototype Program Calls 3
   Using EXTPGM with an Alternate Prototype Name 4

3. **An Alternative to QCMDEXC** **5**
   Prototype for the system() function 5

4. **Subprocedure-style Entry Parameter List for Programs** **7**
   Use a Prototype to Replace *ENTRY/PLIST for Programs 7

5. **Add NOMAIN to the Header Specification of Secondary Modules** **9**
   Use NOMAIN in all Secondary Modules' Source Members 9

6. **Monitoring C Function Runtime Errors** **10**
   Write C Runtime Errors to the Joblog 11
   What about CPF Messages? 13
   RPG IV Declaration for C Runtime CPF Messages 13
   Retrieve CPF Message for C Runtime Functions 13

7. **Use PSDS to Retrieve Job Information** **15**
   Job Information from the PSDS — Helper Subprocedures 16

8. **Use QUALIFIED Data Structures** **17**
   Traditional Data Structures 17
   Qualified Data Structures 17
   Qualified Syntax Use 18

9. **Copy Subfields Between Qualified Data Structures** **19**
   Using EVAL-CORR to Copy a Data Structure 20

10. **Nested Data Structures** **21**
    Nesting Data Structures within One Another 21

11. ***ALL and *ALLX 'xx' — The Repeating Constants** **24**
    Initialize a Field to "Hex Zeros" with *ALLX '00' 25
    Test a Field for a Repeating Pattern 25

12.   Embed Compiler Parameters into Source Members 26
Synchronize Source Statement Numbers with SEU and Debug 26
Use OPTION(*SRCSTMT) to Sequence Compiler Listings 27
Reduce Debug Fatigue with *NODEBUGIO 27
Use OPTION(*NODEBUG) to Avoid F10 Fatigue in Debug 27
Combine Header Specification Options 27
Specify Multiple OPTIONs 27

13.   Avoid "Surprise Initialize" 29
Use INZ to Fix Decimal Data Errors 30

14.   Qualified Externally Described Files (1) 31
Qualified, Externally Described Files 32

15.   Qualified Externally Described Files (2) 33

16.   Calculate the End-of-Month Date 33
Calculate End-of-Month in Fixed Format 33
Calculate End-of-Month in Free Format 34
Get End-Of-Month Subprocedure 34

17.   Using Free-Format Comments in Fixed-Format Code 35
Free-Format Comments in Fixed Format 35

18.   Get Day-of-Week Name 36
GetDayName Subprocedure Source Code 36

19.   Run CL Commands from an FTP Client 38

20.   Put Your Program to Sleep 39
RPG IV Prototype for the sleep() C Runtime Function 39

21.   Use VARYING to Improve Performance 40
VARYING Keyword to Help Improve %SCAN Performance 41

22.   Converting Numeric to Character with %CHAR 42
Convert Numeric to Character 42

23.   Converting Character to Numeric 43
%DEC to Convert Text to Packed Decimal 43
%INT to Convert Text to Integer 43
Convert Character to Number Using RPG xTools's CharToNum 44

24.   Easier Text Concatenation 45
Concatenating Character and Numeric Data 47
Generic Prototype for sprintf() Function 47
Use sprintf() for Concatenation with Substitution Variables 48

25. Create an Auto-Extend User Space **50**
Prototype for QUSCRTUS (Create User Space) API 50
Change User Space Attributes (QUSCUSAT) API Prototype 51
Create User Space and Change Attribute to Auto-Extend 52
Changing Multiple User Space Attributes 53
User Space Attribute Data Structure Templates 54

26. Declare Data Structures as Arrays **55**
Data Structure Arrays — Accessing the Elements 56

27. Initialize Fields to Job Date, System Date, or User Profile **58**
*JOB, *SYS, and *USER Initial Values 58
What about Job Date at Runtime? 59

28. Use C Runtime Functions in RPG **61**
Include the QC2LE Binding Directory to Use C Runtime Functions 61

29. Compare and Ignore Case **61**
Prototype for memicmp() — Compare and Ignore Case 61
Compare Two Fields and Ignore Case 62

30. Free Online Prototypes for APIs, C Functions, MI Instructions **63**
RPG IV Prototype Source Code Web Address 63

31. Checking for Valid Dates with the TEST OpCode **64**
Check a Numeric Field for Valid Date Value 64
Check a Date Variable for a Valid Date Value 65

32. Using the Secret 'X' Edit Code to Convert Numeric to Character **66**
Equivalent MOVEL and EVAL Opcodes Using 'X' Edit Code 68

33. %ADDR — Address of a Variable **69**

34. Understanding API Documentation — Bin(4) Parameters **71**
QUSRTVUS (Retrieve User Space Data) API Documentation 72
QUSRTVUS (Retrieve User Space Data) Prototype 72

35. Understanding API Documentation — Pointer Parameters **73**
QUSPTRUS (Retrieve Pointer to User Space Data) API Documentation 73
QUSPTRUS (Get Pointer to User Space) Prototype 73

36. Better Performance when Accessing User Space Data **75**
QUSPTRUS (Get Pointer to User Space) Prototype 75

37. Integer Data-types — More Efficient than Packed Decimal **77**
Signed Integer Sizes and Ranges — RPG Data-type I 78
Unsigned Integer Sizes and Ranges — RPG Data-type U 78

38.   Sending a Program Message in RPG **79**
Send Program Message (QMHSNDPM) API Prototype (Subset) 80
SNDMSG Subprocedure — QMHSNDPM API Wrapper 81

39.   Retrieve the Function Key Used on a Display File **85**
Use the INFDS Position 369 to Retrieve the Function Key ID Code 86
Function Key Scan Codes 86

40.   Copying More than 64k of Data **88**
Prototype for the C Runtime memcpy() Function 88
Prototype for the MI CPYBYTES Function 88
Copy Big Memory Using Memcpy() 89

41.   Use %XFOOT with %LEN **90**
Length vs. Size 90
Use %XFOOT to Calculate Total Length of All Array Elements 91
Use %XFOOT with VARYING Array Elements 91
Use %XFOOT with %SUBARR to Sum Up Lengths of Elements 1 to 2 92

42.   Use %SUBARR to Subscript Arrays **93**
Sort 50 Elements of a Large Array 93

43.   Use EXTFILE to Avoid Needless Overrides **94**
EXTFILE and EXTMBR to Override Runtime File, Library Member 94
What about Overrides? 94
EXTFILE Syntax 94
Using an Initial Value via *INZSR with EXTFILE 96
Using a Parameter Variable with EXTFILE 96
Module 1: Set up a Variable for EXPORT 97
Module 2: Import the File Name Variable 97

44.   Subprocedure Parameters Rule 1 — Default Behavior **99**

45.   Subprocedure Parameters Rule 2 — Const Parameters **100**
Using CONST on Parameter Definitions 100

46.   Subprocedure Parameters Rule 3 — VARYING **102**
Using VARYING on Parameter Definitions 102
Using VARYING and CONST on Parameter Definitions 102

47.   Subprocedure Parameters Rule 4 — Optional Parameters **104**
Using OPTIONS(*NOPASS) to Declare Optional Parameters 105

48.   Subprocedure Parameters Rule 5 — Skipping Parameters **106**
Use OPTIONS(*OMIT) to Allow Parameter Skipping 106

Test for an Omitted Parameter 107

Testing for Omitted Parameters before V5R1 108

49. Data Structure Templates **109**

Use LIKEDS to Use a Data Structure Template 109

50. Boolean Assignment **112**

Boolean Assignment 113

51. Creating Even-Length Packed Fields **114**

Use PACKEVEN with From/To Column Notation 115

52. Sorting Arrays with SubArrays **116**

Sorting an Array by SubArray Name 116

Cross-footing a SubArray 117

53. Convert between Lower- and Uppercase Letters **118**

Prototype for QlgConvertCase API 119

FRCB_T Data Structure Template for QlgConvertCase API 119

toLower() and toUpper() Subprocedure Wrappers for QlgConvertCase 121

54. Overlapping Data Structures **124**

Overlapping Data Structures 125

Multi-format Files Implemented with Overlapping Data Structures 126

Overlapping Data Structures Using BASED Keyword 127

55. Dynamic Arrays — Dynamically Allocated Array Elements **128**

Dynamically Allocated Array Elements 129

Declare the Array with the BASED Keyword 129

Retrieve a Pointer to a User Space 129

56. Converting Date Formats with the QWCCVTDT API **131**

Prototype for QWCCVTDT API 131

Using QWCCVTDT to Convert Date Format 132

Use QWCCVTDT to Convert Julian Date to Job Date Format 132

Use QWCCVTDT to YYYYMMDD to MMDDYYYY 133

QWCCVTDT Data Structures 133

Data Structures for QWCCVTDT 133

Data Structure for the Time Zone Info Parameter of QWCCVTDT 135

57. Converting Date Formats with the CEExxxx APIs **136**

Converting Non-Standard Date Formats to Real Date Variables 138

Formatting a Date as Words 139

58. Calculated Day of Week — Zeller's Congruence **140**

Zeller's Congruence in RPG IV 140

59. Calculated Day of Week — API Method **141**
CEEDYWK Prototype 141
Get Day of Week Prototype 142
Get Day of Week Procedure Implementation 142

60. LIKE Keyword Misbehavior — Zoned to Packed **144**
Demonstrate LIKE Reverting to Packed Data-type 146

61. Default Data-type: Not So Consistent **147**

62. Debugging Variables that Have Debugger Command Names **149**
Display the Contents of a Field Named EVAL in the Debugger 150

63. Viewing Field Contents in Hex in Debug **151**

64. Display the First Few Bytes During Debug **152**

65. Display Contents of Local Variables with %LOCALVAR **154**

66. Convert Character to Numeric — Using MI **155**
Prototype for _CVTEFN MI Instruction in RPG IV 156
Data Structure for _CVTEFN 157
Named Constants for Data-types Used by _CVTEFN 157
Using _CVTEFN to Convert Varying Character to Numeric 158
Using _CVTEFN to Convert Fixed-length Character to Numeric 159

67. Converting To and From Hexadecimal **160**
Prototypes for Converting To and From Hexadecimal 160

68. Using Decimal Fields as Real-Date Values **162**
Convert an 8-digit Numeric Value to a Real-Date Variable 163
Convert a Real-Date Value to an 8-digit Numeric Value 163
Convert a Real-Date Value to a 10-position Character Value 164

69. Check Object Existence **165**
QUSEC Data Structure Template 165
Check if Object Exists Subprocedure 166

70. Supporting Qualified Object Syntax **168**
ParseObject() Subprocedure Source 169

71. Explained: Bytes Provided, Bytes Available, and Bytes Returned **171**
Bytes Provided — Length of the Data Structure 171
Bytes Returned 172
Bytes Available 173

72. Converting to/from ASCII and Other Character Sets **175**
The iconv() Conversion Environment Handle 176

The iconv() Conversion Structure 175
Prototype for QtqIconvOpen — Open iconv() Environment 177
Prototype for iconv() API 178
Prototype for the iconv_close() API 179
Flowchart of the iconv() Conversion Process *180*
Using iconv() for CCSID/Character Conversion — Complete Example 181

73. Register an Exit Routine for a Program or Service Program **182**
CEE4RAGE Prototype — Register Activation Group Exit Procedure 183
CEE4RAGE2 Prototypes with Conditional Directives 183
Exit Subprocedure Prototype for CEE4RAGE 183
CEE4RAGE2 — Exit Subprocedure Prototype 184
User-Written Exit SubProcedure Skeleton 184

74. Specifying IFS File Names Correctly **187**
Open an IFS File Name trimmed with %TRIMR 188
Properly Specifying IFS File Names and Paths 188
IFS open(), access(), and stat() prototypes with *TRIM 189

75. Checking if IFS Files Exist **190**
Prototype for the C Runtime access() Function 190
Check for IFS File Existence 191

76. RC4 Encryption Using Encryption APIs **192**
Qc3EncryptData API Prototype 192
rc4Encrypt() — Subprocedure to Encrypt Data Using RC4 195

77. Writing Text to the Joblog **197**
Qp0zLprintf API Prototype 198
Joblog Subprocedure 199
Writing to the Joblog with the Joblog Subprocedure 200

78. Reading Save Files with RPG IV **201**
Copy Save File — Example Program 202

79. Encrypting Save Files in RPG IV **204**
Copy Save File with Encryption 205
Copy and Encrypt Save File Command Definition 205
Encrypt a Save File 206

80. Global and Local Variables **209**
Global and Local Variable Name Conflict 210

81.   Create Source Members Used to Create Service Programs **211**
Source Code for the DATERTN Module 212

82.   Binder Source for a Service Program **214**
Binder Source with Hard-Coded Signature 215
Binder Source with New Export 216

83.   Create Binder Language the Easy Way **217**
Results of a RTVBNDSRC Command 217
Binder Source — A Closer Look 218

84.   Linking to a Service Program from an RPG IV Program **219**
What Is a Binding Directory? 220
Specifying a Binding Directory 220

85.   Swap Bytes — Big Endian to Little Endian in RPG IV **222**
Original Big Endian 32-bit Data 223
First Step — Swap Byte 1 with 2, and 3 with 4 223
Second Step — Swap 2-Byte Words 223
SwapByte Subprocedure — Convert Big Endian to Little Endian 224

86.   Dumping the Call Stack with Qp0zDumpStack **225**
Prototype for the Qp0zDumpStack API 225
Dumping the Call Stack from within a Program 225
Formatted Call Stack Dump Output 226

87.   Using Subprocedure Return Values **227**
Define a Subprocedure Return Value 227
Using a Returned Value 228

88.   How Does the %EDITC (Edit Code) Built-in Function Work? **229**

89.   Solid Parameter Testing **231**
Testing Parameter Count with %PARMS() 231
Testing for Skipped Parameters 233

90.   Create ASCII Text Files on the IFS **234**
Creating an ASCII Text IFS File 234
Reopening an IFS File as Text 235
IFS API Prototypes 235
Figurative Constants Used by IFS APIs 236
IFS API Prototypes for RPG IV 236
CrtASCIIFile (Create ASCII File) Subprocedure 237

91. High-level Math in RPG IV **239**
CEE Math API Prototypes 240
C Math Library — An Alternative to CEE Math APIs 241
C Runtime Math Function Prototypes in RPG IV 241

92. Program Described Print File with Dynamic Spacing **244**
PRTCTL Printer File Keyword and Data Structure 244
Using PRTCTL to Control Printed Output 245
Enhanced PRTCTL Data Structure 246

93. Aligning or Centering Text in a Character Field **248**
Left- or Right-Justifying Text 248
Centering Text 249
Using the CENTER Text Subprocedure 250

94. Debug a Batch Job **251**
A Faster Way to Enter the Job Number 252

95. Find and Replace with Regular Expressions **254**
REGCOMP — Compile a Regular Expression String 255
REGCOMP Control Flags 255
REGCOMP Return Values 256
REGEXEC — Search Using Regular Expression 256
REGFREE — Release the Regular Expression Work Buffer 256
REGERROR — Retrieve Regular Expression Errors 256
RegComp() Parameters 258
RegExec() Parameters 259

96. Use DLTOVR when Using OVRDBF OVRSCOPE(*JOB) **261**
OVRDBF OVRSCOPE(*JOB) Corresponds to DLTOVR LVL(*JOB) 261

97. Use a FOR Loop to Allow Multiple Exit Points **262**
Traditional Nested Logic 262
Using a FOR Loop with LEAVE 263
About the FOR OpCode 263

98. Source-level Debugger for Legacy RPG III **265**

99. Set and Get Environment Variables from within RPG IV **266**
Prototypes for PUTENV and GETENV APIs 266
Two Environments 268
CL Access to the Environment 269
Additional Environment API Prototypes 270
Environment APIs 270

100. Simple Scan with Ignore Upper/Lowercase 272
   Use Nested %XLATE Inside %SCAN 272

101. Set the CLASSPATH for Java within RPG IV 274
   Retrieve the Existing CLASSPATH 275
   Scan the New CLASSPATH for %CLASSPATH% 275
   Replace %CLASSPATH% with the Old CLASSPATH 276
   Set the CLASSPATH Environment Variable 277
   SetClasspath() Subprocedure Implementation 278

Epilogue 279

Appendix: Source Member RPGTNT in QCPYSRC *281*

   1. **QUSEC — The API Error Data Structure** 281

   2. **OBJD0100 — Return Structure for QUSROBJD API** 281

   3. **Data Structures Used by QWCCVTDT API** 282

   4. **iconv()-Related Conversion APIs and Data Structures** 283

   5. **CEE4RAGE and CEE4RAGE2 Prototypes** 283

   6. **Regular Expression Base Data-types** 284

   7. **REGEX_T Data Structure Template** 284

   8. **REGMATCH_T Data Structure Template** 285

   9. **Regular Expression Named Constants** 285

   10. **Retrieve Environment Variable (RTVENVVAR)** 286

Conventions Used in this Book

To facilitate the use of variable names and field definitions, a shorthand style is sometimes used to describe a field's attributes. For example, in the paragraphs through this book, the following is used to identify a packed decimal variable:

Packed(x,y)

where *Packed* is the abbreviation for "Packed Decimal," x is the declared length of the field, and y is the number of decimal positions.

The following summary illustrates the other styles of variable declaration shorthand used throughout this book.

- Char(x) — Character
- VChar(x) — Varying Character
- Signed(x,y) — Zoned Numeric
- Int(1) — Integer: 3i0
- Int(2) — Integer: 5i0
- Int(4) — Integer: 10i0
- Int(8) — Integer: 20i0
- UINT(1) — Unsigned Integer: 3u0
- UINT(2) — Unsigned Integer: 5u0
- UINT(4) — Unsigned Integer: 10u0
- UINT(8) — Unsigned Integer: 20u0
- Float(4) — Single Precision Floating Point: 4F
- Float(8) — Double Precision Floating Point: 8F
- Packed(x,y) — Packed Decimal
- Pkd(x,y) — Packed Decimal
- Date(x) — Date variable, where x is the date format

The terms *character variable* and *numeric variable* are often used to refer to a field name or data structure name. The word *variable* should be interpreted as referring to a field name or a data structure name or both:

"The first parameter of the QUSROBJD API must be a *character variable*."

The terms *character value* and *numeric value* are often used to refer to field names, literals, or expressions, such as the valid choices for a parameter of a built-in function:

"The first parameter of the %EDITC built-in function must be a *numeric value*."

To get the latest updates, tools, and information, visit www.RPGTNT.com.

1 Prototype Everything

Prototypes are the basis for call operations in RPG IV. Without prototypes you cannot call a program, subprocedure, or API using either free format or hybrid fixed format. The old call/parm opcodes have been deprecated in RPG IV and should no longer be used.

A *prototype* is simply a declaration of "stuff" used by the compiler. At compile-time, the compiler uses the prototype to check the syntax in your call to a program, subprocedure, or API. It does this to ensure that the data for the parameters of the call are specified correctly.

A prototype begins with the so-called *PR statement.* This is a Definition specification that identifies the name of the prototype and optionally, the name of the program or subprocedure being called, as follows:

```
D GetBalDue      PR            7P 2
```

As illustrated, the prototype name in positions 7 to 21 of the Definition specification indicates the name of the prototype and *not* the name of the subprocedure that is evoked when the prototype is called. **Without additional coding, a prototype defaults to a subprocedure with the same name as the prototype.** Therefore, the prototype in the example above is used to call a subprocedure named GETBALDUE.

But what about when a different subprocedure should be evoked when GETBALDUE is called?

The EXTPROC keyword must be included in the prototype when a subprocedure whose name is different from the prototype is being called. For example, if the subprocedure to be evoked is named RTVCSTBAL, the following prototype statement could be used:

```
D GetBalDue      PR            7P 2   EXTPROC('RTVCSTBAL')
```

Subprocedures and programs may be prototyped. To control whether a program or subprocedure is evoked when the prototyped is called, specify the EXTPGM for program calls and EXTPROC for subprocedure calls.

If the EXTPROC and EXTPGM keywords are not specified, EXTPROC is implied, and the name of the prototype is used as the name of the subprocedure to evoke. The EXTPGM keyword indicates that a program is being called:

```
D GetBalDue      PR            7P 2   extPgm('CMBALDUE')
```

Here, the EXTPGM keyword indicates that a program named CMBALDUE is evoked when the prototype GETBALDUE is called. The sole parameter of EXTPGM is the name of the program being prototyped. This parameter is optional and, if omitted, defaults to the name of the prototype.

Other than inspecting the EXTPGM/EXTPROC keywords of a prototype, there is no way to distinguish between a program call and a subprocedure call.

The subprocedure name on the EXTPROC keyword and the program name on the EXTPGM keyword must be enclosed in quotes and *are* case sensitive. It is very common to have subprocedure names consisting of mixed upper- and lowercase letters; however, virtually *all* program names are specified in uppercase.

When writing subprocedures, the compiler creates an external name for the subprocedure using the name specified on the EXTPROC keyword of the corresponding prototype. If EXTPROC is not specified, the prototype name is used after it is converted to all uppercase.

To define a subprocedure name with upper-, lower-, or mixed-case letters, specify the subprocedure name on the EXTPROC keyword:

```
D GetBalDue      PR           7P 2  EXTPROC('GetBalDue')
```

In this example, the subprocedure name assigned to our subprocedure is 'GetBalDue'. If EXTPROC('GetBalDue') were not specified, the subprocedure name would be 'GET-BALDUE'.

Most prototypes created for RPG IV subprocedures use all-uppercase names. Consequently, the EXTPROC keyword is frequently omitted from prototypes. When prototyping subprocedures for APIs—such as those from the Unix-style APIs, C functions, or MI instructions—the majority of them use either mixed-case or all-lowercase names. The EXTPROC keyword must be used to ensure that the correct API name is prototyped.

Following a PR statement, the parameters for the program or subprocedure are specified. These are similar to specifying subfields of a data structure but often include several additional keywords, such as CONST, VALUE, and OPTIONS. For example, the QCMDEXC API (see Tip #2) would be prototyped as follows:

Simple Prototype for the QCMDEXC API

```
D QCMDEXC        PR           EXTPGM('QCMDEXC')
D   cmdString            32702A  Const OPTIONS(*VARSIZE)
D   nCmdLen              15P 5  Const
D   dbcsFlag               3A  Const OPTIONS(*NOPASS)
```

2 Prototyping a Call to a Program

In addition to subprocedures, programs may have a prototype created for them. This allows them to be called using natural expression syntax or used in free-format RPG IV.

Prototyped programs can be called using the CALLP opcode or in /free syntax by specifying the prototype name along with its parameters enclosed in parentheses:

```
/free
    callp qcmdexc('ADDLIBLE XTOOLS' : 15);

    qcmdexc('RMVLIBLE XTOOLS' : 15);
/end-free
```

To prototype a program, create a prototype in the same way you would for a subprocedure. To indicate that a program and not a subprocedure is being called, specify the EXTPGM keyword, as follows:

Use EXTPGM to Prototype Program Calls

```
D QCMDEXC         PR                      EXTPGM
D   cmdString               32702A        Const OPTIONS(*VARSIZE)
D   nCmdLen                 15P 5 Const
D   dbcsFlag                    3A        Const OPTIONS(*NOPASS)
```

The QCMDEXC API is prototyped above. Note the EXTPGM keyword on the first line. This indicates that a program is to be called. The name of the program being evoked by this prototype is the same as the prototype name. To call QCMDEXC using this prototype, use the CALLP opcode, as follows:

```
C                   callp      qcmdexc('ADDLIBLE XTOOLS' : 15)
```

or in free format:

```
/free
    qcmdexc('ADDLIBLE XTOOLS' : 15);
/end-free
```

The name of the prototype and the name of the program do not need to be the same. When the prototype name is *not* the same as the program being prototyped, specify the program name on the EXTPGM keyword, as follows:

Using EXTPGM with an Alternate Prototype Name

```
D runcmd          PR                    extPgm('QCMDEXC')
D  szCmdStr                    32702A   Const OPTIONS(*VARSIZE)
D  nCmdLen                     15P 5    Const
D  dbcsFlag                        3A   Const OPTIONS(*NOPASS)
```

Note that in the example above, the prototype name is RUNCMD but the EXTPGM keyword identifies QCMDEXC as the program to call.

To call QCMDEXC using this prototype, specify it as follows:

```
C                   callp      runcmd('ADDLIBLE XTOOLS' : 15)
```

or

```
/free
     runcmd('ADDLIBLE XTOOLS' : 15);
/end-free
```

Perhaps a more conventional (and easier) way to call QCMDEXC would be to declare a variable length field and store the command in that field. Then pass the variable length field to the program when it is called, as follows:

```
D runcmd          PR                    extProc('QCMDEXC')
D  szCmdStr                    32702A   Const OPTIONS(*VARSIZE)
D  nCmdLen                     15P 5    Const
D  dbcsFlag                        3A   Const OPTIONS(*NOPASS)

D cmd             S            1024A    Varying

 /free
   cmd = 'addlible xtools';
   runcmd(cmd : %len(cmd));
 /end-free
```

In the example above, the %LEN built-in function is used to calculate the length of the command string; this is used as the second parameter of the call to RUNCMD.

3 An Alternative to QCMDEXC

An alternative to QCMDEXC is the system() function. This function is a C runtime interface that may be called from RPG IV. There are differences between system() and QCMDEXC:

- There is no parameter 2 on system()—meaning that the length of the command string is determined by the system() interface itself rather than requiring it to be calculated in advance.
- When a MONITOR/ON-ERROR handler is used, a call to QCMDEXC will evoke the ON-ERROR handler when an error occurs while processing the CL command. A call to system() does not evoke the ON-ERROR handler when an error occurs in processing the CL command.

The prototype for system() follows:

Prototype for the System() Function

```
D system          PR              10I 0 extProc( 'system' )
D   cmdString                        *    Value Options( *String )
```

The system() function, as prototyped above, may be called using the so-called hybrid syntax in RPG IV, as follows:

```
C                   callp     system('ADDLIBLE XTOOLS')
```

or in free format, as follows:

```
/free
    system('ADDLIBLE XTOOLS');
/end-free
```

To use this or any C runtime function, the Binding Directory named QC2LE must be included on the BNDDIR parameter when the source member is compiled. See Tip #28 for information on including the QC2LE Binding Directory in RPG IV programs.

Most people prefer to specify the BNDDIR keyword on the Header specification in the source member, as follows:

```
H BNDDIR('QC2LE')

/IF DEFINED(*CRTBNDRPG)
H DFTACTGRP(*NO)
/ENDIF

D cpfmsg          S              7A    Import('_EXCP_MSGID')
D system          PR            10I 0 extProc( 'system' )
D  cmdString                      *   VALUE OPTIONS( *String )

/free
    if (system('ADDLIBLE XTOOLS') <> 0);
      if (cpfmsg = 'CPF2103');
        // ignore this message
      elseif (cpfmsg <> *BLANKS);
        // Something didn't work!
      endif;
    endif;
/end-free
```

Here, the BNDDIR('QC2LE') keyword is specified. In addition, the C runtime library's _EXCP_MSGID variable is imported, and its value is assigned to the field named CPFMSG. After a call to system(), it returns either zero or non-zero. If non-zero is returned, the CL command failed. If a CPF message is issued, it is returned in the CPFMSG variable.

4 Subprocedure-style Entry Parameter List for Programs

Legacy applications accepted input parameters — commonly referred to as *ENTRY/PLIST* — by using the PLIST and PARM statements in fixed-format Calculation specifications, as follows:

```
D maxRecs         S              10I 0

C       *ENTRY      PLIST
C                   Parm                    startDate        7
C                   Parm                    endDate          7
C                   Parm                    maxRecs
```

RPG quietly added a method to declare an entry parameter list for programs when it added subprocedures to the language back in version 3.2 and 3.7 of the operating system. Instead of the traditional *ENTRY/PLIST statements, a new method that replaces these statements with a Prototype and Procedure Interface is available. The name of the Prototype and Procedure Interface must be the same as the program name and must appear at the top of the Definition specifications, as follows:

Use a Prototype to Replace *ENTRY/PLIST for Programs

```
      //  SRCFILE(QRPGLESRC) SRCMBR(PRTAGING)
H OPTION(*NODEBUGIO:*SRCSTMT)
FCUSTOMER   IF    E         K DISK

D PrtAging        PR                  EXTPGM('PRTAGING')
D  startDate                  7A      Const
D  endDate                    7A      Const
D  maxRecs                   10I 0    Const

D PrtAging        PI
D  startDate                  7A      Const
D  endDate                    7A      Const
D  maxRecs                   10I 0    Const
```

Specify the EXTPGM keyword with the program's name on the Prototype to replace *ENTRY/PLIST.

The entry parameter list for the program PRTAGING is specified using a Prototype and Procedure Interface instead of the old-fashioned *ENTRY/PLIST. The prototype must appear before the procedure interface. The EXTPGM keyword on the prototype is not strictly required; however, my experience is that it always works when EXTPGM(*myPgmName*) is specified.

In addition, if you want to call PRTAGING from another RPG IV program, you should store the prototype in its own external source member (sometimes called a "/copy member" or "copybook") and then /COPY or /INCLUDE that source member into the caller's source member.

One major benefit from using this syntax is that data structures and arrays may be declared as parameters much more easily.

If a parameter is a data structure, the LIKEDS keyword can be used to define the parameter (see Tip #49 for more details).

5 Add NOMAIN to the Header Specification of Secondary Modules

When a source member is compiled, a huge amount of unnecessary RPG Cycle code is included in the compiled *MODULE object. This extra code is required for the main program module but not for any of the so-called secondary modules. Secondary modules are those that are used to create a multi-module program.

To avoid the overhead of the RPG Cycle in these secondary modules and reduce the final size of the program, add the NOMAIN keyword to the Header specification of all secondary modules in a program.

Use NOMAIN in All Secondary Modules' Source Members

```
 H NOMAIN
```

Do *not* add NOMAIN to the primary or "main" module *or* to programs that are made up of only one module.

The same thing can be applied to creating modules for Service Programs. When creating a *SRVPGM (Service Program), there is no situation where using this extra RPG Cycle code is required. Therefore, always use the NOMAIN keyword on the Header specification for all source members used in a service program.

6 Monitoring C Function Runtime Errors

When a C runtime function is used in RPG IV (and more and more applications are using C runtime functions), it can add a great deal of functionality to the application. When that function fails, retrieving and determining the error can be a completely new experience to RPG IV programmers.

To understand how to trap and handle errors that occur when a C function is used in RPG IV, you have to understand how this is accomplished in C and many other languages.

Unlike RPG IV, the C language doesn't really have the concept of an opcode. Instead, virtually everything that is accomplished in C is done through *functions*. A function is identical to a subprocedure in RPG IV. For example, to copy data from one text field to another, the MOVEL or EVAL opcodes are used in RPG IV. In C, the strcpy() or memcpy() functions are used. Copying numeric values from one field to another is virtually identical in C and RPG IV.

When using C runtime functions, there are two methods for detecting error conditions:

- Inspect the runtime error code value.
- Inspect the global C runtime CPF message variable.

The runtime error code is returned to a program by calling the errno() function. Normally in C this is provided through a macro, but RPG doesn't have macros, so it makes a function available. To retrieve the C runtime error code, two declarations need to be specified, as follows:

```
D errno           PR              *   extProc('__errno')

D nErrNo          S              10I 0 Based(pErrNo)
```

In the example above, the '__errno' function is prototyped. It has no parameters, so one line of code is all that's needed to prototype it. Calling this function returns a pointer to the most current error code generated from a call to another C runtime function; for example:

```
D errno              PR                *   extProc('__errno')

D nErrNo             S             10I 0 Based(pErrNo)
 /free
       if  (open64('/home/cozzi/notes.txt') = -1);
          pErrNo = errno();
       endif;
 /end-free
```

In this example, the open64() function is used to open a file named NOTES.TXT. If the open fails, –1 is returned by the open64(), and you must use errno() to retrieve the error number (i.e., reason code). This number in and of itself is not very useful unless you're an experienced C programmer. In fact, the error code numbers are not documented in the printed or PDF manuals. The only way to determine what they are is to open the ERRNO source member in the H source file in the QSYSINC library. That's SRCFILE(QSYSINC/H) SRCMBR(ERRNO). And yes, the source file name is just the letter *H*.

To make more sense of the error number returned by a call to errno(), another function can be used. This second function, strerror(), retrieves the text description for any error number, as follows:

```
D errno             PR                *   extProc('__errno')
D strerror          PR                *   extProc('strerror')
D  errno                         10I 0 Value

D nErrNo            S             10I 0 Based(pErrNo)
D errMsg            S            128A   Varying

 /free
       if  (open64('/home/cozzi/notes.txt') = -1);
          pErrNo = errno();
          errMsg = %str(strerror(nErrNo));
       endif;
 /end-free
```

In this example, the strerror() prototype is added. It accepts an integer parameter and returns a text string with the description of the error number. Since C text strings are different from RPG character fields, the RPG IV built-in function %STR is used to convert the results of strerror() into RPG-readable data. The message description is then copied to the ERRMSG field.

To simplify retrieving and recording the C runtime error messages, the LOGERRNO() subprocedure is provided. This subprocedure retrieves the current errno() value, retrieves the text description of the error number (if one is returned), and then writes both the number and its text to the joblog, as follows:

Write C Runtime Errors to the Joblog

```
P LogErrNo        B                      Export
D LogErrNo        PI           10I 0

D prt2Joblog      PR           10I 0 extProc('Qp0zLprintf')
D  szFormat                    *     Value OPTIONS(*STRING)
D                              10I 0 Value OPTIONS(*NOPASS)
D                              *     Value OPTIONS(*STRING:*NOPASS)

D errno           PR           *     extProc('__errno')
D strerror        PR           *     extProc('strerror')
D  errno                       10I 0 Value

D nErrNo          S            10I 0 Based(pErrNo)

  /free

     pErrNo = errno();
     if (pErrNo = *NULL);
         return 0;
     endif;

     prt2Joblog('%d - %s'+x'25': nErrNo : strerror(nErrNo));

     return nErrNo;

  /end-free

P LogErrNo        E
```

In the example above, the LOGERRNO subprocedure begins by calling the errno() function. If a valid result is detected, the error number is used on a subsequent call to strerror() to retrieve the error's text description. Both the error number and the text description are written to the joblog using a call to the Qp0zLprintf() API (see Tip #77). And finally, the error number is returned to the caller.

Using the LOGERRNO subprocedure can streamline C runtime error handline, as follows:

```
D nErrNo          S            10I 0

  /free
        if (open64('/home/cozzi/notes.txt') = -1);
           nErrNo = LogErrNo();
           // perform error recovery here, if necessary
        endif;
  /end-free
```

What about CPF Messages?

Sometimes C runtime functions produce a traditional CPF error message. This is notably true when calling the system() function to run CL commands (see Tip #3).

After a CL command has been performed, the exported '_EXCP_MSGID' variable can be tested for a traditional 7-position CPF exception/error message ID. To declare this variable in RPG IV, an IMPORT variable must be specified as follows:

RPG IV Declaration for C Runtime CPF Messages

```
 D cpfmsgid         S             7A    IMPORT('_EXCP_MSGID')
```

The IMPORT keyword is used to link the RPG IV variable with the imported variable. In this case, the C runtime library has exported the '_EXCP_MSGID' variable and our program imports it. At runtime, the CPFMSGID field is used to access the data in '_EXCP_MSGID.'

The name of the variable in RPG IV is irrelevant, so be sure to use a name that can be used consistently throughout all applications.

If a single name isn't possible, avoid redundant declarations by creating a subprocedure (in its own module) that returns the value of the '_EXCP_MSGID' variable. Then call that subprocedure to retrieve the CPF message. This allows you to avoid declaring the IMPORT variable in any of your own application code; for example:

Retrieve CPF Message for C Runtime Functions

```
 H   NOMAIN  BNDDIR('QC2LE')

 D cpfmsgid         S             7A    IMPORT('_EXCP_MSGID')

 P getcpfmsgid      B                   Export
 D getcpfmsgid      PI            7A

 C                  return   cpfmsgid

 P getcpfmsgid      E
```

In the example above, the subprocedure named GETCPFMSGID is defined. GETCPF-MSGID retrieves the value of the '_EXCP_MSGID' variable and returns it to the caller as a 7-position character value. An example of the typical use of the GetCPFMsgID() subprocedure follows.

```
H  NOMAIN  BNDDIR('QC2LE')

/include rpgtnt/qcpysrc,errno

D system          PR          10I 0 extProc( 'system' )
D  cmdString                    *   Value Options( *String )

/free
      if (system('ADDLIBLE RPGTNT') = 1);
        if (GetCFPMsgID() = ' CPF2103');
          // Lib already on list... continue
        endif;
      endif;


P getcpfmsgid     B                    Export
D getcpfmsgid     PI          7A

C                 return      cpfmsgid

P getcpfmsgid     E
```

In the example above, the ADDLIBLE command is performed by calling the system() C runtime function. If the CL command fails, the GetCPFMsgID() subprocedure is called. If CPF2103 is returned, then the library was already on the library list, and nothing else is necessary. Obviously, additional CPF message validations could be performed.

Error coding in RPG IV for non-RPG IV functions isn't always as straightforward as RPG IV native exception/error handling techniques. But in some cases, it can actually be easier to check a return code than to use a series of MONITOR groups, *PSSR, %ERROR() or any of the other techniques available.

7 Use PSDS to Retrieve Job Information

The *program status data structure* (PSDS) is available to all programs and contains information that is often needed in today's applications. Some of the information stored in the PSDS includes the last CPF message ID, Job Name, Job Number, User Profile, and the Program name and the Library from which the program is loaded.

```
D PSDS            SDS
D   PGMNAME            *PROC
D   CPFMsgID                7A    Overlay(PSDS:40)
D   runtimeLib             10A    Overlay(PSDS:81)
D   JobNbr                  6A    Overlay(PSDS:264)
D   JobName                10A    Overlay(PSDS:244)
D   JobUser                10A    Overlay(PSDS:254)
```

To access the subfields of the PSDS, the following syntax may be used.

```
/free
    if %subst(JobUser:1:1) = 'Q';
       joblog('System User Profiles may not be used.');
       return;
    endif;
/end-free
```

The PSDS has to be initialized when the program starts. While the overhead required to initialize the PSDS is relatively insignificant, it is lengthier than having no PSDS in the program or having a short (80 bytes or less) PSDS.

Each module of a program or service program that includes a PSDS performs redundant code that initializes the PSDS. Initialization is performed when the first subprocedure in the module is called—this is done once per module.

To avoid unnecessary redundancy, specify the PSDS in one module for each program or service program you create. Then create a subprocedure that returns the PSDS information to its caller and also calls that subprocedure when PSDS information is needed.

The following source member includes a PSDS data structure along with a subprocedure that returns some of the PSDS information to the caller. This source member could be used in any program or service program where PSDS information is needed. (Note that the PSDS data structure in the following example is "qualified." For more information on Qualified Data Structures, see Tip #8.)

Job Information from the PSDS—Helper Subprocedures

```
H NOMAIN OPTION(*NODEBUGIO:*SRCSTMT)
H Copyright('(c) 2007 Robert Cozzi, Jr.')

D PSDS            SDS                    Qualified
D  PGMNAME           *PROC
D  CPFMsgID                      7A     Overlay(PSDS:40)
D  runtimeLib                   10A     Overlay(PSDS:81)
D  JobNbr                        6A     Overlay(PSDS:264)
D  JobName                      10A     Overlay(PSDS:244)
D  JobUser                      10A     Overlay(PSDS:254)

 /INCLUDE RPGTNT/QCPYSRC,rpgtnt

P GetJobID        B                      Export
D GetJobID        PI                     LikeDS(JobName_T)
D  JobName                      10A      OPTIONS(*NOPASS)
D  JobNbr                        6A      OPTIONS(*NOPASS)
D  JobUser                      10A      OPTIONS(*NOPASS)

D myJobInfo       DS                     LikeDS(JobName_T)
 /free
   if %parms() >= 1;
      jobName = psds.jobname;
   endif;
   if %parms() >= 2;
      jobNbr  = psds.jobnbr;
   endif;
   if %parms() >= 3;
      jobUser = psds.jobuser;
   endif;

   myJobInfo.name = psds.jobname;
   myJobInfo.nbr  = psds.jobnbr;
   myJobInfo.user = psds.jobuser;

   return myJobInfo;
 /end-free
P GetJobID        E

P GetJobName      B                      Export
D GetJobName      PI             10A
C                     return    psds.jobname
P GetJobName      E

P GetJobNbr       B                      Export
D GetJobNbr       PI              6A
C                     return    psds.jobnbr
P GetJobNbr       E

P GetJobUser      B                      Export
D GetJobUser      PI             10A
C                     return    psds.jobuser
P GetJobUser      E
```

8 Use QUALIFIED Data Structures

In V5R1, RPG IV added support for Qualified Data Structures. This caused a significant change in how RPG programmers thought about data structure usage as well as subfield naming conventions.

Before Qualified Data Structures, names of data structure subfields had to be distinctive—that is, each subfield name had to be unique within the entire source member. With Qualified Data Structures, uniqueness of subfield names is no longer an issue—subfield names of qualified data structures need to be unique only within their parent data structure.

To illustrate, let's look at two data structures in a traditional RPG IV source member:

Traditional Data Structures

```
D MyStuff         DS
D  Item                           5A
D  Desc                          30A
D  Price                          7P 2

D YourStuff       DS
D  Item2                          5A
D  Desc2                         30A
D  Price2                         7P 2
```

To convert these data structures into Qualified Data Structures, the QUALIFIED keyword is added to the first line of their declaration, as follows:

Qualified Data Structures

```
D MyStuff         DS                        Qualified
D  Item                           5A
D  Desc                          30A
D  Price                          7P 2

D YourStuff       DS                        Qualified
D  Item                           5A
D  Desc                          30A
D  Price                          7P 2
```

That's it! They are now qualified data structures.

Note that since subfield names of different qualified data structures do not need to be unique, the *2* suffix has been dropped from the subfields of the YOURSTUFF data structure.

The subfields of Qualified Data Structures have different rules from regular subfields:

- Subfield Names must be referenced using qualified syntax.
- Subfield Names are considered unique to the data structure.
- Subfield Names may be reused either as subfield names in other Qualified Data Structures or as standalone field names.

Qualified Syntax Use

To access the subfields of a Qualified Data Structure, *Qualified Syntax* is required. This syntax is simply the data structure name, followed by a period, followed by the subfield name, as follows:

```
C                        eval      myStuff.price = 12.50
C                        if        myStuff.item = yourstuff.item
C        myStuff.Item    Chain     ItemRec
C                        eval      myStuff.price = yourstuff.price
C                        else
C                        eval      myStuff.price = ITMPRICE
C                        endif
```

Qualified syntax may be used in /free (free format) syntax or in traditional RPG columnar locations such as Factor 1, Factor 2, and the Result field. In free format, there are no restrictions on number of qualification levels or length of the name. In traditional syntax, there are two import restrictions:

- The qualified name must physically fit into the Factor 1, Factor 2, or Result field.
- Only one-level qualifications are supported—that is, *x.y* is supported but *x.y.z* is not supported.

Qualified subfields may also be specified on Input and Output specifications.

9 Copy Subfields Between Qualified Data Structures

In v5.4 of the operating system, a new RPG IV opcode is available. This opcode allows the subfields of one data structure to be copied to the subfields of a second data structure based on subfield name. Normally when data structures are copied (using EVAL or MOVEL), a *byte copy* is performed. The EVAL-CORR opcode copies by using subfield names rather than locations. (COBOL programmers may be familiar with this capability from the MOVE CORRESPONDING operation in COBOL.)

The EVAL-CORR opcode can be specified in /free syntax or by using traditional syntax:

```
C                         eval-corr save_Cust = custmast

/free
        EVAL-CORR    targetDS = sourceDS;
/end-free
```

The first EVAL-CORR opcode copies the subfields from the CUSTMAST data structure to the corresponding subfields of the SAVE_CUST data structure. The second /free EVAL-CORR copies the subfields of the SOURCEDS data structure to the corresponding subfields of the TARGETDS data structure.

The subfields are matched up by subfield name and copied regardless of their location in the source or target data structures. In addition, the subfield attributes can be different—that is, the fundamental data-type must match (such as numeric-to-numeric or character-to-character), but the specific data-type and field lengths may be different. In other words, zoned may be copied to packed, varying-length fields may be copied to fixed, and dates in one date format can be copied to dates of another date format.

EVAL-CORR works only with Qualified Data Structures; non-Qualified data structure will generate a compile-time error.

Using EVAL-CORR to Copy a Data Structure

```
D ItemDesc       DS                    Qualified
D  Price                        7P 2  Inz(1.45)
D  QtyOH                        5P 0  Inz(22)
D  QtyBO                        5P 0  Inz(33)
D  Nbr                          5A    Inz('Hello')
D  shipDate                      D    DatFmt(*ISO)
D                                     Inz(D'2006-11-09')

D OrderInfo      DS                    Qualified INZ
D  Nbr                         10A
D  Price                        7S 2
D  QtyOH                        5S 0
D  ShipDate                      D    DatFmt(*USA)
D  QTYBO                        5S 0

 /free
        eval-corr  OrderInfo = ItemDesc;
 /end-free
```

In the example above, the subfields in the target data structure ORDERINFO have the same name as those in the source data structure ITEMDESC. However, the ITEMDESC data structure has packed decimal subfields while the ORDERINFO data structure has zoned decimal subfields. In addition, the length of the NBR subfield is longer in the ORDERINFO data structure, and the SHIPDATE subfield has a different date format.

All these variations are supported by EVAL-CORR, and the assignment/copy is successful—that is, the data is copied in a similar way to copying each field individually with the EVAL operation. Thus, even though some of the subfield attributes are different, the assignment is performed as intended.

10 Nested Data Structures

The LIKEDS and LIKEREC keywords provide the ability to create Qualified Data Structures based on the format of existing data structures or record formats:

```
D CL_Date        DS
D   Century              1S 0
D   Year                 4S 0
D   Month                2S 0
D   Day                  2S 0

D myDate         DS                  LikeDS(CL_DATE)
```

This is extremely valuable to RPG IV development, but it doesn't stop there. RPG IV also supports data structures within data structures. These are known as Nested Data Structures and, strictly speaking, they are simply qualified data structures within qualified data structures —that is, a subfield of a qualified data structure may also be another qualified data structure:

Nesting Data Structures within One Another

```
D CustOrder      DS                  Qualified Inz
D   CustNo               7P 0
D   OrdNbr               7P 0
D   OrdDate                  LikeDS(CL_Date)
D   BalDue              11P 2
```

In the example above, the CUSTORDER data structure is a typical data structure, and it is Qualified. The first two subfields, CUSTNO and ORDNBR, and the last subfield, BALDUE, are traditional subfields. However, the third subfield, ORDDATE, is declared using the LIKEDS keyword, and this creates a nested data structure.

Nested Data Structure allows a subfield to be declared as a data structure—that is, the subfields from the CL_DATE data structure are used as subfields of the CUSTORDER.ORDDATE subfield. When compiled, the CUSTORDER data structure is expanded as follows:

```
D CustOrder       DS                        Qualified Inz
D  CustNo                          7P 0
D  OrdNbr                          7P 0
D  OrdDate                             Qualified ──┐        ┌──────────────┐
D   Century                       1S 0 ───────────────────▶│  Expanded    │
D   Year                          4S 0                      │ CL_DATE structure │
D   Month                         2S 0                      └──────────────┘
D   Day                           2S 0
D  BalDue                        11P 2
```

The subfields from CL_DATE have been inserted after ORDDATE. The Qualified keyword, which is implied by a LIKEDS keyword, is also inserted. These new subfields are accessible using qualified syntax:

```
nYear = CustOrder.OrdDate.Year;
```

The YEAR subfield is qualified to its parent data structure, ORDDATE. ORDDATE, which itself is a subfield, is further qualified to *its* parent data structure, CUSTORDER.

There is no practical limit to the number of levels for nested data structures. Although the RPG limit of 99 nesting levels on just about any "nested" component (parens, IF statements, expressions, etc.) seems to apply to nested data structures as well.

Now the crazy part: *You can actually declare a nested data structure as an array.*

```
D Contact         DS                        Qualified
D  Name                          30A
D  phone                         10S 0 Dim(3)
D  email                         64A   Dim(3)

D Customer        DS                        Qualified Inz
D  CustNo                         7P 0
D  Contact                             LikeDS(CL_Date) Dim(6)
D  Addr                          30A
D  Addr2                         30A
D  City                          20A
D  State                          2A
```

In this example, there are 6 elements of the CONTACT subfield in the CUSTOMER data structure. This provides the ability to hold up to 6 contacts—name, phone numbers, and email addresses. The cool thing is that the CONTACT data structure's PHONE and EMAIL subfields are also arrays of 3 elements each. This means we can have up to 6 contacts per customer with up to 3 phone numbers or email addresses for each contact.

So how do you get to the second phone number of the 3rd contact? By using Qualified syntax, as follows:

```
bestNbrToCall = customer.contact(3).phone(2);
```

This retrieves the second phone number of the third contact.

Nested data structures allow you to move beyond using the OVERLAY keyword in data structure definitions by providing the ability to declare a data structure subfield as a data structure itself.

Nested-data-structure syntax *may* be used in free format and in the Extended Factor 2 syntax. It may *not* be used with traditional opcodes in Factor 1, Factor 2, or in the Result field. It is also not supported in input or output specifications.

11 *ALL and *ALLX 'xx'— The Repeating Constants

Figurative Constants such as *BLANKS* and *ZEROS* have been widely used. But most programmers overlook *ALL*, which is a very useful figurative constant. *ALL is provided in two versions:

- One replicates a literal—specified in *character* notation—matching the corresponding variable's size.
- The other replicates a literal—specified in *hexadecimal* notation—matching the corresponding variable's size. The actual value is converted to normal characters by the compiler.

The first version allows you to copy one or more characters repeatedly to the target field or to compare a field to a repeated pattern of characters. For example, to simulate *BLANKS using *ALL, you would specify *ALL' ' (*ALL followed by a blank inside single quotes).

Any series of characters may be specified following *ALL. For example, to fill a field with the letter *Q*, use *ALL'Q' on the right side of the assignment statement. If *ALL'QRST' is specified, the pattern *QRST* is repeated in the target variable. For example, if the target is 10 positions in length, then *QRST* is repeated as *QRSTQRSTQR*.

The second version allows you to build a character using hexadecimal notation. The *ALL figurative constant followed by the letter *X* (e.g., *ALLX) plus a quoted pair of hexadecimal letters or numbers can be used to build any of the 256 EBCDIC characters. But this is not limited to a single character; multiple hexadecimal characters may be specified.

*ALL and *ALLX may be used in Calculation specifications as well as the Initial Value for any field:

Initialize a Field to "Hex Zeros" with *ALLX '00'

```
D comData          S              255A   Inz(*ALLX'00')

    //  Alternatively, copy the value at runtime
C                       eval      comData = *ALLX'00'
```

To test a field for a repeating pattern of one or more characters, simply use *ALL or *ALLX in conjunction with the IF (or another conditional statement):

Test a Field for a Repeating Pattern

```
D comData          S              255A   Inz(*ALL'. ')

C                       if        comData = *ALL'. '
C                       eval      comData = *ALLX'00'
C                       endif
```

12 Embed Compiler Parameters into Source Members

One the benefits of RPG IV over RPG III and other languages is that compiler parameters from the CRTBNDRPG and CRTRPGMOD commands and a few from the CRTPGM command may be specified directly in the source member.

The *H specification*, which is often referred to as the *Header Specification*, has space in positions 7 to 80 where various controls or compiler parameters may be specified. For example, to add the activation group name *QILE* for the program, the ACTGRP keyword may be specified on the Header specification as follows:

```
H  ACTGRP('QILE')
```

The only difference between specifying the compiler parameter on the Header specification verses the actual CRT*xxx* command is that so-called user-supplied values—such as QILE—must be enclosed in single quotes and normally must be in all uppercase (with a few exceptions). For example, ACTGRP('qile') is *not* valid, but actgrp('QILE') *is* valid.

Compiler parameter on the Header Specification are merged with those specified on the actual compiler. Header specification keywords have priority over any override compiler parameters.

Synchronize Source Statement Numbers with SEU and Debug

When RPG IV was introduced, the compiler sequenced source statements for the benefit of the compiler listing. This provided uniqueness when external definitions or /COPY members were imported.

The problem with this feature was that it became extremely difficult to match the line number from the compiler listing back to the original source member statement line number. So IBM added the OPTION(*SRCSTMT) keyword to force the compiler to use the same line numbers on the compiler listing as in the source member. This means that line 210 in the source member is referenced as line 210 by the compiler listing.

To use OPTION(*SRCSTMT), specify it on the Header specification as follows:

Use OPTION(*SRCSTMT) to Sequence Compiler Listings

```
H OPTION(*SRCSTMT)
```

Reduce Debug Fatigue with *NODEBUGIO

If you've ever debugged an RPG IV program and were stepping through your code using the debugger's F10 (Step) function, you may have run into this problem. If you come across a READ operation to a database or display file and that file is Externally Described, the next F10 will bring you to the top of the Input specifications for the file and position you at the first field in the file. The next F10 positions you to the second field, and so on. For large or small database files, this can be annoying, particularly if you don't care about the value of the input fields.

RPG allows you to avoid this situation. Simply include the OPTION(*NODEBUGIO) keyword in the Header specification for the source member. Almost magically now, when you approach the READ operation while debugging and press the infamous F10 key, you are taken to the next executable line of code and *not* to the top of the Input specifications.

Use OPTION(*NODEBUGIO) to Avoid F10 Fatigue in Debug

```
H OPTION(*NODEBUGIO)
```

Even when no Files are declared in a source member, OPTION(*NODEBUGIO) is allowed—however, it has no effect. This is helpful for creating a standardized Header specification that may be used to /COPY into most source members.

Combine Header Specification OPTIONs

While the OPTION keyword may seem like a "singular" control, it actually supports multiple options at one time. Specify multiple options within the same OPTION keyword by separating each option with a colon. A typical OPTION keyword might include *SRCSTMT and *NODEBUGIO as follows:

Specify Multiple OPTIONs

```
H OPTION(*SRCSTMT : *NODEBUGIO)
```

The compiler keywords most often used on a Header specification include—but are not limited to—the following:

- OPTION(*NODEBUGIO : *SRCSTMT)
- BNDDIR
- DFTACTGRP(*NO)
- ACTGRP
- OPENOPT(*INZOFL)
- EXTBININT

13 Avoid "Surprise Initialize"

Legacy code is often the cause of the infamous Decimal Data Error periodically raising its ugly head. In my experience, this is usually caused by blanks or X'40' characters being stored in numeric fields, which often are actually numeric subfields of a Data Structure.

Fixing this problem can be easy if you simply initialize the data structure. To do this, add the INZ keyword to the Data Structure, and you're done. I have personally corrected around 80 percent of decimal data error problems I've encountered by simply adding the INZ keyword to the Data Structure declaration.

The INZ keyword on the Data Structure declaration specification causes its subfields to be set to zero for numeric fields, to blanks for character fields, and to the oldest (earliest) date for date/time fields. Without the INZ keyword, Data Structures—and therefore all of their subfields—are initialized to blanks.

Use INZ to Fix Decimal Data Errors

```
D MyStuff         DS                       INZ
D   ItemNo                      5P 0
D   Price                       7P 2
D   Desc                       30A
```

Blanks in data structures cause decimal data errors when the data structure contains non-character subfields.

14 Qualified Externally Described Files (1)

With the introduction of Qualified Data Structures (see Tip #8), IBM quietly added the ability to qualify input file fields and, by doing so, they sped up I/O operations.

By converting an Externally Described file to a Qualified File, the I/O operation is performed in one operation rather than a series of internal "MOVE/MOVEL" operations for each input field. To declare a Qualified File, specify the following:

- An externally described file.
- A PREFIX keyword on the File specification identifying a Qualified Data Structure.
- A Qualified, Externally Described Data Structure.

The key component here is to specify the PREFIX keyword on the File Description specification with a data structure name followed by a period; for example:

```
FCUSTMAST  IF   E           K DISK     Prefix('CM.')
```

The data structure name on the PREFIX keyword must be enclosed in quotes, be specified in all uppercase letters, and be followed by a period.

When a PREFIX keyword is used in this way, qualified field names are generated (e.g., CM.CUSTNO). To define the Data Structure named CM that is associated with the CUST-MAST File specification, a Qualified Externally Described Data Structure must be declared:

```
FCUSTMAST  IF   E           K DISK     Prefix('CM.')

D CM            E DS                    EXTNAME(CUSTMAST)
D                                       QUALIFIED
```

In the example above, the Qualified Data Structure (see Tip #8) named CM is declared. Its format (i.e., subfield) is derived from the external definition for the file named CUSTMAST. This means that all the fields from CUSTMAST are included as subfields for the CM data structure.

The PREFIX('CM.') keyword on the File specification associates the input buffer of the CUSTMAST file with the CM data structure. Hence, all input fields must be referred to using Qualified Syntax. In fact, read operations for CUSTMAST are automatically mapped into the CM data structure.

Qualified, Externally Described Files

```
FITEMMAST    IF    E              K DISK      Prefix('IM.')

D IM               E DS                       ExtName(ITEMMAST)
D                                             Qualified
 /free
       read ItemRec;
       dow NOT %EOF()
         if im.QtyOH <=0;
             joblog('Item %s out of stock.':im.item);
         endif;
         if im.backOrd > 0;
             joblog('Item %s is on backorder.':im.item);
         endif;
         if im.price <= 0;
             joblog('Warning item %s has no price.':im.item);
         endif;
         read ItemRec;
       enddo;
     *inlr = *ON;
 /end-free
```

When this technique is applied, the rule of Qualified Data Structure syntax also applies. Since the file is mapped to a qualified data structure, its input fields are renamed to IM.*xxxxxx*, where *xxxxxx* is the original field name.

The input fields must be referred to using only qualified syntax; they are no longer considered stand-alone fields.

The types of files that can use this technique include Input, Input-Add, Update, and Update-Add. Files declared as Output-only cannot use this technique.

15 Qualified Externally Described Files (2)

Qualified data structures aren't limited to data structures—you can also use them as qualified Input fields to a given input file name. Thus, you can have multiple declarations of the same file in the same program and avoid input buffer/field name conflicts. Here's how it works:

```
FCUSTMAST  IF   E            K DISK    PREFIX('CM.')
FCUSTMAST1 IF   E            K DISK    PREFIX('LGL.')
F                                      RENAME(CUSTREC : CUSTLGL)

D CM             DS                    LikeRec(CUSTREC)
D LGL            DS                    LikeRec(CUSTLGL)
D save           DS                    LikeRec(CUSTREC)
```

The Compiler uses the CUSTMAST file name to import the external definition for the CUSTMAST file. The LIKEREC keyword is used to define the format of the CM, LGL, and SAVE data structures. Data structures created by the LIKEREC keyword are Qualified Data Structures and inherit a subfield for each input field in the associated Input record format. The format name specified on LIKEREC must be from a file declared on the File specifications in this source member.

In the example above, the CM and SAVE data structures will have identical formats, whereas the LGL data structure matches the format of the CUSTMAST1's CUSTLGL record format.

The PREFIX('CM.') keyword indicates that the CUSTMAST file's fields should be mapped to a Qualified Data Structure named *CM*. Note that when this technique is applied, the prefix value must be enclosed in quotes, specified in all uppercase letters, and followed by a period.

The PREFIX('LGL.') keyword indicates that the CUSTMAST1 file's fields should be mapped to a Qualified Data Structure named 'LGL.' CUSTMAST1 is a logical file built over the CUSTMAST file and contains many, if not all, of the same field names as CUSTMAST.

When data is read from either the CUSTMAST or CUSTMAST1 files, it is automatically mapped into the CM or LGL data structures, respectively. A side-effect of this technique is that I/O performance is slightly improved. Normally, RPG copies input fields to the input buffer one field at a time. Using Qualified Externally Described files forces it to copy the entire buffer into the program in one operation.

16 Calculate the End-of-Month Date

In several types of applications, the end-of-month date is important. It's often used to determine when to run month-end reports, close the current month's books, or determine if a payment is past due.

Calculating the end-of-month date for any given date can be easily accomplished in RPG IV. One way is to use traditional fixed-format opcodes such as ADDDUR, EXTRCT, and SUBDUR (in that order). The other way uses built-in functions on one line of code. Either method is effective; both run with negligible differences in performance.

The formula for calculating the last day of the month is as follows:

- Add 1 month to the desired date X, giving a new date Y.
- Extract the day number D, from date Y.
- Subtract D days from date Y giving the end-of-month date.

These three steps can be performed in traditional RPG IV as follows:

Calculate End-of-Month in Fixed Format

```
D day              S               5I 0
D nextMonth        S                 D    DatFmt(*ISO)
D endOfMonth       S                 D    DatFmt(*ISO)
D myDate           S                 D    Inz(*SYS)

C       myDate       AddDur    1:*Months    nextMonth
C                    Extrct    nextMonth:*D day
C       nextMonth    SubDur    day:*Days    EndOfMonth
```

In the example above, the field named MYDATE contains the date that is used to determine the end-of-month date.

On the first line, one month is added to MYDATE (a date field), giving NEXTMONTH (also a date field). If MYDATE is D'2006-11-15', then NEXTMONTH becomes D'2006-12-15'.

On the second line, the day of the month is extracted from NEXTMONTH and stored in DAY. This day is extracted from NEXTMONTH rather than from MYDATE because it could vary between those months. For example, if the original date is January 30, 2006, then adding one month would result in a new date of February 28, 2006. (If in step 3 we extracted the day from MYDATE, 30 would be returned instead of the correct value, which is 28.)

On the third line, the day of the month is subtracted from NEXTMONTH. This returns the last day of the previous month, which is also the last day of the month of the date we original specified.

If free format is preferred, you can perform this algorithm in one statement. The use of the %MONTHS, %DAYS, and %SUBDT built-in functions allows the end-of-month routine to be performed in one expression, as follows:

Calculate End-of-Month in Free Format

```
D  myDate          S              D   Inz(*SYS)
D  EOM             S              D
 /free

    eom = (myDate+%months(1))
          %days(%subdt(myDate+%months(1):*DAYS));
 /end-free
```

The date variable *EOM* is assigned the end-of-month date. The starting date is specified in MYDATE. This expression performs the same tasks as the original fixed-format method. Either method may be used.

A GETEOM (retrieve end-of-month) subprocedure can be created using either of these two methods. This subprocedure accepts an input date and returns the end-of-month date for the input date, as follows:

Get End-Of-Month Subprocedure

```
P GetEOM           B                    Export
D GetEOM           PI             D      DATFMT(*ISO)
D  inDate                         D      Const DATFMT(*ISO)

 /free
    return (inDate+%months(1))
           %days(%subdt(inDate+%months(1):*DAYS));
 /end-free
P GetEOM           E
```

This subprocedure is a good argument for a macro language in RPG IV. In many other languages, I could have created a macro that would expand to insert the date into the expression. The expanded code would appear in-line in the program rather than in a sub-procedure.

17 Using Free-Format Comments in Fixed-Format Code

When free-format syntax was introduced to RPG IV, an alternate syntax for comments was also introduced. But unlike free-format source code, free-format comments are not required to be enclosed in /free and /end-free compiler directives.

Here's an example of free-format comments being used in free-format source code:

```
D Notes            S             4000A    Varying

/free
    // These are some comments
    // More comments here
    if A = B;  // Inline comments too!
       bEqual = *ON
    endif;
/end-free
```

Comments may appear anywhere in a free-format source line. However, once the free-format comments appear, no other data is recognized on that line. Therefore, they may appear on the same line *following* a free-format statement but not *preceding* them on the line.

Free-format comments may also be intermixed within fixed-format statements—that is they are not required to be stuffed between /FREE and /END-FREE directives:

Free-Format Comments in Fixed Format

```
    // Declare Lillian Date field
D nDays            S             10I 0

    // Calculate days since Oct 14 1582
C    InputDate      SubDur      BaseDate        nDays:*DAYS

    // Pass the duration to the OS/400 API.
    // Calculate the day of the week.
C                   CALLP       CEEDYWK(nDays: nDayOfWeek :*OMIT)

    // Return the day of week to the caller.
C                   return      nDayOfWeek
P GetDayOfWeek     E
```

18 Get Day-of-Week Name

Often the name of the day of the week is needed for reports, output displays, and web pages. Fortunately, OS/400 includes an API that can format the date in many ways, including returning a simple name of the day of the week.

The CEEDATE API is used to format a date as words. To convert a date into the name of the day of the week, we need to pass to the API the number of days since October 14, 1582 (the so-called "Lillian date") and a formatting string. The API returns the name of the day of the week:

GetDayName Subprocedure Source Code

```
P GetDayName      B                    Export
D GetDayName      PI           10A
D  inputDate                    D      Const DATFMT(*ISO)
D  rtnDayName                  10A     OPTIONS(*NOPASS)

D BaseDate        S             D      INZ(D'1582-10-14')
D nDayOfWeek      S            10I 0
D nDays           S            10I 0
D szDay           S            10A

C                 TEST(E)                  inputDate
C                 if          %ERROR
C                 return      'Invalid'
C                 endif

C     inputDate   SubDur      baseDate       nDays:*DAYS

C                 CallP       CEEDATE(nDays:'Wwwwwwwwwz':szDay:*OMIT)
C                 if          %parms()>= 2
C                 eval        rtnDayname = szDay
C                 endif
C                 return      szDay
P GetDayName      E
```

In the above example, the input date is tested to verify that it is a valid date. Then it calculates the Lillian date for the input date (i.e., the number of days since October 14, 1582). That Lillian date is passed as the first parameter to the CEEDATE API.

The second parameter is a formatting code. The format 'Wwwwwwwwwz' indicates that the Day-Of-The-Week Name is to be returned. The day name is returned to the szDAY field specified on the third parameter. That day name is subsequently returned to the caller.

The CEEDATE API accepts many formatting codes, ranging from entire date as words to the abbreviated day name; for example:

Format String	Example Output
YYMMDD	880516
YYYYMMDD	19880516
YYYY-MM-DD	1988-05-16
<JJJJ> YY.MM.DD	Showa 63.05.16
<CCCC> YY.MM.DD	MinKow 77.05.16
MMDDYY	050688
MM/DD/YY	05/06/88
ZM/ZD/YY	5/6/88
MM/DD/YY	05/06/1988
MM/DD/Y	05/06/8
DD.MM.YY	09.06.88
DD-RRRR-YY	09- VI-88
DD MMM YY	09 JUN 88
DD Mmmmmmmmmm YY	09 June 88
ZD Mmmmmmmmmz YY	9 June 88
Mmmmmmmmmz ZD, YYYY	June 9, 1988
ZDMMMMMMMMZYY	9JUNE88
YYMMDDHHMISS	880516204229
YYYYMMDDHHMISS	19880516204229
YYYY-MM-DD HH:MI:SS.999	1988-05-16 20:42:29.046
WWW, ZM/ZD/YY HH:MI AP	MON, 5/16/88 08:42 PM
Wwwwwwwwwz, DD Mmm YYYY, ZH:MI AP	Monday, 16 May 1988, 8:42 PM

19 Run CL Commands from an FTP Client

Have you ever needed to run a CL command from within an FTP client when you were connected from a PC or Linux box to your iSeries or System i5? There *is* a way.

FTP clients usually support the RCMD command. This command allows you to run commands on the target/remote site from within an FTP session. For example, to run the ADDLIBLE QGPL command, the following FTP statement could be used:

```
>>   RCMD   ADDLIBLE QGPL
```

If the FTP client doesn't directly support RCMD, the FTP QUOTE command can be used. To use QUOTE to run RCMD, specify the RCMD as the parameter to QUOTE, as follows:

```
>>   QUOTE RCMD ADDLIBLE QGPL
```

The FTP QUOTE command conveys the rest of the statement that follows the QUOTE command to the remote server. If the server supports the statement, it is processed accordingly. So between iSeries systems, use RCMD, but between a PC and an iSeries, you may need to use QUOTE RCMD.

20 Put Your Program to Sleep

Inevitably, there will be times when performance isn't taken into consideration for a section of a program. For example, if a record is locked and you would like to give the user the opportunity to try to access the record again, you may want to wait 2 to 30 seconds before attempting another record access.

There are several inefficient ways to accomplish a planned hold or *wait period* in RPG IV. One common yet very poor method involves looping in a Do loop for several thousand iterations. This is arguably the worse kind of delay-loop technique, as it not only delays the current user's job, it also eats up CPU cycles and system resources, consequently impacting every other active job on the system.

A better approach is to use the system's interrupt capabilities and put the job to sleep for the desired wait period. There are two efficient techniques to accomplish this: the sleep() C runtime function or the waittime() MI built-in. My preference is the C runtime function, as it is the easier to use.

Both these functions avoid eating up valuable CPU resources. In fact, there should be virtually no CPU utilization as a result of using either the sleep() or waittime() functions.

As with any C or MI function, a prototype must be created before you can use it. The sleep() function from the C language prototype follows:

RPG IV Prototype for the sleep() C Runtime Function

```
D sleep           PR              10U 0 extProc('sleep')
D   milliSecs                     10U 0 value
```

Once prototyped, call sleep(*xxxx*)—where "*xxxx*" is the number of seconds for which you want your program to sleep—from within RPG IV. To sleep for 2 seconds, specify a value of 2000, as follows:

```
callp  sleep(2000);
```

21 Use VARYING to Improve Performance

Fixed-length character fields have been around forever. With RPG IV, new varying-length fields were introduced. These new fields allow you to store character data in the same way as fixed-length fields *except* the fields keep track of their "current" length.

By tracking their own length, VARYING fields can help out with optimization by informing RPG IV's opcodes of its current length. That way, they perform their task only on the current length instead of the entire field. This is particularly useful with the so-called "string" built-in functions—%SCAN, %XLATE, %CHECK, and so on—as well as simple assignment statements (e.g., EVAL operations).

For example, assume you have a 4,000-byte character field. Scanning, translating, comparing, clearing that field always occurs on all 4,000 bytes. But when a VARYING field that is defined as 4,000-bytes in length is used, only its current length is scanned, translated, compared, or cleared. If its current length is 15, only 15 bytes are manipulated instead of the entire 4,000.

This in and of itself isn't a huge performance benefit; however, when it is compounded several thousand times in a loop or other routine, it matters very much. So when processing many database records or processing subfile or web browser (HTML) output in a loop, adding the VARYING keyword to a character field can improve performance.

VARYING fields are also compatible with the DB2/400 VARLEN keyword. Database files with fields that have the VARLEN keyword automatically map to VARYING fields in RPG IV.

A couple of points about VARYING fields:

- The entire length of the field is allocated by the compiler at startup.
- A 5U0 (2-byte integer) hidden prefix is stored with the field. It contains the current length of the field.
- When the current length of the field is shortened, the current length is changed but the data is not changed.
- When the current length of the field is increased, the current length is changed, and the bytes following the previous current-length position are cleared to the new current length.

To illustrate VARYING fields, the following 10-position VARYING field named VTEXT occupies 12 bytes of memory. This comprises its 2-byte integer prefix and the 10 bytes of the field itself. If it were initialized to the value 'Cozzi', it would be declared as follows:

```
D VText            S              10A    Varying Inz('Cozzi')
```

This field would have the following memory structure:

Memory/Byte Positions											
1	2	3	4	5	6	7	8	9	10	11	12
Data Positions ⟶		1	2	3	4	5	6	7	8	9	10

Current Length		**Data**									
		C	o	z	z	i					
0	0	C	9	A	A	8	4	4	4	4	4
0	5	3	6	9	9	9	0	0	0	0	0

The following illustrates declaring and using a 4,000-position VARYING field with the %SCAN built-in function.

VARYING Keyword to Help Improve %SCAN Performance

```
D Notes            S             4000A    Varying
    /free
        notes = 'Customer was very happy with the +
                 product and will tell their friends.';
        if (%scan('not happy' : notes) > 0);
          bHappyCust = *ON;
        endif;
    /end-free
```

In the example above, the %SCAN built-in function runs substantially faster thanks to the NOTES field being defined as a VARYING field. Only the current length, about 70 bytes, is scanned. If the entire 4,000 bytes were to be scanned, it would (obviously) take more time.

Most opcodes and built-in functions take advantage of VARYING fields. Every opcode that supports traditional fixed-length fields also supports VARYING-length fields.

22 Converting Numeric to Character with %CHAR

In /free RPG IV syntax and with the EVAL operation, the question of how to convert numeric to character keeps coming up. In traditional fixed-format RPG, the MOVE opcode was used, plain and simple—but what about /free?

RPG IV includes the %CHAR built-in function. This built-in function converts just about any non-character data-type to character, and it does it extremely easily.

The syntax is *myData* = %char(*myNumVal*). This converts the numeric value in the myNumVal field to character(s) and stores the value, left-justified and zero-suppressed, in the myNumVal field.

%CHAR also strips off leading zeros and left-justifies the result. It will include a negative sign if applicable but not a positive sign. In addition, the right side of the decimal notation always retains its zeros. So if the value being converted is declared as a 9P4 value, the right side of the decimal always includes 4 digits.

Convert Numeric to Character

```
D price           S              7P 2 Inz(12.50)
D szText          S             10A

    // Convert to Character: szText = '12.50'
C                 eval      szText = %char(price)

    // Or in /free syntax, as follows:
 /free
    szText = %char(price);
 /end-free
```

23 Converting Character to Numeric

In /free RPG IV syntax and with the EVAL operation, the question of how to convert numeric data from text format to true numeric variables is an everyday challenge. In OS/400 v5r2, RPG IV's %DEC and %INT built-in functions were updated to allow you to convert from character data to true numeric.

%DEC to Convert Text to Packed Decimal

The %DEC built-in function allows you to convert a numeric string into a true numeric value. You must specify the length and decimal positions for the resulting value as the second and third parameters of %DEC. The bad news is that these parameters must be hard-coded, as follows:

```
D price            S              7P 2

       price = %dec(szText : 7 : 2);
```

In this example, the character field szText contains a numeric string (such as '200.50'). The %DEC built-in function converts that value to a 7-digit packed value with 2 decimal positions. The result is assigned to the PRICE field, which is defined as Packed(7,2).

%INT to Convert Text to Integer

The %INT built-in function allows you to convert any numeric value to an integer. This value can be an existing numeric value or it can be a numeric text string, as follows:

```
D qty              S              5P 0

       qty = %int('250');
```

The numeric text string '250' is converted to an integer and copied to the QTY field. The numeric text string '250' could have just as easily been stored in a character field.

Note that both %DEC and %INT built-in functions have additional functions—such as converting a number or field declared with decimals to a whole number or formatting the specific length of a work field in an expression—but that's a topic for another conversation.

If you're lucky enough to have a license to RPG xTools (www.rpgxtools.com) on your system, you have nearly 200 easy-to-use subprocedures already installed. Among them is CharToNum(), which, when given a number stored in a character variable, returns that number as a numeric value. The syntax for CharToNum() follows:

Convert Character to Number Using RPG xTools's CharToNum

```
 H BNDDIR('XTOOLS/XTOOLS') OPTION(*SRCSTMT:*NODEBUGIO)
  /INCLUDE XTOOLS/QCPYSRC,convert
 D price           S               7P 2
 D szText          S              10A   Inz('12.50')

    // Convert to numeric: price will equal 12.50
 C                   eval      price = charToNum(szText)
```

The charToNum() subprocedure in RPG xTools uses the CVTEFN MI instruction (see Tip #66) to perform the conversion. It can often do a better job than the %DEC or %INT built-in functions. If you don't have RPG xTools, use %DEC or %INT or see Tip #66 for details on using CVTEFN directly.

24 Easier Text Concatenation

In RPG, to create a text message from various pieces of information—such as a customer number, invoice number, or balance due—along with a text string, the plus sign is normally used as follows:

```
D CustNo          S              7P 0 Inz(12345)
D msg             S             50A

C                 eval          msg = 'Customer ' + %char(custNo) +
C                                     ' not found.'
```

This is much easier in RPG than in most other languages—especially CL, where concatenating numeric data with character strings is painful.

But concatenation can be made even easier. The sprintf() API allows data to be concatenated based on a formatting string. If you specify the field that will receive the text, a formatting string, and the values you want to embed in that formatting string, then sprintf() does the work for you:

```
sprintf(%addr(msg):'Customer %d not found.':custno);
```

The example above may not seem any easier than traditional RPG IV concatenation methods, but it *is* more flexible. As new elements are introduced to the concatenation, it handles them easily, whereas with traditional RPG IV, complexity increases as more elements are introduced to the concatenation. In addition, the programmer can see the layout of the resulting string with the substitution tokens inserted, which is not possible with traditional RPG IV syntax.

The sprintf() API is a C runtime function that allows a set of data to be concatenated much more easily than using other methods. In RPG IV, it can provide some simplicity when repetitive strings need to be created with substitution variables. For example, the following string is used with sprintf() to produce a message that is sent to the user:

```
'Item %d (%s) inventory is %d units.'
```

This is used by sprintf() as a substitution pattern or *format string*. The format string contains substitution variables that are identified with a percent sign and data-type. For example, %d is used for decimal substitutions, and %s is used for text strings (character values). There are many others, but these two can be used for nearly every type of substitution necessary in business applications.

To illustrate: Assume the following is being used for substitution values:

```
1205
'The Modern RPG Language'
2150
```

The output created by sprintf() using these values and the above formatting string would be as follows:

```
'Item 1205 (The Modern RPG Language) inventory is 2150 units.'
```

The first and third items are numeric values; the second is a text string. To specify them along with the formatting code and return variable on sprintf(), it would appear as follows:

```
sprintf(%addr(msg) : fmtString : ItemNo : desc : QTYOH);
```

While the first and second parameters of sprintf() are consistent, the substitution values can be numeric in one situation and character in another. This is a problem when using sprintf() in RPG IV.

RPG IV does not support an "any type" parameter (at least not until V5.5 of OS/400), but sprintf() does. With RPG IV, each type of parameter has to be declared with a specific data-type. This limits what can be conveyed to sprintf(), perhaps even requiring a distinct prototype for each possible combination of substitutions used in each program. Not a great solution.

However, RPG IV includes the %CHAR built-in function. This built-in function can convert just about anything to a text string. This means we can create a single prototype for sprintf() and use it generically with %CHAR implemented to convert non-character parameters to text.

The sprintf() API parameters are as follows:

- The address of a return variable—the field specified on this parameter receives the formatted text string
- A formatting string— a character string that includes text and formatting codes used as placeholders for substitution data
- One or more substitution values—the data being inserted into the formatting string

The formatting string (second parameter) accepts a dozen or so different formatting codes. But the two most used codes are %s (for text strings) and %d (for decimal data).

Concatenating Character and Numeric Data

```
H BNDDIR('QC2LE')

D sprintf         PR            10I 0 extproc('sprintf')
D pOutput                        *    Value
D szFmtString                    *    Value OPTIONS(*STRING)
D usrprf                         *    Value OPTIONS(*STRING:*NOPASS)
D age                           10I 0 Value OPTIONS(*NOPASS)

D Greeting        C                   Const('Hello %s, you are %d +
D                                             years old.')
D msg             S             50A
D usrprf          S             10A   Inz('Bobby')
D age             S              3P 0 Inz(18)

 /free
     sprintf(%addr(msg):Greeting : %trimR(usrprf) : age);
     joblog(msg);
     *inlr=ON;
     return;
 /end-free
```

The sprintf() function is prototyped with two substitution parameters: USRPRF and AGE. When sprintf() is called, it creates a text string that is copied to the MSG field. That string is written to the joblog using the joblog() subprocedure (see Tip #77). The resulting text string written to the joblog would be as follows:

```
Hello Bobby, you are 18 years old.
```

This is great, but it still requires that a unique prototype be created for the sprintf() API for this situation. Creating a unique prototype for each use of sprintf() is certainly not optimal.

Instead, a generic prototype must be created for sprintf(). This prototype needs to have common substitution/replacement parameters so that it works correctly with RPG IV, as follows:

Generic Prototype for sprintf() Function

```
D sprintf         PR            10I 0 extProc('sprintf')
D szRecvVar                      *    Value
D szFormat                       *    Value Options(*STRING : *NOPASS)
D                                *    Value OPTIONS(*STRING : *NOPASS)
D                                *    Value OPTIONS(*STRING : *NOPASS)
D                                *    Value OPTIONS(*STRING : *NOPASS)
D                                *    Value OPTIONS(*STRING : *NOPASS)
D                                *    Value OPTIONS(*STRING : *NOPASS)
D                                *    Value OPTIONS(*STRING : *NOPASS)
D                                *    Value OPTIONS(*STRING : *NOPASS)
D                                *    Value OPTIONS(*STRING : *NOPASS)
D                                *    Value OPTIONS(*STRING : *NOPASS)
D                                *    Value OPTIONS(*STRING : *NOPASS)
D                                *    Value OPTIONS(*STRING : *NOPASS)
```

The prototype for sprintf() specified has a return variable for the first parameter, a formatting code for the second parameter, and several substitution variable parameters.

Since the substitution parameters are OPTIONS(*NOPASS), only the number of the substitution parameter necessary to complete the specific use of sprintf() for any given situation will need to be specified.

Also, since the substitution parameters are OPTIONS(*STRING), the substitution values (parameters 3 through *n*) must be in character format. This means we need to convert any non-character data to character before passing it to this API. To do that, %CHAR or %EDITC can be used.

 TIP   Specifying *NOPASS on the OPTIONS keyword with sprintf() is the key to having it work properly. *Not* specifying OPTIONS(*NOPASS) on one or more of the parameters can cause unexpected results.

The sprintf() function works by inserting the substitution value into the format string in chronological order. The first %s is replaced with the first substitution parameter (e.g., parameter 3), the second %s is replaced with the second substitution parameter (e.g., parameter 4), and so on.

Use sprintf() for Concatenation with Substitution Variables

```
D Greeting        C                       Const('Hello %s %s you are %d +
D                                              years old and have +
D                                              worked here for %s days.')
D msg             S             60A
D fName           S             10A       Inz('Bobby')
D lName           S             10A       Inz('Cozzi')
D age             S              3P 0     Inz(18)
D days            S             10I 0
D startDate       S               D       Inz(D'2006-01-02')

 /free
     days = %diff(%date():startDate:*DAYS);
     sprintf(%addr(msg): Greeting : %trimR(fname):
                     %TrimR(lName) :
                     %char(age):%char(days));
         joblog(msg);
         *inlr=ON;
         return;
 /end-free
```

In this example, the four substitution values are embedded in the substitution string as %s.

The FNAME field is passed, followed by the LNAME field, followed by the AGE field wrapped in %CHAR, and followed by the DAYS field also wrapped in %CHAR.

If you want to use one of the substitution values in more than one location, you can do so by inserting the relative location into the substitution symbol followed by a dollar sign:

```
/free
   sprintf( %addr(msg): '%1$s equals %1$s but is not equal to %2$s':
                        'AAA':'BB');
/end-free
```

The example above results in the MSG field containing the following:

```
'AAA equals AAA but is not equal to BB'
```

25 Create an Auto-Extend User Space

The User Space is an interesting object. User Spaces have been around on this architecture for nearly 20 years, and yet many people still don't know how to create them or why they would use them. In fact, the underlying object on which User Spaces are based was the first object created for this architecture back in the mid-1970s.

The reason most people don't know how to create user space objects is that OS/400 never shipped with a CL command to create this type of object. There is a DLTUSRSPC command, but no CRTUSRSPC command. Some people have created their own user-written CRTUSRSPC command (one is included in RPG xTools).

The User Space is becoming more popular lately because RPG IV allows you to use it for dynamic memory allocation, which in turn allows you to create dynamically sized arrays, data structure arrays, and dynamic memory allocations without actually using the precious (and expensive) system RAM or *main storage*, as we like to call it.

User Spaces are arguably the most optimized objects on the system. They have the ability to automatically grow from a few bytes in length up to 16MB, which is their limit. This allows you to store information in a user space and not worry about the size of the user space—it automatically (and seemingly magically) grows as necessary.

To create a user space, the QUSCRTUS API is used. It creates a user space and sets the User Space's default properties or *attributes*. The following is the prototype for QUSCRTUS:

Prototype for QUSCRTUS (Create User Space) API

```
D QusCrtUsrSpace  PR                    extPgm('QUSCRTUS')
D  UsrSpace                     20A     Const
D  ExtAttr                      10A     Const
D  nSize                        10I 0   Const
D  InitValue                     1A     Const
D  PubAuth                      10A     Const
D  szTextDesc                   50A     Const
D  Replace                      10A     Const
D  api_error                            LikeDS(QUSEC_T)
D                                       OPTIONS(*VARSIZE)
D  bSysDomain                   10A     Const OPTIONS(*NOPASS)
```

Using this API to create a user space requires several parameters, but once a prototype is created, specifying values for those parameters is relatively easy:

```
D mySpaceName     DS                    Qualified
D  UsrSpace                    10A      Inz('MYUSRSPC')
D  LibName                     10A      Inz('QGPL')

 /free
    CallP(e)   QusCrtUsrSpace(mySpaceName:
                  'MYSTUFF' : 6000 : X'00' :
                  '*ALL' : 'Bob''s Stuff' :
                  '*YES' : apiErrorDS);
 /end-free
```

In this example, a user space named MYUSRSPC is created in the QGPL library. The extended object attribute is 'MYSTUFF'. This attribute is visible using the DSPOBJD CL command and is stored just like the RPGLE attribute of an RPG IV program or the PF attribute of a database file.

The user space's initial length is set to 6,000 bytes and is initialized to X'00'. Any character can be used to initialize the user space. Most programmers tend to use blanks (X'40') but hex zeros (X'00') are much more efficient than any other character, including blanks. The object's text description is set to 'Bob's Stuff', and the Replace object parameter is '*YES'. Specifying '*YES' for the Replace parameter is just like specifying REPLACE(*YES) when (re)compiling a program.

If the user space needs to be auto-extending, then the QUSCUSAT (Change User Space Attributes) API is to be called. For some reason, this attribute can't be set when initially creating a user space.

The prototype for the QUSCUSAT API is as follows:

Change User Space Attributes (QUSCUSAT) API Prototype

```
D QusChgUsrSpaceAttr...
D                      PR              extPgm('QUSCUSAT')
D  RtnLibName                  10A
D  UsrSpace                    20A      Const
D  USAttr                      64A      OPTIONS(*VARSIZE)
D  api_error                            LikeDS(QUSEC_T)
D                                       OPTIONS(*VARSIZE)
```

This API can change several attributes of a user space simultaneously or individually. Each attribute is specified in a data structure. For example, to set the Auto Extend attribute, the following data structure is used:

```
D usAutoExt       DS                    Qualified
D  nRecdCount                 10I 0     Inz(1)
D  nAttrKey                   10I 0     Inz(3)
D  nAttrLen                   10I 0     Inz(1)
D  bExtend                     1A       Inz('1')
```

The first subfield, nRecdCount, is the number of User Space Attribute "records" you have included in this data structure. To change the Auto-Extend attribute, we only need one record.

The second subfield, nAttrKey, contains the attribute key for the attribute being changed. To change the Auto Extend attribute, a key value of 3 is required.

The third subfield, nAttrLen, indicates the length of the value specified for the attribute being changed. The user space Auto Extend attribute is 1 byte long, so this field is initialized to 1.

The fourth subfield is the user space attribute value being applied. For Auto Extend, this field is a 1-byte character field. Setting this field to '1' *enables* the user space's Auto Extend attribute. A value of '0' *disables* the Auto Extend attribute.

To change the size of the user space, the following data structure is used:

```
D usSize          DS                        Qualified
D   nRecdCount                  10I 0 Inz(1)
D   nAttrKey                    10I 0 Inz(1)
D   nAttrLen                    10I 0 Inz(4)
D   nNewSize                    10I 0 Inz(12000)
```

The second subfield, nAttrKey is set to 1 (the key used to indicate User Space size), and the fourth field is changed to an integer (10i0). The new size of the user space must be specified in the nNewSize subfield.

All user space objects are created with a fixed length. To set the auto-extend attribute, the QUSCUSAT APIs must be called after they are created, as follows:

Create User Space and Change Attribute to Auto-Extend

```
D userSpaceAttr   DS                        Qualified
D   nRecdCount                  10I 0 Inz(1)
D   nAttrKey                    10I 0 Inz(3)
D   nAttrLen                    10I 0 Inz(1)
D   bExtend                      1A   Inz('1')

D apiErrorDS      DS                        LikeDS(QUSEC) Inz
D rtnLib          S           10A

 /free
    QusCrtUsrSpace('MYUSRSPC   QGPL':
                   'MYSTUFF' : 6000 : X'00' :
                   '*ALL' : 'Bob''s Stuff' :
                   '*YES' : apiErrorDS);

    QusChgUsrSpaceAttr(rtnLib : 'MYUSRSPC   QGPL' :
                       userSpaceAttr : QUSEC);
 /end-free
```

In this example, the name of the user space is passed on the second parameter and followed by the USERSPACEATTR data structure. This data structure contains the elements necessary to set on the user space's auto-extend attribute, as follows:

- nRecdCount — Number of User Space Attributes being modified.

- nAttrKey — Identifier that indicates which key is being modified. To change the auto-extend attribute, they key of 3 is needed.

- nAttrLen — Length of the data being used for the attribute's new value. Since auto-extend is a yes/no value (i.e., a logical '1' or '0'), the length is set to 1.

- bExtend — Indicates if the auto-extend attribute is being turned on or turned off. A value of '1' means *turn on* auto-extend; '0' means *turn off* auto-extend.

Changing Multiple User Space Attributes

It is relatively easy to set up a data structure for each of the user space attributes and then a master data structure with nested data structures. This allows you to change any of the user space attributes as follows:

```
D newAttr          DS                    Qualified
D   attrCount              10I 0 Inz(3)
D   size                         LikeDS(QUSKeySize_T) inz(*LIKEDS)
D   initValue                    LikeDS(QUSKeyInit_T) inz(*LIKEDS)
D   autoExt                      LikeDS(QUSKeyAuto_T) inz(*LIKEDS)
```

The data structure NEWATTR contains a subfield named ATTRCOUNT that identifies the number of user space attributes being changed. This value varies based on the nested data structures being specified. In the example above, three (3) attributes are being changed: the size, initial value, and the auto-extend attribute.

The SIZE, INITVALUE, and AUTOEXT subfields are nested data structures—that is, they are qualified data structures *inside* the NEWATTR data structure. If you want to modify only the auto-extend attribute of the user space, only the AUTOEXT subfield should be specified:

```
D newAttr          DS                    Qualified
D   attrCount              10I 0 Inz(1)
D   autoExt                      LikeDS(QUSKeyAuto_T) inz(*LIKEDS)
```

Note that the ATTRCOUNT subfield is now set to 1 instead of 3, and only AUTOEXT is specified.

The nested subfields are based on data structure templates that I created. They are defined as follows:

User Space Attribute Data Structure Templates

```
D QUSKeySize_T    DS                      Qualified
D   keyID                       10I 0 Inz(1)
D   len                         10I 0 Inz(%size(QUSKeySize_T.value))
D   value                       10I 0 Inz

D QUSKeyInit_T    DS                      Qualified
D   keyID                       10I 0 Inz(2)
D   len                         10I 0 Inz(%size(QUSKeyInit_T.value))
D   value                        1A   Inz(X'00')

D QUSKeyAuto_T    DS                      Qualified
D   keyID                       10I 0 Inz(3)
D   len                         10I 0 Inz(%size(QUSKeyAuto_T.value))
D   value                        1A   Inz('1')
```

To set the auto-extend attribute, declare the NEWATTR data structure as previously illustrated and then set the VALUE subfield of the AUTOEXT nested structure:

```
/free
      newAttr.autoExt.value = '1';

      qusChgUserSpaceAttr(rtnLib : 'MYUSRSPC   QGPL':
                          newAttr : apiError);
/end-free
```

Changing the initial value and the auto-extend attribute simultaneously is just as easy:

```
D newAttr         DS                      Qualified
D   attrCount                   10I 0 Inz(2)
D   autoExt                           LikeDS(QUSKeyAuto_T) inz(*LIKEDS)
D   initValue                         LikeDS(QUSKeyInit_T) inz(*LIKEDS)

 /free
      newAttr.autoExt.value = '1';
      newAttr.initValue.value = X'00';

      qusChgUserSpaceAttr(rtnLib : 'MYUSRSPC   QGPL':
                          newAttr : apiError);
 /end-free
```

26 Declare Data Structures as Arrays

Multiple-occurrence data structures have long been a standard for traditional RPG programs. But recently, RPG was updated, and multiple occurrence data structures were deprecated and replaced with *Data Structure Arrays*.

This new RPG IV feature—Data Structure Arrays—allows you to declare a data structure and then, by adding the DIM keyword, to turn it into an array. One additional feature is that Data Structure Arrays must be Qualified Data Structures. This means that the QUALIFIED keyword must be specified or implied on data structures when the DIM keyword is used. Data structures (which are implicitly qualified, and hence the QUALIFIED keyword is implied) are data structures declared using the LIKEDS or LIKEREC keyword. In these situations, LIKEDS or LIKEREC along with DIM is correct, whereas DIM by itself is incorrect.

The advantage of Data Structure Arrays is that the elements of the array can be accessed directly. Therefore, unlike the OCCURS keyword and corresponding opcode, data structure array elements can be directly accessed through an array index. In addition, since data structure arrays are qualified, their subfields must be addressed using qualified syntax as follows:

```
myDS(x).subfield;
```

The data structure named MYDS is specified along with an array index (X). A period is used to qualify the data structure array to the desired subfield name.

Assume you have an order form or on-line shopping cart that can handle up to 30 line items. A data structure of the following layout could be used to store those line items:

```
D LineItems       DS                      Dim(30) Qualified
D   ItemNo                      5I 0
D   Price                       7P 2
D   QtyOrd                      5I 0
```

The LINEITEMS data structure is both a data structure and an array, hence the Data Structure Array title. To access the elements of a data structure array, a FOR loop can be used, as follows:

Data Structure Arrays — Accessing the Elements

```
D LineItems       DS                          Dim(30) Qualified Inz
D   ItemNo                       5I 0
D   Price                        7P 2
D   QtyOrd                       5I 0

D x               S             10I 0
D totPieces       S              5I 0
D totOrder        S             11P 0

 /free
    for x = 1 to %elem(LineItems);
       if (LineItems(x).QtyOrd > 0);
          totPieces += LineItems(x).QtyOrd;
          totOrder  += LineItems(x).Price * LineItems(x).QtyOrd;
       endif;
    endfor;
 /end-free
```

In the example above, field X is used as a counter for the FOR loop. Each iteration through the FOR loop increments X by 1. When X is used as the index for the LINEITEMS Data Structure Array, it allows direct access to the individual "occurrences" (i.e., elements) of the array and subsequently to the subfields.

As already mentioned, Data Structure Arrays must be qualified *either* implicitly *or* explicitly—but not both. There is some rather anal RPG IV syntax that doesn't allow the QUALIFIED keyword to be used when LIKEDS or LIKEREC is specified (as it is implied) but require it when DIM is specified. The three different methods to declare a Qualified Data Structure, whether are not they are Data Structure arrays, follow:

```
D Lines           DS
D   ItemNo                       5I 0          QUALIFIED is implied
D   Price                        7P 2          with LIKEDS and LIKEREC
D   QtyOrd                       5I 0          and is required with DIM.

D LineItem1       DS                           LikeDS(LINES)  Dim(30)

D LineItem2       DS                           LikeRec(ITEMREC) Dim(30)

D LineItem3       DS                           QUALIFIED Dim(30)
D   ItemNo                       5I 0
D   Price                        7P 2
D   QtyOrd                       5I 0
```

Here, the data structure LINES is a regular non-qualified data structure. It is used as a template later in this example. The LINEITEM1 data structure is declared using the LIKEDS and DIM keywords. Since LIKEDS implies that the data structure is qualified, the QUALIFIED keyword may not be used. In fact, if it is used, a compile-time error is issued.

The LINEITEM2 data structure is declared using the LIKEREC and DIM keywords. Since LIKEREC implies that the data structure is qualified, the QUALIFIED keyword may not be used.

The LINEITEM3 data structure is a regular data structure with subfields defined in line. Since the data structure is an array (the DIM keyword is specified), the QUALIFIED keyword is required. If QUALIFIED is not specified, a compile-time error is issued.

27 Initialize Fields to Job Date, System Date, or User Profile

Retrieving the current date or time in a program has been the sole capability of the TIME opcode until RPG IV added the ability to initialize a field to the current system or job date or time.

The figurative constants *SYS and *JOB allow you to initialize a date or time field to the current system or job date or time. The *USER figurative constant was introduced simultaneously with *SYS and *JOB. It initializes a field with the current user profile.

- INZ(*SYS) — Initializes the variable to the Current System Date or Time
- INZ(*JOB) — Initializes the variable to the Job's Date
- INZ(*USER) — Initializes the variable to the User Profile

In a subprocedure, you may initialize a local variable named TODAY to *SYS. Thereafter, each time that subprocedure is called, the local variable is initialized to the current system date. This can be useful in service programs that remain active for long periods, such as jobs that run over multiple days or whenever the system date is needed instead of the job date returned via UDATE.

*JOB, *SYS, and *USER Initial Values

```
D jobDate         S               D   Inz(*JOB)
D Today           S               D   Inz(*SYS)
D UserID          S             10A   Inz(*USER)
```

Built-in functions were also added to allow runtime access to the job date or system date.

- %DATE() — Returns the current system date
- %TIMESTAMP() — Returns the current system date/time stamp
- %TIME() — Returns the current system time

The TIME opcode continues to be a good choice when the system date/time is needed. However, TIME is used only in traditional RPG IV syntax and not in free format.

What about Job Date at Runtime?

With the introduction of %DATE, the system date can finally be retrieved at runtime without resorting to the TIME opcode. The irony of that is that the %DATE returns only the system date, not the job's run date. So while one feature was added, it appears on the surface that something is missing: job date.

To retrieve the current runtime Job Date, an RPG artifact named *UDATE* must be used:

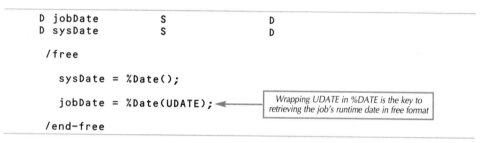

```
D jobDate         S              D
D sysDate         S              D

 /free

   sysDate = %Date();

   jobDate = %Date(UDATE);

 /end-free
```

Wrapping UDATE in %DATE is the key to retrieving the job's runtime date in free format

UDATE is wrapped in %DATE. This converts the non-date UDATE value to a real-date value and copies it to JOBDATE, which is declared as a date variable.

%DATE(UDATE) is all that's needed to retrieve the job's runtime date. If you prefer the 4-digit year version of *DATE, it works as well and results in the same value.

28 Use C Runtime Functions in RPG

The C language is certainly considered to be very powerful and is loaded with the C equivalent of RPG's subprocedures, known as *functions*. Many of these functions can be used directly by RPG without calling a C program, provided you know the secret.

To use any C function in RPG IV, you need to do two things:

- Prototype the C function in RPG IV syntax
- Specify the C runtime library's binding directory QC2LE when compiling the RPG IV source member: BNDDIR('QC2LE')

Prototyping C functions for use in RPG can be a challenge. The author maintains a website at www.rpgiv.com. The downloads page of this website contains many prototypes for the C runtime library.

However, even with the prototypes, unless you include the C runtime binding directory, your source member won't bind (i.e., finish the second phase of the compile process). The binding directory name is QC2LE, and it may be included in the source member using the BNDDIR keyword on the Header specification.

The binding directory is a system object and not a symbolic name; therefore, **it must be specified within single quotes and in all uppercase letters or it will not be located**. BNDDIR('QC2LE') is valid; BNDDIR('qc2le') is invalid. The following is the correct syntax for including the QC2LE binding directory in an RPG IV source member on the Header Specification:

Include the QC2LE Binding Directory to Use C Runtime Functions

```
H BNDDIR('QC2LE')
```

When a binding directory is specified on the Header specification, it is added to any other binding directories specified on additional BNDDIR keyword(s) on this Header specification. In addition, any BNDDIR parameter entries on the CRTPGM or CRTBNDRPG commands are added to the binding process.

29 Compare and Ignore Case

RPG is a great language for processing data, but (surprisingly) it lacks some fundamental features from its specification. For example, when comparing two variables, RPG compares them based on exact matches while ignoring trailing blanks. The case of the letters contained in the variables is taken into account when comparing. But how does one perform a *non*-case-sensitive comparisons in RPG?

One way is to use a C language runtime library function. That function is memicmp(), and may be called from within RPG programs by adding its prototype to the source member. The prototype for memicmp() is as follows:

Prototype for memicmp() — Compare and Ignore Case

```
D memicmp         PR              10I 0 extProc('__memicmp')
D  pValue1                         *     Value
D  pValue2                         *     Value
D  nCompLen                      10U 0 Value
```

This prototype uses the EXTPROC keyword to identify the procedure being called. In this case, the name is '__memicmp.' Note the 2 underscore characters prefixing the name. These underscores are required only in the prototype. To use any C language runtime function, the BNDDIR('QC2LE') keyword must be included on the Header specification of the source member (see Tip #28).

This memicmp() function compares one value to another for the given length. Unlike native RPG compare functions, memicmp() compares the two values for the number of characters specified on the nCompLen parameter. RPG ignores trailing blanks when comparisons are made, but memicmp() does not. Therefore, the letter *A* followed by 3 blanks is not equal to *A* followed by no blanks. Calculating the data length without trailing blanks is a must with this function.

The memicmp() function uses the address of the variables being compared. This is easy to specify: simply wrap the fields in the %addr(varname) built-in function instead of specifying them by themselves. For more information on using the %ADDR built-in function, see Tip #33.

The memicmp() procedure begins comparing the values byte by byte while ignoring case differences. If the two values are equal, memicmp() returns 0. If they are not equal, a non-zero is returned (the position of the first character that didn't match).

Compare Two Fields and Ignore Case

```
H BNDDIR('QC2LE') OPTION(*SRCSTMT)

D memicmp          PR              10I 0 extProc('__memicmp')
D  pValue1                          *    Value
D  pValue2                          *    Value
D  nCompLen                        10U 0 Value


D myName           S               32A   Inz('Robert Cozzi')
D oldName          S               20A   Inz('robert cozzi')

 /free
   if (memicmp(%addr(myName):%addr(oldName)): +
             %Len(%TrimR(myName)) = 0);
     //  They are the same! :)
   else;
     //  They are not the same! ;(
   endif;
 /end-free
```

30 Free Online Prototypes for APIs, C Functions, MI Instructions

Certainly prototyping OS/400 APIs can be a challenge, given the cryptic nature of the documentation. C functions are an even bigger challenge to prototype in RPG, not to mention MI Instructions.

A website maintained by the author contains free downloads that include the prototypes for many APIs, dozens of C runtime functions, and several MI Instructions. They are prototyped in RPG IV syntax and are ready to use. The website address is as follows:

RPG IV Prototype Source Code Web Address

```
www.rpgiv.com
```

Visit www.rpgiv.com and click "Downloads" to view a list of the source members available for download.

31 Checking for Valid Dates with the TEST OpCode

Many routines have been written to test date fields for valid dates. RPG IV makes this task incredibly easy by providing a single opcode to test any type of date or time variable for a valid value.

The TEST opcode can safely check a variable for a valid date or time value. The variable need not be a Date or Time data-type however.

There is a trick to successfully using TEST to check for a valid date. When checking a non-Date data-type field, specify the "DE" operation extenders as follows:

Check a Numeric Field for Valid Date Value

```
D nDate            S              8S 0 Inz(02312006)

 /free

     test(de) *USA nDate;
     if %error();
        if %status() = 112; // Bad date!
           // Do something with the bad date.
        endif;
     endif;

 /end-free
```

The "D" extender is only used when character or numeric fields are being tested for a valid date.

However, when checking a real-date data-type field, do *not* specified the "E" operation extender by itself:

Check a Date Variable for a Valid Date Value

```
D Today            S                   D    Inz(*SYS)

 /free

     test(e) today;  ◄──────    The "D" extender is not allowed when testing a true date
     if %error();                data-type. A compile-time error is issued if it is used.
        if %status() = 112; // Bad date!
          // Do something with the bad date.
        endif;
     endif;

 /end-free
```

In addition, the date format is normally specified when a non-date data-type variable is tested, and it may not be specified when a real-date data-type variable is being checked.

To summarize, specify the date format and "D" extender on the TEST operation when testing a numeric or character field that contains "date" information. Specify only the TEST operation (no extender, no date format) when testing real-date data-type variables.

32 Using the Secret 'X' Edit Code to Convert Numeric to Character

Moving to free format RPG or the so-called hybrid syntax (using EVAL and the extended Factor 2) can be frustrating if you're trying to do certain tasks. Some things that we took for granted in traditional fixed-format RPG are not always obvious in free format, and sometime it's downright difficult.

The MOVE and MOVEL opcodes are not supported in free format and cannot be directly converted. Typically multiple lines of code or nested built-in functions need to be specified to accomplish in free format what can be done in one MOVE opcode.

One such conversion is between numeric and character data. The MOVE and MOVEL opcodes implicitly convert from numeric to character.

Certainly the %CHAR, %EDITC, and %EDITW built-in functions provide some level of conversion. But what is not obvious is a direct conversion from the MOVE and MOVEL operations (between character and numeric data-types) and a free format equivalent. How do you move a numeric value to a character variable and avoid any editing symbols, including thousands and decimal notation, currency symbol and negative sign?

Here is an example of moving a numeric value to character using the traditional fixed-format RPG MOVE opcode:

```
D numValue        S              5P 2 Inz(32.50)
D myData5         S              5A

C                 MOVE     NumValue      myData5
```

What's the free format equivalent? The mysterious 'X' edit code does this for you, as follows:

```
/free
    evalR myData5 = %editC(numValue : 'X');
/end-free
```

%EDITC(numValue : 'X') provides a similar conversion in free format to that of the MOVE opcode.

Use the %EDITC built-in function and the 'X' edit code with the EVAL opcode to simulate the MOVE operation or with EVALR to simulate the MOVE operation.

The 'X' edit code causes the numeric value to be converted to text. The number of digits generated is equivalent to the length of the field being moved. If the value in the field is negative, the sign is assigned to the right-most digit of the result. This sets the top half of the right-most byte to X'D' (B'1101') instead of the normal X'F' (B'1111'). For example, a negative value causes a zero to appear as a right-bracket and the number 1 to appear as the letter J. If the value is positive, then the numbers appear as they normally would.

If a numeric field is 5 positions in length with 2 decimal positions, and contains the value 32.50, as illustrated below, the result of editing this value with edit code 'X' is as follows:

```
D numValue          S             5P 2 Inz(32.50)

D myData4           S             4A
D myData5           S             5A
D myData6           S             6A
 /free
         myData4 = %editC(numValue : 'X');
         myData5 = %editC(numValue : 'X');
         myData6 = %editC(numValue : 'X');
 /end-free
```

• myData4 = '0325'

• myData5 = '03250'

• myData6 = '03250 '

If the field contains a negative value, such as −32.50 the result of editing with edit code 'X' would be as follows:

```
D numValue          S             5P 2 Inz(-32.50)

D myData4           S             4A
D myData5           S             5A
D myData6           S             6A
 /free
         myData4 = %editC(numValue : 'X');
         myData5 = %editC(numValue : 'X');
         myData6 = %editC(numValue : 'X');
 /end-free
```

• myData4 = '0325'

• myData5 = '0325}'

• myData6 = '0325} '

To force right-justified results, use EVALR, as follows:

```
D numValue         S               5P 2 Inz(-32.50)

D myData4          S               4A
D myData5          S               5A
D myData6          S               6A
 /free
        evalR myData4 = %editC(numValue : 'X');
        evalR myData5 = %editC(numValue : 'X');
        evalR myData6 = %editC(numValue : 'X');
 /end-free
```

Remember that the MOVEL and MOVE opcodes are similar to EVAL and EVALR respectively, however they are not identical. The MOVEL and MOVE operations perform a subscripted copy, whereas EVAL and EVALR are assignment statements. The equivalent of EVAL would be a MOVEL(P) (move-left with pad) operation.

Equivalent MOVEL and EVAL Opcodes using 'X' Edit Code

```
D numValue         S               5P 2 Inz(-32.50)

D myData4          S               4A
D myData5          S               5A
D myData6          S               6A

   // Traditional fixed-format to convert Num to Char
C                  MOVEL(P)    NumValue        myData4
C                  MOVEL(P)    NumValue        myData5
C                  MOVEL(P)    NumValue        myData6

   // Hybrid syntax to convert using 'X' edit code
C                  eval        myData4 = %editC(numValue:'X')
C                  eval        myData5 = %editC(numValue:'X')
C                  eval        myData6 = %editC(numValue:'X')

   // Free-format to convert using 'X' edit code
 /free
        myData4 = %editC(numValue : 'X');
        myData5 = %editC(numValue : 'X');
        myData6 = %editC(numValue : 'X');
 /end-free
```

33 %ADDR — Address of a Variable

For decades, RPG programmers have been passing fields between programs as parameter. When tighter integration with other programming languages (e.g., C) was introduced, a new method of passing parameters was also established.

That new parameter-passing method is known as *pass by value*. The original method of passing parameters is known as *pass by reference*. But what does *by reference* mean?

Every field passed as a parameter on a program-to-program call is passed *by reference*. This simply means the compiler passes the memory location or address of the field specified on the parameter to the called program. That way, the called program may modify the parameter's value in its original memory location. This is better for performance and ensures that the value of the field or parameter is always current.

Because of the pass-by-reference implementation RPG programmers have been using, the address of variables has been in use for decades, often without realizing it.

In addition to indirectly referencing the address of a field via parameters, RPG IV includes a way to directly access the address of any field. The %ADDR built-in function returns the memory location or *address* of a field, data structure, array, array element, or data-structure subfield.

The address of a variable can either be used directly via the %ADDR built-in function or it can be copied to a field. The address can only be stored in special fields whose data-type is set up to properly handle a memory address. This data-type is called a *pointer*. In RPG IV, to declare a pointer, use the asterisk (*) data-type, as follows:

```
D custname        S            30A
D ptr             S              *
 /free
     ptr =    %addr(custname);
 /end-free
```

In this example, the address of the CUSTNAME field is retrieved by the %ADDR built-in function. It is stored in the PTR field that has the *pointer* data-type. That pointer variable can be used wherever a pointer is required. You'll see pointers being used mostly with system APIs or C runtime functions.

A pointer variable may contain the valid address of a field or dynamically allocated memory. Allocate memory dynamically using the ALLOC opcode or %ALLOC built-in function. Pointer variables can also contain the address of certain system objects or the data associated with certain system objects. For example, a pointer to a user-space object actually contains the address of the storage associated with the user-space object.

Whenever a parameter of a prototype has a data-type of *pointer*, either a pointer variable or a %ADDR(*varName*) may be specified. In some cases, a field name may be specified, and the compiler will convert it to a pointer (e.g., when OPTIONS(*STRING) is specified on the parameter). To illustrate, let's revisit the prototype for memicmp() function from Tip #29:

```
D memicmp         PR              10I 0 extProc('__memicmp')
D  pValue1                          *   Value
D  pValue2                          *   Value
D  nCompLen                       10U 0 Value
```

The data-type for the first and second parameters indicates that a pointer is required. Since this function is known to *not* modify the content of the data passed to it, we can use the %ADDR built-in function to identify the data we want memicmp() to use.

If memicmp() accepted traditional pass-by-reference parameters, the names of the fields we were passing would be specified for the first and second parameters. Since this function requires pointers for the first and second parameters, the address of the fields must be specified.

%ADDR is used to pass the address of the fields being compared. Surround the field name with %addr(*xxx*) (where *xxx* is the field name), and you have created the address of the field:

```
if  memicmp(%addr(name) : %addr(input) : %len(name)) = 0;
```

34 Understanding API Documentation — Bin(4) Parameters

Whenever you see API documentation that includes a parameter defined as Bin(4), you may think that it equates to the B data-type in RPG. **It does not.** In fact, there are no APIs that require the use of the B data-type.

Bin(4) is an internal IBM-only notation for *binary scalar*. This is an MI (machine interface) term that has been around for 30 years. In RPG and other programming languages, *Bin* should be interpreted as an *Integer*.

The B data-type in RPG IV was deprecated many years ago with the introduction of Integers—that is, data-type *I*.

B data-types do not support the same range of numeric values as the Integer data-type. In fact, you often see Bin(4) miscoded in RPG as a 4B0 value. When this is compiled, it turns into a 2-byte binary field. Why? Because a 2-byte binary field can contain a 4-digit number—hence, *4B0* is stored in 2 bytes.

Instead of the B data-type, use the I data-type whenever you see Bin(4) specified in API documentation. Define the field as follows:

```
D  nStart          S              10I 0
```

In the rare situation where you see Bin(2) specified in API documentation, use

```
D  nStart          S               5I 0
```

The API documentation may identify Bin(4) as INT, INT4 Binary(4), or Integer. All are 10I0 values. Likewise, Bin(2) values are often documented as Binary(2), INT2, Short, and short integer. All are 5i0 values.

If the word *unsigned* is specified, the U data-type is used instead of the I data-type:

```
D  nStart          S              10U 0
```

Synonyms for *unsigned* include UINT, unsigned integer, unsigned int, unsigned long, and UBIN(2) or UBIN(4).

An example of the documentation for a typical parameter of an API follows:

QUSRTVUS (Retrieve User Space Data) API Documentation

Parameter	Description	Input/Output	Type(length)
Required Parameter Group			
1	Qualified user space name	Input	Char(20)
2	Starting position	Input	Binary(4)
3	Length to retrieve	Input	Binary(4)
4	Receiver Variable	Output	Char(*)
Optional Parameter Group			
5	API Error Data Structure	Input/Output	Struct(QUSEC)

To translate this into a prototype, the Binary(4) parameters are converted to 10i0 values, the Char(*n*) parameters (where *n* is the length) are converted to alpha character fields, and the Char(*) parameters are either data structures or large return variables whose length is established by specifying it on another parameter.

One common misconception is that Char(*) parameters are pointers; they are not pointers but rather a synonym for a character parameter of indeterminate length. The prototype for this API follows:

QUSRTVUS (Retrieve User Space Data) Prototype

```
D QusRtvUserSpaceData...
D                     PR                      EXTPGM('QUSRTVUS')
D  szUsrSpace                   20A           Const
D  nStart                       10I 0         Const
D  nLength                      10I 0         Const
D  szRtnData                 65535A           OPTIONS(*VARSIZE)
D  apiErrorDS                                 LikeDS(QUSEC_T)
D                                             OPTIONS(*VARSIZE:*NOPASS)
```

35 Understanding API Documentation — Pointer Parameters

Whenever you see API documentation that includes a parameter defined as PTR(SPP), you may specify a pointer variable for that parameter. For example, the parameters of QUSPTRUS API (Retrieve Pointer to User Space) are documented as follows:

QUSPTRUS (Retrieve Pointer to User Space Data) API Documentation

Parameter	Description	Input/Output	Type(length)
1	Qualified user space name	Input	Char(20)
2	Return pointer	Output	PTR(SPP)
3	API Error Data Structure	Input/Output (optional)	Struct(QUSEC)

The second parameter is PTR(SPP)—this is IBM notation for *space pointer*. A space pointer is used in low-level MI programming. Space pointers have been exposed to traditional programming languages (e.g., RPG IV) in the form of pointers to data—a space pointer points to data storage such as fields, data structures, arrays, or other areas on the system.

QUSPTRUS (Get Pointer to User Space) Prototype

```
D QusPTRUS        PR                  extPgm('QUSPTRUS')
D  szUserspace                  20A   Const
D  pRtnPtr                        *
D  apiErrorDS                         LikeDS(QUSEC_T)
D                                     OPTIONS(*VARSIZE:*NOPASS)
```

The second parameter is specified as a passed-by-reference pointer, because the API is returning the pointer. The API expects a field whose data-type is * (asterisk) so that it can copy the pointer to the user space data into that field. The Input/Output section of the parameter description indicates that this parameter is categorized as Output. Therefore, it should be passed by reference.

Some APIs have a slight variation of pointer-parameter declaration. For example, the C runtime function memicmp() is documented as follows:

```
int  memicmp(void* buf1, void* buf2, unsigned int cnt);
```

The parameters with the void* attribute indicate that a pointer is passed. However, because the word *const* is not specified and only one asterisk is present, the parameters are passed by reference. Therefore, RPG IV prototype may be specified using two different methods.

The first method assumes that the length of the void* parameters are known. For example, if the lengths of the first and second parameters of memicmp() were 256 characters or fewer, the following prototype could be used:

```
D memicmp         PR              10I 0 extProc('__memicmp')
D  pValue1                        256A  OPTIONS(*VARSIZE)
D  pValue2                        256A  OPTIONS(*VARSIZE)
D  nCompLen                       10U 0 Value
```

In this example, the first and second parameters are declared as normal 256-byte passed-by-reference character parameters. This style allows a regular field to be specified for parameters 1 and 2, and the respective field's address is passed to the memicmp() function.

What the API is really looking for, though, is a pointer parameter that is passed by *value*. In RPG IV, that prototype would appears as follows:

```
D memicmp         PR              10I 0 extProc('__memicmp')
D  pValue1                          *   Value
D  pValue2                          *   Value
D  nCompLen                       10U 0 Value
```

When a pointer variable (data-type *) is specified, either the %addr() built-in function or a pointer variable (also data-type *) may be specified for the parameter. The VALUE keyword on the parameter declaration causes the compiler to make a copy of the pointer and pass that copy to the memicmp() API.

All this provides for some pretty flexible methods for calling APIs, but it also adds a level of complexity that may not be as beneficial.

36 Better Performance when Accessing User Space Data

When a user space is used in an RPG IV program, the Retrieve User Space data (QUSRTVUS) API is often used to extract a subset of the data in that user space. Likewise, the Change User Space data (QUSCHGUS) API can be used to modify the content of an existing user space.

It would be much easier if we could simply access the User Space and then, using traditional RPG IV MOVE, MOVEL, and EVAL operations, manipulate it as necessary. Well, you can—but it involves pointers.

The Retrieve a Pointer to a User Space (QUSPTRUS) API allows you to retrieve a pointer to a user space, and then use that pointer to read from or write to the user space. The prototype for QUSPTRUS follows:

QUSPTRUS (Retrieve Pointer to User Space) Prototype

```
D QusPTRUS        PR                    extPgm('QUSPTRUS')
D  szUserspace                   20A    Const
D  pRtnPtr                         *
D  apiErrorDS                            LikeDS(QUSEC_T)
D                                        OPTIONS(*VARSIZE:*NOPASS)
```

This API, while somewhat complex, only requires a few lines of code, as follows:

```
D Undo            DS                        Dim(30) Qualified
D                                           Based(pUndo)
D   custno                        7P 0
D   compname                      35A
D   address                       20A
D   city                          20A
D   state                          2A
D   zipcode                       10A

 /free
     qusptrus('MYSPACE    QGPL' : pUndo : apiError);

     dou  (fKey=F3);
     exfmt  custmaint;
     if      (FKey=Enter);
       x += 1;
       undo(x).custno = custno;
       undo(x).compname = compname;
       undo(x).address = address;
       undo(x).city    = city;
       undo(x).state   = state;
       undo(x).zipcode = zipcode;

       // continue processing the transaction.
     enddo;

 /end-free
```

In this example, a pointer to the user spaced named MYSPACE in QGPL is returned. The pointer is stored in the PUNDO variable. RPG IV automatically implicitly declares this pointer variable because it appears on a BASED keyword (line 2 in the example), so there's no need for the programmer to implicitly declare it.

Once the pointer is returned, the Data Structure Array (see Tip #26) named UNDO has available storage.

The rest of the program is pretty standard—each EXTFMT transaction is posted to the UNDO buffer we recreated. Obviously, you'd have to ensure that not more than %ELEM(undo) transactions were saved.

So what's the big deal? Well, when the program ends, the user space sticks around—it is a real system object. The program could in theory be re-entered by the user, and they could actually undo the previous transactions. All a programmer would need to do is retrieve the previously stored data from the UNDO user space.

User Space objects can be as large as 16MB. They can be a fixed length that can be changed later, or they can be dynamic and automatically grow up to that 16MB in length. This should be enough space for thousands of undo transactions (as illustrated in the example). All the programmer would need to do is increase the number of elements initially specified on the DIM keyword.

37 Integer Data-types — More Efficient than Packed Decimal

What's the fastest numeric data-type on the system? You might be surprised to learn that it is Integer. That's right, contrary to the myth that Packed decimal is the fastest numeric data-type, the Integer data-type is actually the fastest. It is fastest for string operations (such as %SCAN), for looping control (such as the FOR loop), and for array indexes.

Integer is the native data-type for the iSeries and System i5. Unlike System/38, these contemporary systems have modern CPUs in them and perform best with integers. In fact, everything is converted to Integer or Floating point—not to Packed, as some believe.

Use integers for all your work variables that do not require decimal positions.

RPG supports two forms of integer data-types:

- Signed Integers—data-type I
- Unsigned Integers—data-type U

The two perform similarly. One difference is that *unsigned* integers do not recognize negative values—that is, they don't use an extra bit to indicate a negative value—whereas *signed* integers do recognize negative values and use one of their bits to indicate a negative value.

Also, signed integers have a different range of values than unsigned integers. The following two tables illustrate the range of signed and unsigned integers.

Signed Integer Sizes and Ranges — RPG Data-type I

RPG IV Size/Type	Low/High Range	Bytes of Memory Occupied	C and Java Data-type	API Docs
3I 0	–128 to 127	1	char	Bin(1) Binary(1)
5I 0	–32768 to 32767	2	short	Bin(2) Binary(2)
10I 0	–2,147,483,648 to 2,147,483,647	4	long	Bin(4) Binary(4)
20I 0	–9,223,372,036,854,775,808 to 9,223,372,036,854,775,807	8	long long	Bin(8) Binary(8)

Unsigned Integer Sizes and Ranges — RPG Data-type U

RPG IV Size/Type	Low/High Range	Bytes of Memory Occupied	C and Java Data-type	API Docs
3U 0	0 to 255	1	char	UBin(1) UBinary(1)
5U 0	0 to 65535	2	unsigned short	UBin(2) UBinary(2)
10U 0	0 to 4294967295	4	unsigned long	UBin(4) UBinary(4)
20U 0	0 to 18,446,744,073,709,551,615	8	unsigned long long	UBin(8) UBinary(8)

38 Sending a Program Message in RPG

The CL language offers easy commands for sending program messages. To accomplish this in RPG IV requires either calling an API or calling a CL program that runs the SNDPGMMSG command. The complexity of the messaging APIs often prevents people from using them. Another obstacle is that IBM put an extra stack level in programs so that simply using a target program queue of *PRV doesn't always work. But it does work... sometimes. Get the point?

To send a message from RPG IV, the QMHSNDPM (Send Program Message) API is used. When you send messages using this API to a previous invocation (up the call stack), both the Call Stack Entry parameter and the Relative Invocation parameter need to be specified.

The call-stack entry can be set to *, *CTLBDY, *EXT, *PGMBDY, and *PGMNAME. The relative invocation parameter is a numeric parameter that indicates where you want to send the message relative to the call-stack entry. In the API with ILE programs, it is normally set to one higher than you think it should be.

A simple subprocedure wrapper for the QMHSNDPM API can be a bit daunting. With programs comprising modules and subprocedures, setting the correct parameter values can be challenging. Here is the prototype for the QMHSNDPM API.

Send Program Message (QMHSNDPM) API Prototype (Subset)

```
     //  SEND Program Message API Prototype

D QMHSNDPM        PR                      extPgm('QMHSNDPM')
D  szMsgID                       7A       Const
D  szMsgFile                    20A       Const
D  szMsgData                  6000A       Const OPTIONS(*varsize)
D  nMsgDataLen                  10I 0     Const

   **  Message Type may be one of the following:
   **  *COMP    - Completion
   **  *DIAG    - Diagnostic
   **  *ESCAPE  - Escape
   **  *INFO    - Informational
   **  *INQ     - Inquiry.
   **  *NOTIFY  - Notify
   **  *RQS     - Request
   **  *STATUS  - Status
D  szMsgType                    10A       Const

   **  Call Stack Entry (ToPgmQ) may be one of the following:
   **  *        - *SAME
   **  *EXT     - The external message queue
   **  *CTLBDY  - Control Boundary
   **  *PGMBDY  - Program Boundary
   **  *PGMNAME - Program name
   **  *EXT     - External message queue
D  szCallStkEntry...
D                               10A       Const
D  nRelativeCallStackEntry...
D                               10I 0     Const
D  szRtnMsgKey                   4A
D  apiErrorDS                             LikeDS(QUSEC_T)
D                                         OPTIONS(*VARSIZE)
```

A wrapper that calls the QMHSNDPM API to send a message to *PRV can be created to give the caller of the subprocedure the feeling of using the SNDPGMMSG CL command without the command definition—or the overhead of CL.

The wrapper that I've created allows you to send an impromptu message from within RPG IV using parameters similar to that of the SNDMSG CL command. Here is the syntax of this subprocedure:

```
SNDMSG( 'message text' [ : msgtype [ : topgmq ] ] )
```

The *message text* parameter can be any text up to 1,024 bytes long and is required.

The *msgtype* (message type) parameter may be any of the available message types (in all uppercase)—for example, *INFO, *COMP, *DIAG, *ESCAPE, and *STATUS. The default, if unspecified, is *INFO.

The *topgmq* (to program queue) parameter identifies the relative program queue to which the message is sent. If unspecified, it default is *SAME (which is represented internally as '*').

The following call to SNDMSG displays a status message on the screen until it is cleared or another status message is issued.

```
/free
      sndmsg('Searching for past due invoices':'*STATUS');
/end-free
```

Unlike a native RPG IV built-in function, subprocedures are not able to accept user-written special values for parameters. When the '*STATUS' value is used with this subprocedure, the value must be enclosed in single quotes and specified in all uppercase.

One thing I like to use this wrapper for is writing information to the joblog to help with debugging:

```
/free
    Chain custno custmast;
    if NOT %Found();
        sndmsg('Customer ' + %char(custno) + ' Not found.');
    endif;
/end-free
```

The above code logs its message to the joblog at the same invocation level as the caller of the SNDMSG procedure.

There are a couple of additional features of the SNDMSG subprocedure: The TOPGMQ parameter allows you to specify *PRV or *PRVPGM. Specifying TOGPGMQ(*PRV) sends the message to the caller of the procedure that is running SNDMSG. Specifying TOPGMQ(*PRVPGM) sends the message to the previous program. Using SNDMSG('hello' : '*INFO' : '*PRV') from within the main line Calculations of an RPG IV program causes the message to be sent to the current program's PEP (program entry procedure) and not to the previous program. Use *PRVPGM to send messages to the previous program and *PRV to send them to the previous subprocedure.

The SNDMSG subprocedure source code follows.

SNDMSG Subprocedure — QMHSNDPM API Wrapper

```
 H OPTION(*NODEBUGIO:*SRCSTMT)
  /IF DEFINED(*CRTBNDRPG)
 H   DFTACTGRP(*NO) BNDDIR('RPGTNT/RPGTNT')
  /ELSE
 H   NOMAIN
  /ENDIF

  /INCLUDE RPGTNT/QCPYSRC,rpgtnt

 D SndMsg          PR             4A
 D  szMsg                      1024A    Const Varying
 D  szMsgType                    10A    Const
 D                                      OPTIONS(*NOPASS)
 D  szToPgmQ                     10A    Const
 D                                      OPTIONS(*NOPASS)
```

Continued...

…continued

```
/IF DEFINED(*CRTBNDRPG)
/free
  sndmsg('Hello World!' );
  eval *INLR = *ON;
  return;
/end-free
/ENDIF

P SndMsg            B                 Export
**********************************************
**  Send an impromptu message to a pgmq
**********************************************
   //   2006 by Robert Cozzi, Jr.
   //   Origin: www.RPGxTools.com
   //   Permission to use is hereby granted
   //   provided this notice is included
   //   in its entirety.
**********************************************
D SndMsg           PI              4A
D  msg                          1024A  Const Varying
D  szMsgType                      10A  Const
D                                      OPTIONS(*NOPASS)
D  szToPgmQ                       10A  Const
D                                      OPTIONS(*NOPASS)

**********************************************
/include qsysinc/qrpglesrc,qusec
**********************************************
**  Local variables.
D msgType          S                   Like(szMsgType) Inz('*INFO')
D toPgmQ           S                   Like(szToPgmQ)  Inz('*')

D msgid            S               7A  Inz('CPF9897')
D msgf             DS             21
D  MsgFile                        10A  Inz('QCPFMSG')
D  MsgLib                         10A  Inz('*LIBL')
D
D msgData          S            1024A
D nDataLen         S             10I 0 Inz(0)
D nRelInv          S             10I 0 Inz(1)
D nIncInv          S             10I 0 Inz(1)
D RtnMsgKey        S              4A
D myAPIErrorDS     DS                  LikeDS(QUSEC)

C                  eval          myApiErrorDS = *ALLX'00'

C                  if            %Parms()>=2
C                  eval          msgType = szMsgType
C                  if            %subst(msgType:1:1)<>'*'
C                  eval          msgType = '*' + %TrimL(msgType)
C                  endif
C                  endif
```

Continued…

…continued

```
C                     if        %Parms()>= 3
C                     if        szToPgmQ <> *BLANKS
C                     eval      toPgmQ= szToPgmQ
C                     endif
C                     if        toPgmQ = '*SAME'
C                     eval      toPgmQ = '*'
C                     endif
C                     endif

     // Status messages always go ToPgmQ(*EXT)
C                     if        msgType = '*STATUS'
C                     eval      toPgmQ = '*EXT'
C                     endif

C                     if        msgType = '*'
C                     eval      msgType = '*INFO'
C                     endif

     // Get the length of the message to be sent.
C                     eval      msgData = %Trim(msg)
C                     eval      nDataLen = %len(%Trim(msg))

C                     Select
 **   *SAME
C                     when      toPgmQ  = ' '
C                               or toPgmQ = '*SAME'
C                               or toPgmQ = '*'
C                     eval      toPgmQ = '*'
C                     eval      nRelInv = 0
C                     eval      nIncInv = 1
 **   *PRV, *PRVPRC or *PRVPROC
C                     when      toPgmQ = '*PRVPRC'
C                               or toPgmQ = '*PRVPROC'
C                               or toPgmQ = '*PRV'
C                     eval      toPgmQ = '*'
C                     eval      nRelInv = 1
C                     eval      nIncInv = 1
 **   *PRVPGM
C                     When      toPgmQ = '*PRVPGM'
C                     eval      toPgmQ = '*CTLBDY'
C                     eval      nRelInv = 0
C                     eval      nIncInv = 1
 **   *CTLBDY
C                     when      toPgmQ = '*CTLBDY'
C                     eval      nIncInv = 2
 **   *EXT
C                     when      toPgmQ = '*EXT'
C                     eval      nRelInv = 0
C                     endsl

 **   Since we're a relative invocation, and we are
 **   one-level deep, we need to bump up the relative
 **   invocation by the calculated increment.
C                     eval      nRelInv = nRelInv + nIncInv
```

Continued…

…continued

```
C                     callp(e)  QMHSNDPM(msgid    : msgf :
C                                        msgData : nDataLen :
C                                        msgType   :
C                                        toPgmQ    :
C                                        nRelInv   :
C                                        rtnMsgKey :
C                                        myAPIErrorDS)

C                     return    rtnMsgKey
P SndMsg            E
```

39 Retrieve the Function Key Used on a Display File

For decades, programmers have used *response indicators* to signal the Command or Function key pressed by a user. There are two major problems with this approach: it uses an indicator, and there is no indication which of the two keys was actually pressed.

For just as long as there have been interactive programs, there has been the File Information Data Structure or INFDS. The INFDS is assigned to files in RPG and contains information about the status of the file. For Display files, the INFDS is often referred to as the *Workstation Data Structure* or *WSDS*.

Whenever a display file record is returned to the RPG program, the WSDS is updated. In position 369 within the WSDS, "attention identification bytes" is set to the scan code for the function key used to return control to the program. Each of the function keys as well as the other entry keys—such as ENTER, HELP, HOME, PRINT, PageUp, and PageDown—returns a unique scan code that identifies that it was used to return control to the program.

No response indicators are assigned to the key in the DDS when this technique is employed. Only the function key needs to be specified. Of course, if the response indicator is already there, you may certainly ignore it, and everything will work fine. Position 369 of the WSDS is always updated regardless of the use of response indicators in the DDS, as follows:

```
     A                                          INDARA
     A                                          CAØ3 CF12
     A                                          CFØ4
     A                                          CFØ5
     A            R CUSTMAINT                   CLRL(*NO)
```

This is great news, because it not only eliminates the use of an indicator (or ten!), but it also allows you to check for the specific key itself.

Use the INFDS Position 369 to Retrieve the Function Key ID Code

```
FEDITCUST   CF   E              Workstn INFDS(WSDS)

D WSDS            DS
D FKey                         1A   Overlay(WSDS:369)
```

The scan codes that are returned to position 369 have been published in my best-selling RPG IV book, *The Modern RPG IV Language* (from MC Press) for more than a decade; I've reproduced them here in the interest of completeness.

Function Key Scan Codes

```
     *********************************************************
     ** (c) Copyright 1989 - 2003 by Robert Cozzi, Jr.    **
     *********************************************************
     **   Description  . . . . . Function key named constants **
     **   Features . . . . . . . The Scan Code of each     **
     **                          each function key.        **
     *********************************************************
.....DName++++++++++ETDsFrom+++To/L+++IDc.Keywords++++++++++++
     D F1             C              CONST(X'31')
     D F2             C              CONST(X'32')
     D F3             C              CONST(X'33')
     D F4             C              CONST(X'34')
     D F5             C              CONST(X'35')
     D F6             C              CONST(X'36')
     D F7             C              CONST(X'37')
     D F8             C              CONST(X'38')
     D F9             C              CONST(X'39')
     D F10            C              CONST(X'3A')
     D F11            C              CONST(X'3B')
     D F12            C              CONST(X'3C')
     D F13            C              CONST(X'B1')
     D F14            C              CONST(X'B2')
     D F15            C              CONST(X'B3')
     D F16            C              CONST(X'B4')
     D F17            C              CONST(X'B5')
     D F18            C              CONST(X'B6')
     D F19            C              CONST(X'B7')
     D F20            C              CONST(X'B8')
     D F21            C              CONST(X'B9')
     D F22            C              CONST(X'BA')
     D F23            C              CONST(X'BB')
     D F24            C              CONST(X'BC')
     D CLEAR          C              CONST(X'BD')
     D ENTER          C              CONST(X'F1')
     D HELP           C              CONST(X'F3')
     D PAGEUP         C              CONST(X'F4')
     D PAGEDOWN       C              CONST(X'F5')
     D ROLLDOWN       C              CONST(X'F4')
     D ROLLUP         C              CONST(X'F5')
     D PRINT          C              CONST(X'F6')
     D RECBACKSP      C              CONST(X'F8')
     D AUTENT         C              CONST(X'3F')
```

To detect which function key was used to return control to the RPG IV program, compare position 369 of the INFDS to one of these named constants as follows:

```
C                          DOW       FKey <> F3
C                          EXFMT     CustMaint
C                          SELECT
C                          When      FKey = F12
C                          Callp     previous()
C                          When      FKey = F3
C                          exsr      Exit
C                          When      FKey = F5
C                          Callp     Rollback(1)
C                          endSL
C                          endDo
```

In the example above, the FKEY subfield of the WSDS is used to compare against each expected function key. When a match is found, the corresponding routine is called.

40 Copying More than 64k of Data

RPG is a great language for processing data, yet some fundamental features are surprisingly limited. One is the ability to declare a field longer than 64k in length. While this "limit" is adequate for about 95 percent of the applications being developed today, what about the 5 percent that require longer data manipulation? A simple application needing to process HTML or XML could easily need to copy more than 64k of data.

Copying more than 64k of data requires that you use non-RPG functions, such as the C memcpy() (memory copy) or MI cpybytes() (copy bytes) functions. To use these functions in RPG IV, specify the binding directory BNDDIR('QC2LE') on the Header specification (see Tip #28) of the source member in which they will be called, and then prototype them as follows:

Prototype for the C Runtime memcpy() Function

```
D memcpy          PR                     extProc('__memcpy')
D  pTarget                        *      Value
D  pSource                        *      Value
D  nLength                      10U 0    Value
```

Prototype for the MI CPYBYTES Function

```
D cpybytes        PR                     extProc('_CPYBYTES')
D  pTarget                        *      Value
D  pSource                        *      Value
D  nLength                      10U 0    Value
```

Note that there are *two* underscores in front of memcpy() and only *one* underscore in front of CPYBYTES(). Also, the memcpy() function name is in all lowercase, whereas the CPYBYTES() is in all uppercase.

The memcpy() function is the safest to use. However, CPYBYTES() is the fastest. Data being copied with cpybytes() is restricted in that it cannot contain pointers. If it does, the copied pointer values are invalidated.

For example, a data structure or array contains a pointer. When that data structure is copied with memcpy(), it is copied accurately. When copied with CPYBYTES(), the data is copied *but* the pointer integrity at the new location is lost. Copied pointers cannot be used as a pointer.

Since CPYBYTES() avoids checking for pointers in the data being copied, it performs copies faster than memcpy(). For short data sets (fewer than several hundred kilobytes in length), the performance difference between these two functions is negligible.

Both these functions use the address of a variable instead of the variable name itself. This means you need to enclose the variable names in the %addr(*varname*) built-in function (where *varname* is the name of the field or data structure being copied). Alternatively, a pointer variable may be used instead of %addr(*varname*).

Copy Big Memory Using memcpy()

```
H BNDDIR('QC2LE') DFTACTGRP(*NO)

D memcpy          PR                    extProc('__memcpy')
D  pTarget                        *     Value
D  pSource                        *     Value
D  nLength                      10U 0 Value

D ptr             S              *
D parts           S          65535A  Dim(10)

 /free
       ptr = %alloc(%size(parts:*ALL)); // Get some storage

       // Copy the data structure to the new memory.
       memcpy(ptr : %addr(parts) : %size(parts:*ALL));
       // Do something with the data
       dealloc ptr;  // Free up the allocated memory.

       *INLR = *ON;
       return;
 /end-free
```

41 Use %XFOOT with %LEN

To calculate the number of bytes of storage that an entire array occupies, the %SIZE built-in function may be used. Include the second parameter *ALL on %SIZE to retrieve the number of bytes of memory the entire array occupies:

```
D names             S              20A    Dim(5)
D arrSize           S               5U 0

/free
      arrsize = %size(names : *ALL);
/end-free
```

For a character array, this is pretty straightforward. Five elements times 20 bytes per element equals an array size of 100 bytes. But what about arrays with numeric elements?

If an array is defined with 10 elements, and each element is a 9-position packed value, what is the size of the array? For an example, see the following:

```
D qty               S               9P 0 Dim(10)
D bytes             S               5U 0
D allBytes          S               5U 0
/free
      bytes = %size(qty);  // size of a single array element.
      allBytes = %size(qty : *ALL);  // size of entire array.
/end-free
```

Using %SIZE *without* *ALL, the size of a single element is returned. A 9-digit packed field is stored in 5 bytes of storage; therefore, %SIZE(QTY) returns 5. Using %SIZE *with* the *ALL parameter returns the length of the entire array, or 5 times 10 (50) in our example.

Length versus Size

The declared *length* of a packed or integer variable or array element is different from its declared *size*. When the length of an array element is needed, use the %LEN built-in function to return the declared length. When the number of bytes of storage occupied by a field or array element is needed, use the %SIZE built-in function. For an example, see the following:

```
D qty              S                  9P 0 Dim(10)
D Len              S                 10I 0
 /free
    len = %len(qty);
 /end-free
```

The LEN field is set to 9, which is the declared length of the QTY array elements. Unlike %SIZE, the %LEN built-in function does not support an *ALL parameter. Therefore, another approach must be taken, and this is where %XFOOT comes in.

An anomaly of %XFOOT is that if it encloses a %LEN built-in function that further encloses an array, the %XFOOT built-in function will add up the declared lengths of the array elements. For an example, see the following:

Use %XFOOT to Calculate Total Length of All Array Elements

```
D QTY              S                  9P 0 Dim(10)
D totDigits        S                 10I 0
D totSize          S                 10I 0
 /free
    totDigits = %XFOOT(%len(QTY)); // Result is 90
    totSize   = %size(QTY:*ALL);   // Result is 50
 /end-free
```

The %XFOOT built-in function magically adds up the lengths of each of the array elements for the array specified within the %LEN built-in function.

For arrays with character elements, the length and size are identical unless the VARYING keyword is used. In this case, the technique can be used to calculate the current length of each of the variable length elements in the array as follows:

Use %XFOOT with VARYING Array Elements

```
D NAMES            S                 20A  Dim(20) VARYING
D totLen           S                 10I 0
 /free
    names(1) = 'Bob';
    names(2) = 'Bobby';
    names(3) = 'Robert';

    totLen = %XFoot(%len(names));
        // Only elems 1 to 3 have data
        // Elems 4 to 20 are empty
        // totLen is equal to 14
 /end-free
```

Here, the array NAMES has three elements that contain data. Since VARYING fields that do *not* contain data have a current length of zero, only the lengths of the three elements *with* data are cross-footed by %XFOOT.

Another option is the %SUBARR built-in function (added in OS/400 V5R3). This built-in function allows an array to be subscripted, which allows you to add up the lengths of the array elements you want; for example:

Use %XFOOT with %SUBARR to Sum Up Lengths of Elements 1 to 2

```
D NAMES            S               20A    Dim(20) VARYING
D totLen           S               10I 0
 /free
    names(1) = 'Bob';
    names(2) = 'Bobby';
    names(3) = 'Robert';

    totLen = %XFoot(%Len(%subarr(names:1:2)));
         // Only elems 1 to 2 are used
         // totLen is equal to 8
 /end-free
```

In this example, %XFOOT adds up the current lengths of array elements 1 and 2 of the NAMES array. The elements whose lengths are being accumulated are identified in parameters 2 and 3 of the %SUBARR built-in function.

42 Use %SUBARR to Subscript Arrays

Late in the life of RPG IV (not until OS/400 V5R3), the %SUBARR (subscript array) built-in function was added. This built-in function allows a portion of an array (a subset of its elements) to be used just like the array itself. This built-in function "fakes out" any opcode or other built-in function that uses it by making it think it is working with an array of the number of elements specified. Subscripted elements can be cross-footed, sorted, or searched. The syntax of %SUBARR is as follows:

```
%SUBARR( array  : start-element [ : number-of-elements ] )
```

Anywhere an array can be specified (in Calculation specifications), the %SUBARR built-in function can be used. The only exception is with the %LOOKUP*xx*() built-in functions, which already incorporate array subscripting into their own syntax.

The quintessential use for %SUBARR is with the SORTA opcode. If only 50 elements of a 2,000-element array are to be sorted, %SUBARR can help:

Sort 50 Elements of a Large Array

```
D custsales        S              9P 0 Dim(2000)
 /free
     sorta %subarr(custSales:51:50);
 /end-free
```

Elements 51 to 100 of the CUSTSALES array are sorted using SORTA. Elements 1 to 50 and 101 to 2000 are unaltered by the operation.

43 Use EXTFILE to Avoid Needless Overrides

RPG IV allows you to specify file names that the program uses on the File Description specification. The EXTFILE keyword and EXTMBR keyword may be used to specify a runtime file or member name that differs from the compile-time file name. This allows you to avoid issuing OVRDBF commands in CL. However, additional override attributes still require the use of OVRDBF.

EXTFILE and EXTMBR to Override Runtime File, Library Member

```
Fcustomer  IF   E           K DISK    EXTFILE('OELIB/CUSTMAST')
F                                      EXTMBR('DIV7')
```

Here, the file *CUSTMAST* in the OELIB library is opened at runtime. The member that is open is DIV7. Within the RPG source, however, the CUSTOMER file name (positions 7 to 20) is used to access the file.

The file name specified in positions 7 to 20 must exist at compile-time. The compiler uses this file name for the external definition and for all file accesses in the program or module. The actual file being processed, however, is the CUSTMAST file in the OELIB library as specified on the EXTFILE keyword.

What about Overrides?

When EXTFILE is used, the file is opened directly; an override (OVRDBF) command is not used internally to redirect the file. To see which file is open, use the Open Files option on the WRKJOB (Work with Job) display.

If an override is applied to the file name in positions 7 to 20 of the File specification, it is ignored. Overrides to the file name specified on the EXTFILE keyword are applied as usual.

EXTFILE Syntax

The syntax for the EXTFILE keyword is the same as that of a qualified object name used in CL or on Command Entry, as follows:

```
[LIBRARY/ ] FILE
```

The file name may be specified by itself or it may be qualified to a library name. If qualified, the library name must precede the file name, and it must be connected to the file name using a forward slash (/).

The EXTFILE keyword accepts either a literal value enclosed in quotes or a field name. The actual file and library name must be in uppercase; otherwise, a runtime error may be issued.

If a variable is specified, it must be a 21-position, fixed-length character field or data structure. Those 21 positions make it large enough to accept a 10-position file name, a 10-position library name and the 1-byte qualifier (i.e., the forward slash).

The following list contains examples of several valid file name formats for the EXTFILE keyword. If specified as a literal, the file name must be enclosed in quotes; if a variable is specified, the file name may not be quoted.

- 'CUSTMAST'—the file name itself enclosed in quotes
- '*LIBL/CUSTMAST'—the file name qualified to *LIBL and enclosed in quotes
- 'OELIB/CUSTMAST'—the file name qualified to a library name and enclosed in quotes
- *VARNAME*—a field name whose attributes must be 21-positions and character; contains the filename

When a field name is used in the *VARNAME*, the file name must be specified in the field using one of the other three syntaxes. As mentioned, quotes are *not* specified when using a field name.

When a variable is used with the EXTFILE keyword, it must contain a file name before the file is open. If it does not contain the file, a runtime error is generated.

Since the RPG Cycle opens files at a given point in the program start-up code—regardless of whether or not the RPG Cycle is used for program logic—either the field used with EXTFILE must contain the name of the file before the program starts *or* the file must include the USROPN keyword and be opened manually.

To populate the field used by the EXTFILE or EXTMBR keyword with a file or member name before it is opened by the RPG Cycle, you have several options:

- Initialize the field with the file name when the field is defined on the Definition specifications.
- Pass the file and/or member name as parameters and use those parameters as the field names of the EXTFILE or EXTMBR keywords.
- IMPORT the field name used by the EXTFILE or EXTMBR keywords from another module, populating it with the file and/or member name before calling the first subprocedure in the module.

The other choice is to control when the file is opened using the USROPN (User Controlled Open) keyword. Specify USROPN on the File specification for the file that uses EXTFILE or EXTMBR keywords as follows:

Using an Initial Value via *INZSR with EXTFILE

```
FCUSTOMER   IF   E              K DISK      ExtFile(custfile) USROPN

Dcustfile        S              21A

C                     open      CUSTOMER

CSR    *INZSR         BEGSR
C                     eval      custfile = 'OELIB/CUSTMAST'
CSR    ENDINZ         ENDSR
```

In this example, the file name is moved into the CUSTFILE variable at runtime within the *INZSR subroutine. When the Detail Calculations begin (after returning from *INZSR), the file is open via the OPEN opcode.

Another option is to specify the file name in a variable passed as a parameter to the program, as follows:

Using a Parameter Variable with EXTFILE

```
FCUSTOMER   IF   E              K DISK      extFile(custfile)

Dcustfile        S              21A

C      *ENTRY         PLIST
C                     PARM                  CUSTFILE
```

Because references to parameter values are established before the RPG Cycle opens files, file names may be passed to programs as parameters, even when USROPN is not used.

The final option is to specify the file name in a variable that is imported into the module.

In the following example, two source members are created. Each is compiled into a *MODULE and then bound together using CRTPGM. Module 1 exports the CUSTFILE field. CUSTFILE is a 21-position variable that is set to the name of the file to be opened by a subprocedure in Module 2 as follows:

Module 1: Set Up a Variable for EXPORT

```
Dcustfile            S              21A    EXPORT
 /free
    if appCode = 'O';
      custfile = 'OELIB/CUSTMAST';
    elseif appCode = 'A';
      custfile = 'APLIB/CUSTMAST';
    else;
      custfile = 'ARLIB/CUSTMAST';
    endif;
         //  Now call a subproc in the
         //  module that has the EXTFILE keyword.
    CustReport(fromDate : toDate );
 /end-free
```

Here, CUSTFILE is declared as a 21-position character field and is exported by adding the EXPORT keyword to the definition. Then, based on the value of the APPCODE field, the name of the file to be opened is copied to the CUSTFILE field.

The final step is to call the CUSTREPORT() subprocedure:

Module 2: Import the File Name Variable

```
H NOMAIN OPTION(*NODEBUGIO:*SRCSTMT)
FCUSTOMER   IF   E          K DISK      extFile(custfile)
F                                       PREFIX('CM.')

D CM                  DS               LikeRec(CUSTREC)
Dcustfile             S         21A    IMPORT

P CustReport          B                Export
D CustReport          PI
D   startDate                   D      Const DATFMT(*ISO)
D   endDate                     D      Const DATFMT(*ISO)
 /free
      setll startDate customer;
      read customer;
      dow not %EOF();
         // Range check the due date.
         if CM.DUEDATE >= startDate
            and CM.DUEDATE <= endDate;
           printAgingLineItem(CM.CustNo:CM.TRNNBR);
         endif;
         read customer;
      enddo;
      return;
 /end-free
P CustReport          E
```

In our example, the file named CUSTOMER is declared as an Input file and includes the EXTFILE keyword. The field named CUSTFILE is specified as the parameter for that keyword. CUSTFILE is declared on the Definition specifications as a 21-position character field. The IMPORT keyword is also specified. This indicates that the field has actually been declared in another source member. Its memory location (i.e., its address) is imported into this source member rather than being assigned to new storage. Consequently, the field shares its storage location with the field of the same name from Module 1.

When the first subprocedure in Module 2 is called (CUSTREPORT in our example), the mini-RPG Cycle is called and automatically opens the declared files. Since CUSTFILE has already been set to a file name, that file is actually open. Subsequent calls to CUSTREPORT will use the same file regardless of the file in the CUSTFILE field *unless* the file is explicitly closed and then reopened with a new file name.

44 Subprocedure Parameters Rule 1 — Default Behavior

To pass parameters to subprocedures, define the parameter on the subprocedure's procedure interface. This is similar to the way a data structure subfield is declared. In the following example, the MSG parameter is defined on the SNDMSG subprocedure.

```
P SndMsg           B                      Export
D SndMsg           PI              4A
D   msg                          10A

   //   implementation goes here.

P SndMsg           E
```

The MSG parameter is a simple 10-position character value. The default rules for character parameters allow a value to be passed that is at least as long as the parameter definition. Therefore, a parameter that is declared as a 10-position character value accepts fields of 10-bytes or longer. The compiler rejects shorter values.

This rule applies to character parameters of any length, whether 1 byte, 10 bytes, 64k, or any other size.

When a parameter is defined as a numeric value, the default behavior is that the value passed on that parameter must have the same attributes (data-type and length) as the numeric parameter definition. For example, if a parameter is defined as Packed(7,2), only Packed(7,2) values may be specified for that parameter.

Again, this is the default behavior as long as no additional parameter definition keywords—such as VALUE, CONST, or OPTIONS(*VARSIZE)—have been specified.

45 Subprocedure Parameters Rule 2 — CONST Parameters

If the value passed on a parameter to a subprocedure will not be modified by the subprocedure, you can add the CONST keyword to the parameter definition:

Using CONST on Parameter Definitions

```
P SndMsg          B                        Export
D SndMsg          PI              4A
D  msg                         1024A   Const
D  len                          10I 0  Const
  //    implementation goes here.

P SndMsg          E
```

The MSG parameter is declared as a 1024-byte character value and includes the CONST keyword. The LEN parameter is an integer (10i0) and also includes the CONST keyword.

Any parameter that includes the CONST keyword becomes read-only and cannot be modified within the subprocedure. The caller can rest assured that the data passed on the parameter will not be changed by the subprocedure.

There are additional features or advantages when using CONST with parameters:

- The value passed on the parameter may be shorter or longer than the declared length of the parameter.
- Variable-length fields (those declared with the VARYING keyword) may be passed to fixed-length (non-VARYING) parameters and are automatically converted to fixed-length.

- Fixed-length fields (character fields without the VARYING keyword) may be passed to VARYING parameters and are automatically converted to VARYING length fields.
- A quoted character string literal or named constant may be specified for character parameters. Numeric literals or named constants may be specified for numeric parameters.
- An expression, including the return value of another subprocedure, may be specified on the parameter.
- A numeric value specified for a numeric parameter is automatically converted into the format and type of the prototype definition. This allows expressions, literals, and fields of other lengths or numeric data-types to be specified—reducing the number of work fields that are needed.

When I create a subprocedure, I create a habit of including the CONST keyword for each parameter definition *except* those I know will be modified within the subprocedure.

46 Subprocedure Parameters Rule 3 — VARYING

When a character parameter of a subprocedure could be any length, it is often advantageous to make the parameter VARYING. This allows a variable-length field to be passed to the parameter and the length to be determined within the subprocedure using the %LEN() built-in function:

Using VARYING on Parameter Definitions

```
P SndMsg          B                      Export
D SndMsg          PI              4A
D   msg                        1024A      VARYING
  //    subproc implementation goes here.

P SndMsg          E
```

A restriction is introduced when VARYING is used without CONST or VALUE: You are restricted to passing only VARYING fields to VARYING parameters. Since most fields used in RPG are fixed-length, it is a rare situation when a VARYING-only parameter is necessary.

By adding the CONST keyword to a VARYING parameter, you indicate that both varying and fixed-length values are to be passed on the parameter:

Using VARYING and CONST on Parameter Definitions

```
P SndMsg          B                      Export
D SndMsg          PI              4A
D   msg                        1024A      Const VARYING
  //    implementation goes here.

P SndMsg          E
```

The downside to using CONST on a parameter definition is that the parameter becomes read-only; one major benefit is that fixed-length fields or varying-length character fields may be passed on the parameter. Using CONST also allows literals to be passed on the parameter.

When a VARYING parameter is received in the subprocedure, it is a VARYING field. Therefore the %LEN() built-in function can be used to retrieve the length of the value passed on the parameter. When a varying field is passed, the current length of that varying-length field is passed as the parameter length. When a fixed-length field is passed, the length of the that field (its defined length) is used to set the current length of the varying-length parameter. Often when calling a subprocedure, it is advantageous to wrap fixed-length parameter values in the %TRIMR() built-in function to strip the trailing blanks. The data length is used as the current length of the varying parameter.

47 Subprocedure Parameters Rule 4 — Optional Parameters

By default, a parameter of a subprocedure is required. The compiler issues a compile-time error if a parameter is not specified when the subprocedure is called.

To make a parameter optional, the OPTIONS(*NOPASS) keyword must be added to the parameter definition. OPTIONS(*NOPASS) allows the subprocedure to be called without specifying a value for the parameter.

A normal subprocedure with three parameters is defined as follows:

```
P SndMsg          B                         Export
D SndMsg          PI             4A
D   msg                       1024A    Const Varying
D   msgType                     10A    Const
D   toPgmQ                      10A    Const
   //    implementation goes here.

P SndMsg          E
```

In this example, all three parameters are required by the definition of the subprocedure— that is, none of them includes OPTIONS(*NOPASS).

The second and third parameters (MSGTYPE and TOPGMQ), however, are *not* required by this subprocedure. To change their definitions so that they become optional, add the OPTIONS(*NOPASS) keyword:

Using OPTIONS(*NOPASS) to Declare Optional Parameters

```
D SndMsg          PI              4A
D   msg                        1024A   Const Varying
D   msgType                      10A   Const OPTIONS(*NOPASS)
D   toPgmQ                       10A   Const OPTIONS(*NOPASS)
```

The first parameter is required, so it does not include the OPTIONS(*NOPASS) keyword. The second and third parameters are optional and, therefore, contain the OPTIONS(*NOPASS) keyword.

When a parameter contains OPTIONS(*NOPASS), all parameters that follow it are required to include OPTIONS(*NOPASS). This is a key point that is often overlooked—and one that will produce compile-time errors.

If a subprocedure supports (for example) up to 3 parameters and parameter 2 is optional, then, logically, parameter 3 must also be optional. Likewise, if a subprocedure supports 12 parameters and the optional parameters begin with parameter 5, then parameters 5 through 12 must be optional *and* OPTIONS(*NOPASS).

When OPTIONS(*NOPASS) is applied to the second and third parameters of the SNDMSG subprocedure, it allows you to call it using any of the following forms:

- sndmsg('Hello World!');
- sndmsg('Hello World!' : '*INFO');
- sndmsg('Hello World!' : '*INFO' : '*PRV');

The SNDMSG subprocedure may be called with the 1, 2, or 3 parameter specified. It is up to the subprocedure to use the %PARMS() built-in function to determine the number of parameters passed to the subprocedure.

That a parameter is optional does not imply that it may be skipped. If parameter 2 is *not* needed but parameter 3 *is* needed, then parameters 2 and 3 must be specified. For example, the following statement is invalid:

```
sndmsg('Hello World!' :   : '*PRV');
```

By default, skipping a parameter is not allowed. To learn how to define a parameter that can be skipped, see Tip #48.

48 Subprocedure Parameters Rule 5 — Skipping Parameters

An optional parameter is one type of parameter (see Tip #47), but you can also declare parameters that may be skipped—for example, if parameter 2 is *not* needed but parameter 3 *is* needed, you *can* skip over parameter 2 and specify only parameter 3.

To do this, specify OPTIONS(*OMIT) on the parameter(s) you want to skip. This allows you to skip the parameters when they are not needed and specify a value only when they are needed.

Skipped parameters, however, are still required. If parameter 2 is not needed but parameter 3 is needed, a reserved or special value must be passed for parameter 2. That value is referred to as a *null value* or *null pointer*. To specify a null value for a parameter in RPG IV, the *OMIT figurative constant is provided. Simply specify *OMIT for the skipped parameter in place of any real parameter value.

Skipped parameters are officially referred to as an "omitted parameter." Most other languages use a variation of the word "NULL" but RPG IV uses *OMIT as follows:

```
sndmsg('Hello World!' : *OMIT : '*PRV');
```

The value *OMIT is specified for the second parameter. Note that *OMIT is not enclosed in quotes.

Since the SNDMSG subprocedure already includes the *NOPASS option, adding *OMIT to it requires a slightly different syntax:

Use OPTIONS(*OMIT) to Allow Parameter Skipping

```
     P SndMsg              B                    Export
     D SndMsg              PI            4A
     D   msg                          1024A      Const Varying
     D   msgType                        10A      Const OPTIONS(*NOPASS:*OMIT)
     D   toPgmQ                         10A      Const OPTIONS(*NOPASS)
        //   implementation goes here.

     P SndMsg              E
```

The OPTIONS keyword is specified as OPTIONS(*NOPASS:*OMIT). This means that both *NOPASS and *OMIT options are applied to the second parameter. Unlike *NOPASS, however, any parameter may include OPTIONS(*OMIT) without affecting other parameters. So while OPTIONS(*NOPASS:*OMIT) is very common, OPTIONS(*OMIT) is also perfectly acceptable.

To take advantage of this capability inside the subprocedure, test the input parameter for the *OMIT value. To do this (and this is where it gets a bit inconsistent), compare the address of the parameter to *NULL. Yes, ironically, *NULL is used to check for *OMIT parameters. If the parameter's address is equal to *NULL, then *OMIT was specified for the parameter:

```
if %parms() >=2;
   if %addr(msgType) <> *NULL;
      // A value for msgType is specified
   endif;
endif;
```

Before testing the address of the parameter for *NULL, it's important to make sure that the parameter has been specified. After all, most *OMIT parameters are also optional parameters; therefore, you have to make sure a value is specified before attempting to read the address of the parameter.

To make sure the parameter was passed (as *OMIT or a real value), use the %PARMS built-in function. This built-in function returns the number of parameters passed to the subprocedure. A more complete example follows:

Test for an Omitted Parameter

```
P SndMsg         B                       Export
D SndMsg         PI              4A
D   msg                       1024A      Const Varying
D   msgType                     10A      Const OPTIONS(*NOPASS:*OMIT)
D   toPgmQ                      10A      Const OPTIONS(*NOPASS)
 /free
     if %parms() >= 2;
       if %addr(msgType) <> *NULL;
         // A value for msgType is specified
       else;
         // No message type.
       endif;
     else;
       // No message type.
     endif;

P SndMsg         E
```

Testing for Omitted Parameters before V5R1

Before V5R1, %addr(msgType) would not work when a parameter was CONST due to a feature missing from the compiler. This meant that CONST parameters could not have their addresses tested. To circumvent this shortcoming, the CEETSTA API could be used to test a parameter for *OMIT regardless of the type of parameter sent to the subprocedure; for example:

```
 //   Prototype for CEETSTA
    D IsParmOmitted    PR                        extProc('CEETSTA')
    D  bNotOmitted                     10I 0
    D  nParmNum                        10I 0 Const
    D  szParmError                     12A   OPTIONS(*OMIT)

       // SNDMSG Subprocedure Implementation
    P SndMsg           B                         Export
    D SndMsg           PI               4A
    D  msg                           1024A   Const Varying
    D  msgType                         10A   Const OPTIONS(*NOPASS:*OMIT)
    D  toPgmQ                          10A   Const OPTIONS(*NOPASS)

     // Omitted flag for the OPTION(*OMIT) parameter(s).
    D bP2              S               10I 0

     /free
        if %parms() >= 2
           isParmOmitted(bP2 : 2 : *OMIT)
           if bP2 = 1;
              // A value for msgType is specified
           else;
              // No message type.
           endif;
        else;
           // No message type.
        endif;

    P SndMsg           E
```

Here, the CEETSTA API is called to verify if parameter 2 was passed as *OMIT. When running V5R1 or later, the %ADDR(myParm) = *NULL method is preferred.

After calling CEETSTA, the field bP2 contains 0 if *OMIT was passed on the parameter or 1 if a value was specified.

Either of the above techniques should work using V5R1 and later.

49 Data Structure Templates

RPG IV supports declaring a variable based on the attributes of another variable by using the LIKE keyword. Beginning with V5R1, you can accomplish the same thing with data structures by specifying the LIKEDS keyword, as follows:

Use LIKEDS to Use a Data Structure Template

```
D order           DS                        INZ
D  item                          5A
D  qtyord                        5P 0
D  price                         7P 2

D myOrders        DS                     LikeDS(ORDER)
```

The data structure named ORDER is a typical data structure. Another data structure, MYORDERS, is also declared. It is defined based on the ORDER data structure using the LIKEDS keyword.

When this technique is applied, the new data structure (MYORDERS in the example) is defined with the same subfields as the ORDER data structure. In addition, MYORDERS is implicitly declared as a Qualified Data Structure (see Tip #8).

The initial value of the ORDER data structure is not automatically carried over to the MYORDERS data structure. To inherit the initial values of the original data structure, specify the INZ(*LIKEDS) keyword in addition to the LIKEDS keyword, as follows:

```
D myOrders        DS                     LikeDS(ORDER) INZ(*LIKEDS)
```

The subfields of MYORDERS have the same names as those of the ORDER data structure. In our original example, the generated data structure MYORDERS would appear as follows:

```
D myOrders        DS                     QUALIFIED
D  item                          5A
D  qtyord                        5P 0
D  price                         7P 2
```

If INZ(*LIKEDS) is also specified, then the new data structure looks like this:

```
D myOrders        DS               INZ QUALIFIED
D  item                     5A
D  qtyord                   5P 0
D  price                    7P 2
```

The original data structure (ORDER in our example) can be any type of data structure. Its structure is used as a template to create the new data structure. The new data structure is always a Qualified Data Structure regardless of whether the original data structure is qualified. The new data structure includes all the subfields from the original data structure.

It can be useful to create a data structure that is only used as a template for creating other data structures. When a data structure is used in this way, it is referred to as a *Data Structure Template*.

The phrase *Data Structure Template* is often used to refer to the original data structure. The ORDER data structure in our example is used as a Data Structure Template—that is, it is only being used to create new data structures.

Any data structure may be used as a data structure template. Here's an example.

The QlgConvertCase API (see Tip #53) requires a data structure for one of its parameters. That data structure controls both the type of conversion that is performed and the direction of the conversion (to or from uppercase). The data structure that the API uses is named FRCB and could be declared as follows:

```
D FRCB            DS               Align Qualified
D  ReqType                 10I 0 Inz(1)
D  CCSID                   10I 0 Inz(0)
D  CvtTo                   10I 0 Inz(0)
D  Reserved                10A   Inz(*ALLX'00')
```

The four subfields of FRCB are initialized, and the data structure is aligned on a 16-byte boundary (a requirement for this data structure) and qualified. We don't use this data structure directly, but instead we treat it as a format (or data structure template) and use it to create our own FRCB data structure, as follows:

```
D myFRCB          DS               LikeDS(FRCB) Inz(*LIKEDS)
```

While the INZ(*LIKEDS) keyword is optional, it is used in the example above so that the new MYFRCB data structure subfields are correctly initialized. The values stored in the subfields are a critical element to ensuring that the API works properly. The ALIGN keyword is automatically inherited by LIKEDS—specifying it again would be redundant.

If an initial value in the data structure template isn't necessary, you can save some storage and also prevent other programmers from storing information directly in the data structure template by removing its storage allocation.

To avoid allocating storage for a data structure, specify the BASED keyword:

```
D FRCB             DS                        Based(ptr_to_nothing)
D   ReqType                   10I 0
D   CCSID                     10I 0
D   CvtTo                     10I 0
D   Reserved                  10A
```

The BASED keyword causes the storage allocation for the data structure to be controlled by the programmer. RPG IV implicitly declares a pointer variable with the same name as that specified on the BASED keyword. Therefore, a pointer variable named PTR_TO_NOTHING is implicitly declared.

Be sure to use a field name that you are certain hasn't been used elsewhere. Some developers prefer alternatives to the *ptr_to_nothing* name:

```
D FRCB             DS                        Based(NULL)
D FRCB             DS                        Based(ptr)
D FRCB             DS                        Based(null_ptr)
```

Since no storage is allocated for the field or data structure when BASED is used, data may not be stored in the FRCB data structure unless you allocated storage using %ALLOC.

If a new data structure using FRCB as a template is declared, data may be stored in that new data structure. This is possible because the BASED keyword is not inherited by the LIKEDS keyword as follows:

```
D myFRCB           DS                        LikeDS(FRCB) Inz

C                  eval       myFRCB.reqType = 1
C                  eval       myFRCB.CCSID = 0
C                  eval       myFRCB.cvtTo = 0
C                  eval       myFRCB.reserved = *ALLX'00'
```

Every data structure can be used as a data structure template. Data structure templates are easy to use. This technique provides a level of dereferencing that allows modifications to be made much more easily.

50 Boolean Assignment

Conditional assignments or indicator-switching code first appeared in RPG decades ago. In the old RPG II language, to "set on" an indicator a COMP (compare) opcode was used to compare the value of Factor 1 with Factor 2. The result of the comparison set on one of the Resulting Indicators.

Since then, RPG III and RPG IV displaced the COMP opcode with the IF opcode along with other conditional statements. The COMP opcode probably hasn't been used in new RPG source code for more than 20 years; here's a nostalgic example.

```
D AmtDue          S              7P 2 Inz(125.00)
D crdLimit        S              7P 2 Inz(200.00)

C     AmtDue       Comp    CrdLimit                        71
C                  EXFMT   MYDSPF
```

The COMP opcode compares AMTDUE to CRDLIMIT. If AMTDUE is greater, CRDLIMIT indicator 71 is set on. Since all RPG opcodes set off resulting indicators before they perform their task, if AMTDUE is not greater than CRDLIMIT, indicator 71 will be off.

In RPG IV, the above code could be reengineered as follows:

```
D AmtDue          S              7P 2 Inz(125.00)
D crdLimit        S              7P 2 Inz(200.00)

C                  if      AmtDue > CrdLimit
C                  eval    *IN71 = *ON
C                  else
C                  eval    *IN71 = *OFF
C                  endif
C                  EXFMT   MYDSPF
```

In this situation, the indicator is still required, so a conditional statement is used to set it on or off. Unfortunately, this means more lines of code, and thus some developers feel they are writing less readable code than the old RPG II-style COMP operation.

A single EVAL statement can be used to replace the clutter that can appear when an attempt is made to set on an indicator using IF/ELSE/EVAL statements. This is known as *Boolean Assignment.*

Boolean Assignment

```
D AmtDue          S              7P 2 Inz(125.00)
D crdLimit        S              7P 2 Inz(200.00)

C                 eval      *IN71 = (AmtDue > CrdLimit)
C                 EXFMT     MYDSPF
```

The right side of the equal sign (of the EVAL operation) is generating an *ON or *OFF result (true or false condition). That result is assigned to indicator 71. This is effectively accomplishing the same task as the old COMP opcode and doing it in one statement.

With this capability, the indicator can be set on or off based on a much more complex condition than was possible with COMP opcode:

```
D AmtDue          S              7P 2 Inz(125.00)
D crdLimit        S              7P 2 Inz(200.00)
D today           S               D  Inz(*SYS)

C                 eval      *IN71 = (AmtDue > CrdLimit)
C                                   and (dueDate < Today)
C                 EXFMT     MYDSPF
```

The indicator is set on if the amount due is greater than the credit limit and the due date is earlier than today's date.

If you would rather not use numeric indicators, consider using Named Indicators instead. These are fields declared in the RPG IV source member with a data-type of N. These fields are indicators and can be set on or off (assigned *ON or *OFF) and mapped to the indicator buffer of Display or Print files.

51 Creating Even-Length Packed Fields

The use of length notation for field declaration has long since replaced the from/to column notation that RPG programmers used for decades. Declaring packed numeric fields as subfields of data structures has also become much easier:

```
D webOrder1       DS                          Inz
D   item                          4P 0
D   date                          8P 0
D   qty                           9P 0
D   price                         7P 2
```

The length of both character and numeric fields is explicitly declared using *length notation*. This is one of the first RPG IV-style features programmers embrace when moving to RPG IV from RPG II or RPG III.

Often legacy data structures contain from/to column notation. Converting these data structures to length notation may be preferred, but it isn't always an option.

```
D webOrder2       DS                              Inz
D   item                      1      3P 0
D   date                      4      8P 0
D   qty                       9     13P 0
D   price                    14     17P 2
```

In this example, from/to column notation is used instead of the friendlier length notation. Also, because ITEM and DATE were originally even-length packed fields, they had to be declared with the next multiple of packed field sizes. In other words, a Packed(4,0) field uses 3 bytes of storage—the same as a Packed(5,0) field—so positions 1 to 3 are specified. A Packed(8,0) field uses 5 bytes of storage—the same as a Packed(9,0) field—so positions 4 to 8 are specified. But this does not cause these subfields to be declared as even-length packed fields—it declares them as Packed(5,0) and Packed(9,0), respectively. Clearly, this is not what is needed.

To solve this problem, RPG IV includes a keyword that forces packed fields to be declared with an even number of digits. The PACKEVEN keyword indicates that packed fields and array elements that have been declared with from/to column notation are to have an even number of digits. To apply this to the previous example, add the PACKEVEN keyword to the ITEM and DATE subfield declarations, as follows:

Use PACKEVEN with From/To Column Notation

```
D webOrder3      DS                        Inz
D   item                   1        3P 0 packeven
D   date                   4        8P 0 packeven
D   qty                    9       13P 0
D   price                 14       17P 2
```

When the ITEM and DATE subfields are declared, their lengths are Packed(4,0) and Packed(8,0), respectively.

52 Sorting Arrays with SubArrays

RPG IV has a little-known feature that allows you to sort an array by any position of an array's elements. This is known as *SubArrays*.

To use subarrays, create an array as a data structure subfield, and then overlay that array with additional subfields. Those new subfields become subarrays with the same number of elements as the original array, and they occupy the same memory locations as the original array.

A subarray may be specified on the SORTA operation or the %XFOOT built-in function. When used with SORTA, the original array's elements are sorted by the positions of subarray elements. When used with %XFOOT, the positions of the subarray in the original array are totaled.

Sorting an Array by SubArray Name

```
D myDS             DS                     Inz
D arr                                     Dim(30)
D  item                        5A         Overlay(arr)
D  qty                         3S 0       Overlay(arr:*NEXT)
 /free
       SortA  item; // Sort by item number
       SortA  qty;  // Sort by quantity
 /end-free
```

The ARR array has 30 elements. A second subfield named ITEM is declared as a 5-position character field that overlays the ARR subfield. A third subfield, QTY, is declared as a 3-position zoned numeric field that overlays ARR in the next available position. Therefore, the implied length of an element of the ARR array is 5 plus 3—or 8 bytes.

The ARR array does not require its elements to be defined. Its length may be specified, but if it is omitted the compiler calculates the length of the array elements by adding up the sizes of the elements of any overlapping arrays (subfields ITEM and QTY in the example). ITEM and QTY are subarrays of ARR that are implicitly declared as arrays with 30 elements each—the same number of elements as the ARR array.

The following table illustrates the memory layout for a single array element of the ARR, ITEM, and QTY arrays. Remember, there are 30 of these elements.

Location:	1	2	3	4	5	6	7	8
ARR(1)	A	A	A	A	A	9	9	9
ITEM(1)	A	A	A	A	A			
QTY(1)						9	9	9

To sort the ARR array by QTY, specify the following:

```
     C                        sorta     QTY
```

To sort the ARR array by ITEM, specify the following:

```
     C                        sorta     ITEM
```

To sort the entire ARR array, specify the following:

```
     C                        sorta     ARR
```

When the array or one of its subfields is sorted, the entire array element is sorted—that is, when sorting the array by QTY, the elements of ARR are arranged and not just the portion that makes up the QTY array.

Cross-footing or totaling the elements of an array can also take advantage of subarrays. Use the %XFOOT built-in function to summarize the numeric portion of the array, as follows:

Cross-footing a SubArray

```
     /free
       OrderTotal = %xFoot(QTY);
     /end-free
```

The same restrictions and limitations that apply to normal arrays also apply to subarrays.

53 Convert between Lower- and Uppercase Letters

RPG IV has no "compare while ignoring case." RPG IV has no "convert to lowercase." RPG IV has no "convert to uppercase." However, RPG IV *does* have the ability to access APIs that can provide this kind of function.

If your programs run on North American companies only, and you don't worry about converting data between upper and lower case for non-USA character sets, then a simply %XLATE built-in function can be used as follows:

```
D UPPER           C                        'ABCDEFGHIJKLMNOPQRSTUVWXYZ'
D lower           C                        'abcdefghijklmnopqrstuvwxyz'
D MYNAME          S              20A       Inz('Bob Cozzi')

 /free
   //  Convert to lowercase
      myName = %xLate(upper:lower: myName);

 /end-free
```

Many (most?) applications today have to run on systems that may or may not be using the USA character set (CCSID). If this is the case, then the %XLATE built-in function is not good enough. Instead, the QlgConvertCase API should be used.

The QlgConvertCase API performs letter case conversion; it converts to uppercase or to lowercase. Nonalphabetic characters pass through the API unaltered. The API uses CCSID (coded character set identifier) tables to perform the conversion, which is safer than using the XLATE opcode with lowercase and uppercase character patterns.

Specify the CCSID of the data being converted, or set it to 0 (zero) to indicate that the data is in the job's default CCSID. Usually the CCSID is set to zero.

The API uses a Function Request Control Block (FRCB) data structure to reduce the number of parameters that are needed to perform a conversion. The prototype for the QlgConvertCase follows.

Prototype for QlgConvertCase API

```
D QlgCvtCase      PR                        extProc('QlgConvertCase')
D  frcb                                     CONST LikeDS(FRCB_T)
D  inString                       65535A    CONST Options(*VARSIZE)
D  OutString                      65535A    Options(*VARSIZE)
D  nLength                        10I 0     CONST
D  apiError                                 LikeDS(QUSEC_T)
D                                           OPTIONS(*VARSIZE)
```

The first parameter is a FRCB data structure. This data structure has different formats depending on what the API is being used for. For conversions between lower and upper case, the FRCB data structure is defined as follows:

FRCB_T Data Structure Template for QlgConvertCase API

```
D FRCB_T          DS                        Align Qualified
D  reqType                        10I 0     Inz(1)
D  Type_of_Request...
D                                 10I 0     Overlay(ReqType)
D  CCSID                          10I 0     Inz(0)
D  CvtTo                          10I 0     Inz(1)
D  Convert_to_LowerCase...
D                                 10I 0     Overlay(CvtTo)
D  Reserved                       10A       Inz(*ALLX'00')
```

In this data structure, which I've defined as a data structure template (see Tip #49 for information on data structure templates), I have included two long subfield names that more clearly indicate their purpose. These subfields overlay other subfields that have traditionally short names.

The two subfields Type_of_Request and Convert_to_LowerCase are used to control the type of conversion being performed and the direction of the conversion (to or from lowercase). The Type_of_Request subfield should be set to 1 (case conversion) while Convert_to_LowerCase should be set to 1 for conversion to lowercase or to 0 for conversion to uppercase.

The FRCB_T data structure template should not be used directly, but rather it should be used with the LIKEDS keyword to create your own instance of the data structure. Note that the FRCB_T template already has initial values specified, which means INZ(*LIKEDS) will be helpful.

To define your own FRCB data structure, the following can be specified.

```
D myFRCB          DS                        LikeDS(FRCB_T) INZ(*LIKEDS)
```

The FRCB data structure template I've created has initial values to cause a conversion to lowercase. To change this so that it will cause a conversion to uppercase, set the Convert_to_LowerCase subfield to 0:

```
D myFRCB          DS              LikeDS(FRCB_T)
D                                 INZ(*LIKEDS)

 /free
   //  Make the API convert to lowercase
      myFRCB.CvtTo = 1;

   //  Make the API convert to UPPER case
      myFRCB.CvtTo = 0;
 /end-free
```

To perform the conversion, call the QlgConvertCase API and specify the data to be converted, an output field to receive the converted data, and the API error data structure (see item #1 in the Appendix for a description of the QUSEC_T data structure):

```
**   Local variables
D TO_LOWER       C               Const(1)
D TO_UPPER       C               Const(0)
D myFRCB         DS              LikeDS(FRCB_T)
D                                Inz(*LIKEDS)
D myAPIErrorDS   DS              LikeDS(QUSEC_T)
D name1          S          30A  Inz('Robert Cozzi, Jr.')
D name2          S          25A

 /free
      myFRCB.CvtTo = TO_UPPER;
      myAPIErrorDS = *ALLX'00';
      nLength = %len(%trimR(name1));

   //  NAME2 = 'Robert Cozzi, Jr.'
      QlgCvtCase(FRCB : name1: name2:
            nLen : myAPIErrorDS);
   //  NAME2 = 'ROBERT COZZI, JR.'

      return;
 /end-free
```

To wrap this all up in a nice little package, I've created toUpper() and toLower() subprocedures that do just what their names imply. To use them, pass in the data to be converted, an output variable, and the length of the data being converted:

```
D name            S          30A    Inz('Robert Cozzi, Jr.')
D nameL           S          30A
D nameU           S          30A
D nLength         S          10I 0

  /free
      // Calculate length of the data in NAME1.
      nLength = %len(%trimR(name));

      toLower(NAME : nameL : nLength);
      toUPPER(NAME : nameU : nLength);
  /end-free
```

If you move the prototypes for toUpper() and toLower() to a separate source member, you can /COPY the prototypes into your own source members. Then bind to the module or service program that contains the compiled toUpper and toLower subprocedures.

Here is a complete example that may be compiled and run.

toLower() and toUpper() Subprocedure Wrappers for QlgConvertCase

```
H  OPTION(*SRCSTMT:*NODEBUGIO)
 /IF DEFINED(*CRTBNDRPG)
H DFTACTGRP(*NO)
 /ELSE
H NOMAIN
 /ENDIF

 ***********************************************************
 ** Function Request Control Block (FRCB) template.
 ** DO NOT STORE DATA DIRECTLY IN THIS Data Structure.
 ***********************************************************
D FRCB_T          DS                 Align Qualified
D  ReqType                    10I 0
D  Type_of_Request...
D                             10I 0 Inz(1) Overlay(ReqType)
D  CCSID                      10I 0 Inz(0)
D  CvtTo                      10I 0 Inz(1)
D  Convert_to_LowerCase...
D                             10I 0 Inz(0) Overlay(CvtTo)
D  Reserved                   10A    Inz(*ALLX'00')

 ***********************************************************
 ** QSYSINC needs to be installed: It is included with OS/400.
 ** DO NOT STORE DATA DIRECTLY INTO the QUSEC data structure.
 ***********************************************************
 /INCLUDE RPGTNT/QCPYSRC,QUSEC

 ***********************************************************
 **    Prototype for the QlgConvertCase API.
 **    /INCLUDE this if you have it.
 **    You can get it free at: www.rpgiv.com/downloads
 **    Note that we use a shorter name for the prototype.
 ***********************************************************
```

Continued…

...continued

```
D QlgCvtCase      PR                              extProc('QlgConvertCase')
D  ctrlBlock                                      Const LikeDS(FRCB_T)
D  inString                     65535A           Const Options(*VARSIZE)
D  OutString                    65535A           Options(*VARSIZE)
D  nLength                      10I 0            Const
D  apiError                                      LikeDS(QUSEC_T)
D                                                OPTIONS(*VARSIZE)
  ***********************************************************
  ** Put these prototype into a separate source member
  ** and /INCLUDE them into this source member and any
  ** other members that call toLower() or toUPPER().
  ***********************************************************
D ToLower         PR
D  szInput                      65535A           Const Options(*VARSIZE)
D  szOutput                     65535A           OPTIONS(*VARSIZE)
D  nLen                         10I 0            Const

D ToUpper         PR
D  szInput                      65535A           Const Options(*VARSIZE)
D  szOutput                     65535A           OPTIONS(*VARSIZE)
D  nLen                         10I 0            Const
  ***********************************************************

 /IF DEFINED(*CRTBNDRPG)

D name1           S             30A    Inz('Robert Cozzi, Jr.')
D name2           S             25A
D name3           S             25A
D nLength         S             10I 0

 /free
     // calculate length of the data in the NAME1 field.
     nLength = %Len(%trimR(name1));

     toLower(NAME1 : name2 : nLength);
     toUPPER(NAME2 : name3 : nLength);

      // At this point:
      // NAME1 = 'Robert Cozzi, Jr.'
      // NAME2 = 'robert cozzi, jr.'
      // NAME3 = 'ROBERT COZZI, JR.'

     eval *INLR = *ON;
     return;
 /end-free

      //  End of /IF DEFINED(*CRTBNDRPG)
 /endif

P ToLower         B                              Export
D ToLower         PI
D  szInput                      65535A           Const OPTIONS(*VARSIZE)
D  szOutput                     65535A           OPTIONS(*VARSIZE)
D  nLen                         10I 0            Const
```

Continued...

...*continued*

```
  **  Local variables
D TO_LOWER         C                      Const(1)
D TO_UPPER         C                      Const(0)
D myFRCB           DS                     LikeDS(FRCB_T) Inz(*LIKEDS)
D myAPIErrorDS     DS                     LikeDS(QUSEC_T)

 /free
   //  Make the API convert to lowercase
     myFRCB.CvtTo = TO_LOWER;
     myAPIErrorDS = *ALLX'00';
     QlgCvtCase(FRCB : szInput: szOutput:
               nLen : myAPIErrorDS);
       return;
 /end-free

P ToLower          E

P ToUpper          B                      Export
D ToUpper          PI
D  szInput                       65535A   Const OPTIONS(*VARSIZE)
D  szOutput                      65535A   OPTIONS(*VARSIZE)
D  nLen                            10I 0  Const

  **  Local variables
D TO_LOWER         C                      Const(1)
D TO_UPPER         C                      Const(0)
D myFRCB           DS                     LikeDS(FRCB_T) Inz(*LIKEDS)
D myAPIErrorDS     DS                     LikeDS(QUSEC)

 /free
   //  Make the API convert to UPPER CASE
     myFRCB.CvtTo = TO_UPPER;
     myAPIErrorDS = *ALLX'00';
     QlgCvtCase(FRCB : szInput: szOutput:
               nLen : myAPIErrorDS);

       return;
 /end-free

P ToUpper          E
```

54 Overlapping Data Structures

Believe it or not, RPG has been around for several decades, and there is still code running that was written as far back as the 1970s and 1980s. In the early days, file systems were not as powerful as today's database systems (such as DB2).

To figure out what some of these old programs are doing, a bit of program archeology is required. One thing that is occasionally discovered is that these old RPG II-oriented programs often use multi-format files.

Multi-format files are files that contain more than one type of record format. For example, an Order Entry system may use a file that includes both Order Header records and Order Detail records.

Today, when multiple record formats are required, multiple database files (or *tables* if you're an SQL programmer) are created.

When a program uses multi-format files and the program needs to be migrated to RPG IV, the multi-format files can be migrated to a more contemporary interface. That interface is Overlapping Data Structures.

To migrate code from multi-format files to Overlapping Data Structures, two externally described files or two program-described data structures need to be created.

If multiple files are being used, one file needs to be created for each unique format of the original file. If the original file contained two formats (such as Header and Detail records), then you must create two database files. If the original file contains 5 formats, then 5 database files need to be created. An example using a 2-format and 2-file approach follows.

Create the files using DDS. The following DDS may be used to create an Order Header and an Order Detail file.

```
A              R ORDHDR
A                CUSTNO          7P 0
A                ORDNBR          5P 0
A                ORDDATE         8S 0
A                INVNBR          7P 0
A            K ORDNBR

A              R ORDDETL
A                ORDNBR          7P 0
A                LINENO          5S 0
A                ITEMNO          5A
A                QTYORD          5P 0
A                PRICE           7P 2
A            K ORDNBR
A            K LINENO
```

In the RPG program, add an externally described data structure for each file that has been created (two in our example), as follows:

```
D hdr           E DS                    ExtName(OrdHeader)
D detl          E DS                    ExtName(OrdDetail)
```

Determine which of the formats is the longest. Once the longest format is identified (the ORDDETAIL file in our example), declare a pointer variable that is initialized to the address of that data structure:

```
D ptr_data       S              *    Inz(%addr(detl))
```

Then, for the other data structure(s), add the BASED keyword and specify the name of the pointer variable you just declared:

Overlapping Data Structures

```
D hdr           E DS                    ExtName(OrdHeader)
D                                       Based(ptr_data)

D detl          E DS                    ExtName(OrdDetail)

D ptr_data       S              *    Inz(%addr(detl))
```

At this point, both data structures occupy the same memory location. Therefore, whenever data is copied into the HDR or the DETL data structure, the other data structure contains the same data. When data in one data structure is modified, the other is also modified. This is not a copy of the data but rather both data structures occupying the exact same memory space.

To use this technique as a replacement for a multiple format file, declare a program described file, as follows:

```
FOLDFILE    IF   F   63        K DISK
IOLDFILE    NS
I                                1   63   DATA
```

Next, modify the PTR_DATA variable so that it points to the DATA field in the program described file rather than the longest data structure:

```
D ptr_data        S              *   Inz(%addr(DATA))
```

In addition, the DETL data structure (and any others you may have) must be based on the PTR_DATA pointer just like the HDR data structure. Add the BASED keyword to the DETL data structure definition:

```
D detl          E DS              ExtName(OrdDetail)
D                                 Based(ptr_data)
```

If you put everything together correctly, it should look similar to the following:

Multi-Format Files Implemented with Overlapping Data Structures

```
FOLDFILE    IF   F   63        K DISK

D hdr           E DS              ExtName(OrdHeader)
D                                 Based(ptr_data)

D detl          E DS              ExtName(OrdDetail)
D                                 Based(ptr_data)

D ptr_data        S              *   Inz(%addr(data))

IOLDFILE    NS
I                                1   63   DATA
```

Whenever the OLDFILE is read, the data from the file is copied to the input field named DATA. Since the HDR and DETL data structures share the DATA field's memory, they too contain the data read from the file. From that point, select the format (i.e., data structure) you need to use for any given record, and access the subfields accordingly.

To ensure that this technique is less likely to cause field name conflicts, create your data structures as qualified data structures (see Tip #8). Add the QUALIFIED keyword to each of their definitions, as follows:

Overlapping Data Structures Using BASED Keyword

```
D hdr            E DS                ExtName(OrdHeader) QUALIFIED
D                                    Based(ptr_data)

D detl           E DS                ExtName(OrdDetail) QUALIFIED
D                                    Based(ptr_data)
```

Because the data structures are qualified, qualified syntax is required to access the data in their subfields. This allows you to have the same subfield name (such as the ORDNBR subfield in our example) in both data structures and to avoid name collision and compile-time errors.

55 Dynamic Arrays — Dynamically Allocated Array Elements

Normally, the memory required for an array can be excessive. If an array is declared with thousands of elements, the amount of storage required to accommodate the array elements can run into the megabytes. RPG IV only offers arrays with a fixed number of array elements.

All elements of an array are allocated when the program is loaded. This occurs regardless of whether or not those elements are actually used. If the program declares an array with 500 elements and doesn't use the array at all, then all 500 elements are still allocated; if the program only needs 30 elements, all 500 elements are allocated; if it needs 101 elements, all 500 elements are still allocated; and so on.

I created a technique—known as Dynamically Allocated Arrays—for RPG IV that provides an alternative. By dynamically allocating the array elements on demand, storage is preserved and used much more efficiently.

Dynamic memory allocation is not new to programming, but it is relatively new to RPG applications. Rather than use dynamic memory allocation techniques such as ALLOC and REALLOC opcodes, the technique I developed uses a User Space Object to allocate and store the space needed for the array elements. In addition, it seems to run more efficiently than reallocating memory.

A user space must be created before using this technique. This is due to the fact that a pointer to the user space is retrieved; therefore, the user space must already exist.

In addition, the user space must have the auto-extend attribute set. When this attribute is on, the system automatically enlarges the user space size when a program attempts to access data beyond the current size. This allows an array in RPG IV to dynamically allocate its elements on demand and without any complex algorithms. For information on creating a user space with the auto-extend attribute, see Tip #24.

Dynamically Allocated Array Elements

```
D dynArr          DS                        Qualified
D  name                          10A        Inz('RAM_001')
D  library                       10A        Inz('QTEMP')
D myStuff         S               7P 2 Dim(5000) BASED(myPtr)
D I               S              10I 0
D aCount          S              10I 0 Inz(20)
D apiErr          DS                        LikeDS(QUSEC_T) Inz

CSR    *INZSR         BegSR
C                     callp(e)  qusptrus(dynArr: myPtr : apiErr)
C                     if        myPtr = *NULL
       // Bad pointer!
C                     else
       // Everything okay?
       // Then initialize the first 20 elements
C                     for       i = 1 to aCount
C                     eval      myStuff(i) = 0
C                     endif
C                     endif
CSR    EndInz         EndSR
```

The user space named QTEMP/RAM_001 is used as the storage for the dynamic array. This user space has to have been previously created with the auto-extend attribute set on. Let's look more closely at the components of this example.

Declare the Array with the BASED Keyword

```
D myStuff          S               7P 2 Dim(5000) BASED(myPtr)
```

A dynamic array is declared normally but includes the keyword BASED(myPtr) with the name of a pointer variable. The compiler automatically declares this pointer variable if you don't explicitly declare it yourself.

The compiler does not automatically allocate storage for variables associated with the BASED keyword. Instead, it is the programmer's responsibility to allocate the storage. For Dynamic Arrays, storage is allocated by retrieving a pointer to a user space, as follows:

Retrieve a Pointer to a User Space

```
C                     CallP     QusPtrUs(dynoArr : myPtr : apiErr)
```

The QUSPTRUS API retrieves a pointer to a user space. The pointer is specified on the second parameter of the API, and the user space name is specified on the first parameter.

The third parameter is the API error data structure (it can be ignored for this example). The prototype for QUSPTRUS follows:

```
D QusPTRUS        PR                      extPgm('QUSPTRUS')
D  szUserspace                     20A    Const
D  pRtnPtr                           *
D  apiError                                LikeDS(QUSEC_T)
D                                          OPTIONS(*VARSIZE:*NOPASS)
```

The first parameter is the old-fashioned 20-byte object name. The first 10 positions of this parameter must be the name of the user space; the second 10 positions (11 to 20) must contain the library name in which the user space is located. The special values *LIBL or *CURLIB are supported. This user space must have the auto-extend attribute set to '1' in order to work with this technique. For information on how to set the auto-extend attribute of a user space, see Tip #24.

The second parameter should contain the name of the pointer variable (myPtr in the example on page 127) that receives the pointer to the user space.

The third parameter is optional and is the standard API error-data structure.

The user space must exist *before* retrieving a pointer to it—otherwise, the APIERROR parameter of QUSPTRUS will include the CPF error message indicating that the user space object was not found.

Once the dynamic array is declared it, use the array like any other array. Be certain to access only those array elements that have been populated or that are to be populated. Otherwise, corrupt data could result. Be sure to read Tip #42 for information on sub-scripting arrays with the %SUBARR built-in function for more information.

56 Converting Date Formats with the QWCCVDT API

RPG IV easily converts between Date (D) data-type formats. Simply assign one date variable to another, regardless of DATFMT (date format), and the date is converted to the target format.

A lot of database files and RPG programs use numeric fields that contain dates. These legacy date values are typically stored in numeric fields and need to be converted to different date formats—from YYYYMMDD to MM/DD/YYYY, for example.

Dates stored in numeric or character fields may be converted from one format to another using the QWCCVTDT API. This API converts between date formats and can also retrieve the current system date.

To use the QWCCVTDT API, prototype it as follows:

Prototype for QWCCVTDT API

```
D QWCCVTDT        PR                     EXTPGM('QWCCVTDT')
D  inFmt                        10A      Const OPTIONS(*VARSIZE)
D  inDate                       64A      Const OPTIONS(*VARSIZE)
D  outFmt                       10A      Const OPTIONS(*VARSIZE)
D  outDate                      64A            OPTIONS(*VARSIZE)
D  api_error                             LikeDS(QUSEC_T)
```

This API uses input and output data structures to stored the input and output date values. In addition, the input and output date formats are specified before the values (data structures), as follows:

```
QWCCVTDT('input-fmt' : fromDate : 'output-fmt' : toDate : QUSEC_T)
```

One of the most common types of data conversion is to convert the current date to the job's date format. QWCCVTDT can easily handle this, as follows:

Using QWCCVTDT to Convert Date Format

```
D fromDate       DS                    LikeDS(CvtDT17_T)
D toDate         DS                    LikeDS(CvtDT16_T)
D today        . S              D      Inz(*SYS)
D jobDate        S              6S Ø
D apiErr         DS                    LikeDS(QUSEC_T) Inz

 /free
    fromDate = *ALL'Ø';
    toDate   = *ALL'Ø';
    fromDate.date = %char(today:*ISOØ);
    QwcCvtDT('*YYMD': fromDate:'*JOB': toDate : apiErr);
    jobDate = %Int(toDate.date);
 /end-free
```

The system date is automatically stored in the field named TODAY. That date is converted to character and copied into the DATE subfield of the FROMDATE data structure.

The date is then converted to the job's date format by QWCCVTDT and copied into the TODATE data structure. Then the returned date value is converted to numeric by the %INT() built-in function and assigned to the JOBDATE field.

To convert a Julian date to *ISO format, the following example code can be used:

Use QWCCVTDT to Convert Julian Date to Job Date Format

```
D fromJul        DS                    LikeDS(CvtDT16_T)
D toDate         DS                    LikeDS(CvtDT16_T)
D today          S              D      Inz(*SYS)
D jobDate        S              6S Ø
D apiErr         DS                    LikeDS(QUSEC_T) Inz

 /free
    fromJul  = *ALL'Ø';
    toDate   = *ALL'Ø';
    fromDate.century = '1';   // Set century to 2ØØØ
    fromJul.date = 'Ø6127';   // Set date to 127th day of 2ØØ6
    QwcCvtDT('*JUL': fromJul:'*JOB':toDate);
    jobDate = %Int(toDate.date);
 /end-free
```

To convert from an 8-digit date stored in a zoned decimal field (e.g., for a database file) to the traditional USA date format of MM/DD/YYYY, the QWCCVTDT API can be used as follows:

Use QWCCVTDT to YYYYMMDD to MMDDYYYY

```
D fromDate         DS                         LikeDS(CvtDT17_T)
D toDate           DS                         LikeDS(CvtDT17_T)
D today            S                  D       Inz(*SYS)
D usaDate          S                8S 0
D invDate          S                8S 0
D apiErr           DS                         LikeDS(QUSEC_T) Inz

 /free
    fromDate = *ALL'0';
    toDate   = *ALL'0';
    fromDate.date = %char( invdate );
    QwcCvtDT('*YYMD': fromDate:'*MDYY': toDate : apiErr);
    usaDate = %Int(toDate.date);
 /end-free
```

The date is read from a database file (not shown) and stored in the INVDATE field. The INVDATE field definition is illustrated in this example; however, it would normally be defined on an externally described file.

INVDATE is converted to character and copied to the DATE subfield of the FROMDATE data structure. QWCCVTDT is called, and the date is converted to traditional USA format (MMDDYYYY). That new value is converted to numeric by the %INT built-in function and copied to the USADATE field.

QWCCVTDT Data Structures

QWCCVTDT API uses no fewer than 5 data structures. Several formats support 6- or 8-digit date values, but there are others for less traditional date formats. The data structures used by QWCCVTDT are as follows:

Data Structures for QWCCVTDT

```
 **   Use with 6-digit date/time and milli-seconds
 **   Note: Julian dates should be left-justified, blank-filled
D CvtDT16_T        DS                         Qualified
D   century                       1A
D   date                          6A
D   time                          6A
D   milliSeconds                  3A
```

Continued...

...continued

```
             **  Use with 8-digit dates and milli-seconds
             **  Note: Julian dates should be left-justified, blank-filled
        D CvtDT17_T        DS                     Qualified
        D  date                          8A
        D  time                          6A
        D  milliSeconds                  3A

             **  Use with 6-digit dates/century digit and micro-seconds
             **  Note: Julian dates should be left-justified, blank-filled
        D CvtDT19_T        DS                     Qualified
        D  century                       1A
        D  date                          6A
        D  time                          6A
        D  microSeconds                  6A

             **  Use with 8-digit dates and micro-seconds
             **  Note: Julian dates should be left-justified, blank-filled
        D CvtDT20_T        DS                     Qualified
        D  date                          8A
        D  time                          6A
        D  microSeconds                  6A

             **  Use with DOS GetDateTime()
        D DOSGetDateTime_T...
        D                   DS                     Qualified
        D  hours                         3I 0
        D  minutes                       3I 0
        D  seconds                       3I 0
        D  hseconds                      5I 0
        D  day                           3U 0
        D  month                         3U 0
        D  year                          5U 0
        D  UTCOffset                     5I 0
        D  dayOfWeek                     3U 0
```

When a Julian date format (*JUL or *LONGJUL) is specified with these data structures, the Julian date must be left justified and padded with blanks on the right.

In the rare case when you need to use the DOSGetDateTime_T structure, be sure to specify the INZ keyword along with it in order to avoid decimal data errors:

```
        D myDOSTime        DS                     LikeDS(dosGetDateTime_T)
        D                                         INZ
```

The INZ keyword causes the numeric subfields of myDOSTime to be initialized to zero at program start up. Without it, the data structure will contain blanks and cause decimal data errors.

Time zone support was recently added to QWCCVTDT. Using a time zone value requires the use of a different data structure. That data structure follows:

Data Structure for the Time Zone Info Parameter of QWCCVTDT

```
     **   Use when specifying the TimeZone parameter of QWCCVTDT
D  timeZoneInfo_T   DS                    Qualified INZ
D   bytesReturned              10I 0
D   bytesAvail                 10I 0
D   timeZoneTitle              10A
D   reserved                    1A
D   DTS_Indy                    1A
D   UTC_Offset                 10I 0
D   timeZoneDesc               50A
D   timeZoneName               10A
D   timeZoneMsgID               7A
D   timeZoneMsgFile...
D                              10A
D   timeZoneMsgLib...
D                              10A
```

57 Converting Date Formats with the CEExxxx APIs

When nontraditional date formats need to be processed by RPG IV, the language's built-in date-handling routines come up short. They will blow up when a date contains an invalid separator or when it is in a nonstandard format.

A common situation occurs when a date is created in Microsoft Excel or on another platform and is an unusual format or contains a nonstandard separator symbol. For example, the date formats *USA, *ISO, *EUR, and *JIS have a fixed format and a fixed separator symbol—that separator *cannot* be modified. The formats *MDY, *YMD, and *DMY have a fixed format but support several different separator symbols. In addition, all date formats support the "no separator" option when converting to character format.

The separator is specified following the date format itself. If a separator is not specified, the date format's default separator is used. If a zero (0) is specified for the date separator, then no separator is used.

To convert dates contained in character or numeric variables to real-date data-type fields, the value in the character or numeric field must be in one of the standard date formats.

But what happens when the date is not in standard format? For example, a date stored in a character field in *ISO format does not contain a dash as separator. Instead, it contains a forward slash. If this value is used with %DATE to convert it to a real-date data-type, a runtime error will occur. Also the MOVE and MOVEL opcodes would fail.

Normally a character date value can be converted to a real-date data-type variable, as follows:

```
D myDate           S                   D
D ediDate          S                   10A   Inz('2006/06/30')
 /free
       myDate = %date(ediDate : *ISO);
 /end-free
```

This example will fail at runtime because the separator is a forward slash instead of the dash that is required by the *ISO format. A quick look through the available date format does not find anything that supports dates in this format.

To bypass this shortcoming, the CEE*xxxx* low-level APIs can be used. When the RPG compiler detects these "in-line" APIs, their object code is copied into the resulting program or module. The additional overhead of a traditional subprocedure call is not introduced since the code is in line. Consequently, calling these functions can be as fast as or faster than native RPG IV opcodes or built-in functions.

Two CEE*xxxx* APIs will bypass the date format shortcoming in RPG IV. When used together, a character date value can be converted from any date format to any date format. Those APIs are as follows:

- CEEDAYS — Calculate Lillian Date from Character Date
- CEEDATE — Convert from Lillian Date to Character Data

The CEEDAYS API is used to calculate the number of days between the date (in any character format) and October 14, 1582. The benefit of this API over the SUBDUR opcode or the %DIFF() built-in function is that it works with non-date variables that use standard or nonstandard separators. The prototype for CEEDAYS follows:

```
D CEEDAYS         PR                    extProc('CEEDAYS')
D                                       OPDESC
D  inDate                     255A      Const OPTIONS(*VARSIZE)
D  inFormat                   255A      Const OPTIONS(*VARSIZE)
D  nDays                      10I 0
D  apiErrorDS                           LikeDS(QUSEC_T)
D                                       OPTIONS(*OMIT)
```

The CEEDATE API converts a Lillian Date (integer) to a textual date. The integer must contain the number of days since October 14, 1582. The date is returned as a character string in a user-specified format. To format the date as 'DDMMYY' then call CEEDATE with 'DDMMYY' as the date formatting code. The prototype for CEEDATE follows:

```
D CEEDATE         PR                    extProc('CEEDATE')
D                                       OPDESC
D  inDays                     10I 0
D  outFormat                  255A      Const OPTIONS(*VARSIZE)
D  rtnDate                    255A      OPTIONS(*VARSIZE)
D  apiErrorDS                           LikeDS(QUSEC_T)
D                                       OPTIONS(*OMIT)
```

Both of these APIs include a date format parameter. This parameter is a user-defined date format using a combination of simple date formatting codes. The formatting codes include, but are not limited to DD, MM, YY, and YYYY. Anything other text in the formatting parameter is considered separator characters or ignored text.

For example, using the CEEDAYS API, a date format of 'YYYY/MM/DD' can be specified for the previous example date of '2006/06/30'. In this case, the API extracts the date elements and throws away the unimportant data—such as the separators. The number of days since October 14, 1582 is returned, and that value is passed to CEEDATE. CEEDATE converts that value into a valid date format. The following example illustrates these steps in RPG IV.

Converting Non-Standard Date Formats to Real Date Variables

```
D myISODate       S              D   DatFmt(*ISO)
D myDate          S            10A   Inz('2006/06/30')
D nDays           S            10I 0

 /free
             // Convert from custom Excel-style Date format to Lillian
         ceedays(myDate : 'YYYY/MM/DD' : nDays : *OMIT);

             // Convert from Lillian to *ISO format
         ceedate(nDays : 'YYYY-MM-DD' : myDate : *OMIT);

             // Convert the *ISO format value to a real date variable
         myISODate = %date(myDate:*ISO);

 /end-free
```

The call to CEEDAYS is used to calculate the number of days since October 14, 1582. This is the so-called *Lillian Date* used by all CEE*xxxx* date APIs.

Since CEEDAYS allows the format of the textual date to be specified on the second parameter, the nonstandard 'YYYY/MM/DD' date format is specified. This is often the style output to CSV files created with Microsoft® Excel. Any conventional or unconventional date format may be specified.

```
         ceedays(myDate : 'YYYY/MM/DD' : nDays : *OMIT);
```

Once the Lillian Date is returned to the nDAYS parameter, the second API, CEEDATE, is called. It converts the Lillian Date to an *ISO-date-formatted character string—that is, the date is formatted just like an *ISO date but is copied to a character variable. The returned value is stored in the same field (MYDATE in our example) as the original date value.

```
         ceedate(nDays  : 'YYYY-MM-DD' : myDate : *OMIT);
```

Because the returned character string is in *ISO date format, it can (if necessary) be used with the %DATE built-in function or the MOVE/MOVEL opcodes to convert it to a real-date data-type, as follows:

```
         myISODate = %date(myDate:*ISO);
```

Another use for CEEDATE is to convert a Lillian Date into words. This can be used when reports or HTML Web pages need the date in a more human-friendly format. The follow example illustrates how to use CEEDATE to convert a Lillian Date to words.

Formatting a Date as Words

```
D myDate           S              10A     Inz('06/30/2006')
D textDate         S              50A
D nDays            S              10I 0

 /free
          ceedays(myDate : 'MM/DD/YYYY' : nDays : *OMIT);

          ceedate(nDays  : 'Wwwwwwwwwz, Mmmmmmmmmz DD, YYYY' :
                    textDate : *OMIT);

          //  textDate contains 'Friday, July 30, 2006'

 /end-free
```

A character field containing a *USA-style date value is converted to a printable format using CEEDATE. The formatting code 'Wwwwwwwwwz, Mmmmmmmmmz DD, YYYY' uses a sequence of W and M letters to indicate the name of the day of the week (Wwwwwwwwwz) and month name (Mmmmmmmmmz). In addition, several commas and other characters may be embedded in the formatting string. These commas and any other rogue text are passed through to the output value. If all-uppercase day or month names are desired, specify the pattern in all uppercase. In addition, removing the trailing "z" from the day or month pattern outputs fixed-length names—the text following the day or month name will not be concatenated with blanks trimmed.

For more information on the formatting-code parameter, see the online API documentation for the CEEDATE API.

58 Calculated Day of Week — Zeller's Congruence

There are almost as many routines available to calculate the day of the week as there have been days since the millennium. However (unfortunately), RPG IV does not include a built-in function that calculates the day of the week.

While there are various algorithms available—including some that use a "divide by 7" calculation—virtually all of them have a somewhat restricted range of dates for which they produce correct results. Almost the only exception is Zeller's congruence—a century-old algorithm that accurately calculates the day of the week. I've converted this algorithm to RPG IV and have included it below.

Zeller's Congruence in RPG IV

```
P GetDayZ          B                        EXPORT
D GetDayZ          PI             10I 0
D  inDate                          D    CONST DATFMT(*ISO)

D nDay             S              10I 0
D nMonth           S              10I 0
D nYear            S              10I 0

 /free
     nDay   = %subdt(inDate:*DAYS);
     nMonth = %subdt(inDate:*MONTHS);
     nYear  = %subdt(inDate:*YEARS);

     if nMonth < 3;
        nMonth += 12;
        nYear  -= 1;
     endif;

     return %REM( %div((13*nMonth+3):5) +
             nDay + nYear + %div(nYear:4) -
             %div(nYear:100) + %div(nYear:400) : 7 )
 /end-free
P GetDayZ          E
```

You call this subprocedure to calculate the day of the week for today's date by specifying the following:

```
/free
    day = GetDateZ( %Date() );
/end-free
```

The GetDayZ() subprocedure is called with %DATE() as its parameter. This passes the current system date to the subprocedure. The day of the week is calculated and returned by the GetDayZ() subprocedure. The day of the week is then copied to the DAY variable.

59 Calculated Day of Week — API Method

There are so many APIs available to RPG IV that there is really no one person who remembers them all. One such API is CEEDYWK. This API is an ILE built-in. ILE built-in APIs are APIs whose object code is inserted into the compiled object directly. Normally, a call to an API inserts a call to a routine in a service program or a stand-alone program.

ILE built-ins (as they are called) work a little differently. Rather than insert a call to a subprocedure or program, the actual object code for the API itself is inserted directly in line into the compiled object. This avoids the overhead of a program or subprocedure call.

The prototype for the CEEDYWK API used by the GETDAYOFWEEK subprocedure is shown below.

CEEDYWK Prototype

```
D CEEDYWK           PR               10I 0 extProc('CEEDYWK')
D  nDays                             10I 0 Const
D  nRtnDayOfWeek                     10I 0
D  ioFeedBack                        12A   OPTIONS(*OMIT)
```

The first parameter of CEEDYWK is the number of days since October 14, 1582. This may seem a bit of an odd value, but it gives the API a known duration to do its calculation.

The second parameter of CEEDYWK must be a variable that is defined as a 4-byte integer (10i0) value. This variable receives the day of the week.

The third parameter is an I/O error feedback parameter that is normally specified as *OMIT and ignored.

To calculate the days since October 14, 1582, use either the SUBDUR opcode or the %DIFF built-in function and then pass that day-counter to CEEDYWK, as follows:

```
nDays_Since = %diff(myDate:D'1582-10-14':*DAYS);
ceedywk( nDays_Since : nDayOfWeek : *OMIT);
```

The %DIFF built-in function is used to calculate the difference in days between the current date and October 14, 1582.

The third parameter indicates the type of duration being calculated (*Days, *Months, *Years). In this case, the number of days is desired, so *DAYS is specified.

The number of days since October 14, 1582 is passed to the CEEDYWK API. The API calculates the day of the week from that value and returns it as a value of 1 to 7.

Example: A prototype for a subprocedure named GetDayOfWeek() that simplifies calling CEEDYWK follows.

Get Day of Week Prototype

```
D GetDayOfWeek    PR              10I 0
D  inDate                          D   CONST DATFMT(*ISO)
```

GetDayOfWeek accepts a date in any date format, automatically converts it to *ISO format, and then calculates the day of the week as a value 1 to 7, with Sunday = 1, Monday = 2, and so on. The subprocedure implementation itself is only two lines of calc specifications:

Get Day of Week Procedure Implementation

```
P GetDayOfWeek    B                    EXPORT
D GetDayOfWeek    PI              10I 0
D  inDate                          D   CONST DATFMT(*ISO)

    // Base date is based on date the calendar changed.
D BaseDate        C                     Const(D'1582-10-14')
D nDayOfWeek      S               10I 0
/free
    ceedywk(%diff(inDate:BASEDATE:*DAYS) : nDayOfWeek:*OMIT);
    return nDayOfWeek;

  /end-free
P GetDayOfWeek    E
```

Certainly this subprocedure makes retrieving the day of the week with CEEDYWK more readable. Using it to retrieve the day of the week allows much more readable code to be used:

```
/free
        nDayOfWeek = GetDayOfWeek(%date());
    /end-free
```

Presto!—the day of the week for the current system date is calculated.

60 LIKE Keyword Misbehavior — Zoned to Packed

The LIKE keyword works like this: When a derived field is defined using the LIKE keyword, it inherits the attributes (i.e., length, data-type, VARYING, and ALIGN keywords) of its reference field or data structure.

It is true that the LIKE keyword inherits the attributes (including the data-type) of the original field. However, when the original field (called the Referenced Field) is defined on Input specifications only (externally described or program described), then the resulting or derived field is defined as packed.

When a zoned decimal field from an Input specification is brought into a program by the compiler, the compiler converts that zoned decimal field to packed decimal. Don't believe me? Look at a field definition for a zoned decimal field that has been brought in from an externally described file. If the field is defined as Zoned(6,0), the compiler redefines it as Packed(6,0).

When the LIKE keyword is used to create a derived field from an Input zoned decimal field, the resulting derived field's data-type is packed, not zoned. Why? Because the compiler has already converted that zoned field to packed decimal. Consequently, the new LIKE derived field is also packed.

```
D myZoned            S                      Like(iZoned)

IINPUT      NS
I                                    S    1    6  ØiZoned
I                                    P    7   10  ØiPacked
```

The derived field named MYZONED is defined as Packed Decimal even though its reference field, IZONED, is a Zoned Decimal field. This is due to the fact that the compiler converts all numeric fields declared on Input specifications to Packed Decimal. Since IZONED is converted to Packed Decimal, MYZONED ends up being Packed Decimal as well.

To resolve this issue, redefine the input field in another Definition specification using the Zoned Decimal data-type.

```
D iZoned          S              6S 0
D myZoned         S                   Like(iZoned)

IINPUT      NS
I                              S   1   6 0iZoned
I                              P   7  10 0iPacked
```

This forces the field definition of the IZONED field to be Zoned Decimal. Any derived fields that reference it (using the LIKE keyword) are also Zoned Decimal.

A similar problem also exists for date fields. All date fields are converted to *ISO format regardless of their format in the database file.

Always redefining zoned Input fields can be a tedious thing to remember. An alternative to redefining each zoned decimal field by hand is to include the file in the program as an externally described data structure. When this is done, the record format of the file is used to create a data structure layout. All the fields of the file are generated as data-structure subfields using their original data-types (no conversion to packed decimal is performed).

Example: The CUSTMAST file contains several fields—2 are zoned decimal and the other fields are of various data-types and lengths:

```
  **      DDS for CUSTMAST database file
A           R CUSTREC
A             CUSTNO       7P 0
A             COMPNAME    30A
A             ORDDTE       8S 0    ┌──────────────────────┐
A             SHIPDTE      8S 0    │ Zoned Decimal fields  │
A             ADDRESS     30A      └──────────────────────┘
A             CITY        20A
A             STATE        4A
A             ZIPCODE     10A
A             PHONE       11P 0
A             EMAIL       64A         VARLEN(32)
```

This CUSTMAST file can be used to create a data structure. Then the zoned numeric fields ORDDTE and SHIPDTE can be referenced to create derived fields that retain the Zoned Decimal data-type.

```
  **  RPG IV excerpt that uses CUSTMAST as a Data Structure
D CUST           E DS            ExtName(CUSTMAST)
D orderDate        S             Like(ORDDTE)
D shipDate         S             Like(SHIPDTE)
```

The ORDERDATE and SHIPDATE fields are stand-alone fields and not part of the CUST data structure, and they are defined as zoned decimal. The data structure named CUST does not necessarily need to be referred in the program as we are only using the field definitions and not the fields themselves.

The LIKEREC keyword is not the same as EXTNAME. LIKEREC creates a QUALIFIED data structure using the current format of an Input file. Because the compiler converts zoned numeric fields to packed decimal, the derived data structure generated by LIKEREC will also contain packed decimal field definitions.

The following example demonstrates how Zoned Decimal fields defined on Input specifications (program described or externally described) are converted to Packed Decimal by the compiler. Then, when they are used as a reference field to create derived fields, those derived fields also become Packed Decimal.

Demonstrate LIKE Reverting to Packed Data-type

```
       **   Example Physical File DDS for EXTERN.
A            R EXTERNREC
A              XZONED          6S 0
A              XPACKED         7P 0

       **   Example RPG IV Source
       **   Demonstrates LIKE keyword usage.
FEXTERN    IF   E             DISK
FINPUT     IF   F   64        DISK

D myZoned            S              6S 0
D myPacked           S              7P 0

       // This field ends up as Zoned.
D lZoned             S                        Like(myZoned)
       // This field ends up as Packed.
D lPacked            S                        Like(myPacked)

       // All four of these fields end up as Packed.
D liZoned            S                        Like(iZoned)
D liPacked           S                        Like(iPacked)
D lxZoned            S                        Like(xZoned)
D lxPacked           S                        Like(xPacked)

IINPUT      NS
I                              S   1    6 0iZoned
I                              P   7   10 0iPacked
```

All four of these fields are defined as PACKED

61 Default Data-type: Not So Consistent

When defining a field in RPG IV, long-time RPG programmers tend to leave off the data-type. While the merits of this programming practice can be debated, continuing to practice this technique in RPG IV can create unexpected results.

> What's the default data-type for numeric fields in RPG IV?
> Answer: It depends.

There are four areas of RPG where a variable may be defined: the Input specifications, Data Structure Subfields, Stand-alone fields, and (if you still have legacy code) in the Calculation specifications.

Each of these areas allows the data-type to be omitted when declaring a variable. In the case where numeric variables are being defined, this can be disastrous.

The following list contains the areas of RPG where variables may be defined and, for numeric variables, the default data-type that the language uses.

- Input Specifications — ZONED
- Data Structure Subfields — ZONED
- Stand-alone Fields — PACKED
- Calc Specification-defined Fields — PACKED

Here's an example of this ambiguity when declaring numeric variables with an implicit or default numeric data-type.

```
D acctno           S              7  0
D myDS             DS                          What are the data-types
D  acctno                         7  0           for these fields?

IINPUT     NS
I                                1   7 ØACCTNO
C                  Z-ADD   Ø            ACCTNO            7 0
```

Here are the same variables declared with their default data-type explicitly specified. Note that they do not default to the same data-type in each declaration.

```
D acctno          S              7P 0

D myDS            DS
D   acctno                       7S 0

IINPUT     NS
I                               1    7S0ACCTNO

C                   Z-ADD    0            ACCTNO          7 0
```

No Data-type allowed—
always Packed

Always specify the data-type when writing RPG IV, regardless of your historical coding habits.

62 Debugging Variables that Have Debugger Command Names

Using the full-screen debugger for RPG IV and ILE CL programs can be fun, but it can also be frustrating. If you are debugging a program that includes variables with the same name as that of one of the Debugger's line commands, you often receive a syntax error when trying to view the contents of those variables.

For example, if a legacy application has been converted to RPG IV, a field with the name EVAL (the same as the Debugger's EVAL command) could exist. Perhaps the field contains the current evaluation rating of a product.

Normally, if you attempt to view the contents of the EVAL field using the EVAL command or by positioning the cursor on the field name and then pressing F11, the following message is displayed.

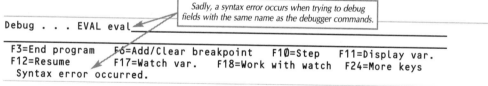

```
                                  Sadly, a syntax error occurs when trying to debug
                                  fields with the same name as the debugger commands.
 Debug . . . EVAL eval

 F3=End program   F6=Add/Clear breakpoint   F10=Step   F11=Display var.
 F12=Resume       F17=Watch var.   F18=Work with watch   F24=More keys
   Syntax error occurred.
```

So how *do* you display fields with the same names as Debug commands or identifiers?

The answer is %VAR(). Wrap the field name in %VAR(), and the Debugger knows that it is a field name.

Display the Contents of a Field Named EVAL in the Debugger

```
Debug . . . EVAL %VAR(eval)_____

 F3=End program   F6=Add/Clear breakpoint   F10=Step   F11=Display var.
 F12=Resume       F17=Watch var.  F18=Work with watch  F24=More keys
  EVAL = 4.6
```

In this example, the EVAL command is used to display the contents of the field named EVAL. Without %VAR(), the debugger thinks EVAL is a debugger command and issues a syntax error.

To view a list of Debugger functions (such as %VAR), press F1 (help) on the Debugger command line. A Help window will appear. In the Help window, page down until you see the link to the "RPG language examples." Position the cursor to the left of that link and press Enter. The list of Debugger functions for RPG IV will be displayed.

63 Viewing Field Contents in Hex in Debug

The full screen debugger has several ambiguous features (such as the one featured in Tip #65). Another is the ability to view the content of a variable or data structure in hexadecimal notation.

Normally, to view the contents of a field, the cursor is positioned somewhere on the field name, and the F11 key is pressed. This actually issues an EVAL command to display the field's contents:

```
                                    ┌─────────────────────────────────────┐
                                    │ When a field contains unusual characters, it is │
                                    │ displayed as a blank or reverse image box.      │
                                    └─────────────────────────────────────┘
  Debug . . . EVAL ifsAttr

  F3=End program   F6=Add/Clear breakpoint    F10=Step    F11=Display var.
  F12=Resume       F17=Watch var.  F18=Work with watch     F24=More keys
    IFSATTR = ' '.
```

Here, the content of the IFSATTR field is displayed. The Debugger's EVAL command is either explicitly or implicitly run to display a field's value. While the EVAL command does a good job displaying regular fields, it doesn't know what do with characters in the field that are less than X'40'. Often it simply inserts a "green box" character, which indicates an unexpected character value.

To display a field's content in hexadecimal, you must manually type in the EVAL command followed by the field name, then suffix the field name with a :x sequence. This causes the EVAL operation to display the field's value in hexadecimal, as follows:

```
                                ┌──────────────────────────────────────────┐
                                │ To display the field's content in hexadecimal, add │
                                │ the :x suffix to the field on an EVAL command.      │
                                └──────────────────────────────────────────┘
  Debug . . . EVAL ifsAttr:x

  F3=End program   F6=Add/Clear breakpoint    F10=Step    F11=Display var.
  F12=Resume       F17=Watch var.  F18=Work with watch     F24=More keys
      00000       4040.... ........ ........ ........   -  .............
```

 TIP To avoid typing in the EVAL command, use the F11 key to automatically display the field's content; then press the F9 key to retrieve the previous Debugger command. This retrieves the EVAL command. At this point, move the cursor over, and type in the suffix.

64 Display the First Few Bytes During Debug

The Debugger supports several suffixes for the EVAL (display field content) command, including

- eval field:C — Display the value in character notation
- eval field:S — Display the value in character using C-style null-terminated string notation
- eval field:X — Display the value in hexadecimal notation

All suffixes support an optional *Length* parameter; for example:

```
Debug . . . EVAL ifsAttr:x_1_____

F3=End program    F6=Add/Clear breakpoint    F10=Step    F11=Display var.
F12=Resume          F17=Watch var.  F18=Work with watch  F24=More keys
   00000      40...... ........ ........ ........   -    ..............
```

The length parameter controls the number of characters displayed when the EVAL command is performed. At least one space *must* appear between the suffix and the length parameter.

You might think that you can simply add the length parameter to the EVAL command without specifying a suffix (such as *:c*).

Well, you can't.

There are additional suffix options depending on the language being debugged, but in practice, all suffixes seem to work in all languages.

When a Data Structure is display during a debug session, each of the data structure's sub-fields are display along with their content. For example, to display a data structure named MYDS, the EVAL MYDS command is used. The results could be as follows:

```
> EVAL myDS
  MYDS.QTYORD = 009.
  MYDS.ITEM = 'AAABB'
  MYDS.PRICE = 00032.50
  MYDS.DESC = 'HDV Video Tape       '
```

This is probably the desired effect most of the time. *But*—what if you want to look at the content of the data structure without viewing its subfields? How do you treat the data structure as one large field?

When debugging, display a data structure's content directly without displaying its subfields by typing the EVAL command followed by the name of the data structure and then adding the :c suffix to the data structure name. This causes the EVAL command to display the data structure's value as a character string, as follows:

```
Debug . . . EVAL myDS:C _____

F3=End program   F6=Add/Clear breakpoint   F10=Step   F11=Display var.
F12=Resume          F17=Watch var.  F18=Work with watch  F24=More keys
MYDS:C = '009AAABB     HDV Video Tape      '
```

This causes the entire data structure to be displayed as one long character string.

To display a portion of the data structure, specify the number of bytes you want to display immediately following field suffix. For example, to display the first 10 bytes, do the following:

```
Debug . . . EVAL myDS:C  10 _____

F3=End program   F6=Add/Clear breakpoint   F10=Step   F11=Display var.
F12=Resume          F17=Watch var.  F18=Work with watch  F24=More keys
MYDS:C = '009AAABBCD'
```

The first 10 bytes of the data structure are displayed.

65 Display Contents of Local Variables with %LOCALVAR

Stepping into a subprocedure (Shift-F10) while debugging can help determine the cause of a nagging problem in your code. But while in that subprocedure, the Debugger allows you to display all the local variables (fields, arrays, and data structures) declared in that subprocedure.

In debug, stop at a breakpoint where a call to a subprocedure appears and use the Step-Into command key (F22/Shift-F10) to continue debugging the subprocedure. The Debugger will stop on the first line of the subprocedure (normally the P specification). Use F10 (Step) to continue to the first Calculation specification in the subprocedure.

Once the Debugger has entered the subprocedure, you can display a list of all the local variables along with their content by displaying %LOCALVAR Debugger function via the EVAL command:

```
Debug . . . EVAL %LOCALVAR _____

 F3=End program    F6=Add/Clear breakpoint    F10=Step    F11=Display var.
 F12=Resume        F17=Watch var.  F18=Work with watch  F24=More keys
```

The Debugger displays each local variable along with its current value when the "EVAL %LOCALVAR" command is run on the Debugger's command line.

66 Convert Character to Numeric — Using MI

Using MI inside of RPG IV is probably one the least-used features of RPG IV. The subprocedures of any ILE module may be called from any other programming language. You simply need to prototype the interface in the caller's language: If you're calling C from RPG IV, you need to prototype the C language functions/subprocedures in RPG IV syntax. Likewise, when calling MI, you need to prototype the MI function in RPG IV syntax.

One MI instruction, _CVTEFN (Convert External Form to Numeric), helps convert numeric data contained in a character field to numeric. This MI instruction is used by the system to convert numeric input fields from a Display file to the packed, zoned, or integer format used by the Input specification of an RPG IV program. This MI instruction seems to be very efficient.

Numeric data from contemporary user interfaces (such as Web browsers) are also displayed and entered as character text. Convert this data to numeric so the RPG IV program can handle it correctly. If the data is simply numeric data with no edit symbols, comma, or currency symbol, then a standard %DEC() built-in function will perform the conversion well. If the value is strictly digits and nothing else—including no decimal point—then a standard %INT() built-in function will perform the conversion nicely.

When the data coming into the RPG IV program is from an EDI or CGI (Web) transaction or from a comma-separated value (CSV) file, the %DEC and %INT built-in functions may not be good enough.

This is where _CVTEFN is beneficial. The _CVTEFN MI instruction allows you to define the input and output format of the data. Pass it the character string containing a numeric value in text format along with the desired output format. The _CVTEFN does the conversion for you.

To use _CVTEFN, specify the type of formatting the numeric text contains. For example, it may contain a comma, a period, and a currency symbol. It doesn't matter if the value actually contains these symbols, but if there's any chance it could, _CVTEFN needs to know about it. In other words, *this parameter is required.*

The following diagram illustrates converting a 12-position character field that contains a number with a dollar sign, a comma, and a decimal point to Packed(7,2) format.

The RPG IV prototype for the _CVTEFN function follows:

Prototype for _CVTEFN MI Instruction in RPG IV

```
D cvtefn          PR                  extProc('_CVTEFN')
D  rtnValue                      *    Value
D  returnAttr                         Const
D                                     LikeDS(DPA_T)
D  charData                 256A      Const
D  charDataLen              10U 0     Const
D  editMask                   3A      Const
```

The first parameter of _CVTEFN is the address of a packed, zoned, or integer variable that will receive the converted numeric value. This variable must match the type, length, and decimal positions specified on the second parameter.

The second parameter is the attributes of the return value (first parameter). It is a data structure called "DPA Template" (identified below) that indicates the format of the resulting value—that is, the value returned to parameter 1. Parameter 1 must be the address of a variable whose attributes match that of the DPA Template settings.

The third parameter is a character variable or literal. It contains the text form of the value being converted. The _CVTEFN function accepts a value of up to 32,767 bytes for this parameter. However, in practice, the 256-byte parameter definition (included in the prototype above) is more than adequate.

Trailing blanks should be removed from this parameter value using %TRIMR() or something similar. Leading blanks are ignored by _CVTEFN, but it may be safer to trim off both trailing and leading blanks before passing the value to _CVTEFN.

The fourth parameter is the length of the data passed on the third parameter. The data length—not the field length—should be specified for this parameter.

The fifth parameter is a 3-position edit mask. The first byte must contain the character used as the currency symbol. The second byte must contain the character used as the thousands separator (i.e., the comma on North American systems), and the third byte must contain the character used as the decimal notation (i.e., a period on North American systems). A null value is allowed for this parameter, which means passing *OMIT instead of a 3-byte text string. A typical 3-byte string passed to this parameter follows:

```
'$,.'
```

As mentioned, the second parameter is a data structure based on the DPA Template. This data structure, converted to RPG IV, would appear as follows:

Data Structure for _CVTEFN

```
D DPA_T           DS                      Qualified ALIGN
D  dataType                     1A
D  type                         1A   Overlay(dataType)
D  result_size                  5I 0
D   decPos                      3I 0 Overlay(result_size)
D   length                      3I 0 Overlay(result_size:*NEXT)
D   len                         3I 0 Overlay(length)
D  Reserved1                   10I 0 Inz(0)
D  Reserved2                    1A   Inz(X'00')
```

The following is a description of the subfields of the DPA_T data structure.

- dataType — The hex code that identifies the data-type of the variable passed on the first parameter of _CVTEFN
- type — Alias for the dataType subfield
- decPos — The number of decimal positions for the result
- length — The size of the numeric field
- len — Alias for the length subfield
- Reserved1 — An integer that ends the data structure
- Reserved2 — A one-byte pad character to make the data structure 8 bytes long; like most reserved fields, it needs to be initialized to all-hexadecimal zeros, hence INZ(*ALLX'00') is specified

There are additional subfields that are used for convenience. For example, the RESULT_SIZE subfield is used to map the decimal positions and field length into two 1-byte integers.

The data-type used by _CVTEFN must be in MI hexadecimal-notation data-type. To simplify how these data-types are specified, the following named constants may be used.

Named Constants for Data-types Used by _CVTEFN

```
D T_INT         C                        Const(X'00')
D T_UINT        C                        Const(X'0A')
D T_UNS         C                        Const(X'0A')
D T_Integer     C                        Const(X'00')
D T_Float       C                        Const(X'01')
D T_Zoned       C                        Const(X'02')
D T_Signed      C                        Const(X'02')
D T_Pkd         C                        Const(X'03')
D T_Packed      C                        Const(X'03')
```

The data-type stored in DPA_T.dataType *must be* one of the above values. For example, if the output should be packed decimal, then the T_Packed constant should be used.

Using _CVTEFN to Convert Varying Character to Numeric

```
H BNDDIR('QC2LE') OPTION(*NODEBUGIO:*SRCSTMT)
H DFTACTGRP(*NO) ACTGRP(*NEW)

     // Include the prototype for _CVTEFN and DPA_T DS
   /INCLUDE rpgtnt,qcpysrc,rpgtnt

D szChar          S             12A    Varying Inz('$1,234.50-')
D myNumValue      S              7P 2
D myCVT           DS                    LikeDS(DPA_T)
C                 eval       *INLR = *ON
  /free
      myCvt = *ALLX'00';      // Clear the data structure.
      myCvt.type = T_Packed;  // Set data-type to packed.
      myCvt.length = 7;       // Set length to (7,2)
      myCvt.decPos = 2;

         // Do the conversion
      cvtefn(%addr(myNumValue) : myCVT :
             szChar : %len(szChar) : '$,.');

      return;
  /end-free
```

In this example, the text field SZCHAR contains the value '$1,234.50–'. This text string is converted to a Packed(7,2) value by the _CVTEFN function.

The data structure MYCVT is set to hex zeros (X'00') so that all the subfields are properly initialized. The data-type is set to T_Packed (X'03'), the length is set to 7, and the number of decimal position is 2.

Using _CVTEFN to Convert Fixed-length Character to Numeric

```
H BNDDIR('QC2LE') OPTION(*NODEBUGIO:*SRCSTMT)
H DFTACTGRP(*NO) ACTGRP(*NEW)

    // Include the prototype for _CVTEFN and DPA_T DS
  /INCLUDE rpgtnt,qcpysrc,rpgtnt

D szChar          S            25A Inz('  $1,234.50-  ')
D myNumValue      S             9P 2
D myCVT           DS                LikeDS(DPA_T)
D nLen            S            10I 0

C                eval       *INLR = *ON

  /free
      myCvt = *ALLX'00';        // Clear the data structure.
      myCvt.type = T_Packed;  // Set data-type to packed.
      myCvt.length = %len(myNumValue); // Set length to 9
      myCvt.decPos = %decpos(myNumValue); // Set decppos to 2

      nLen = %len(%Trim(szChar)); // Get length sans blanks
          // Do the conversion
      cvtefn(%addr(myNumValue) : myCVT :
             %Trim(szChar) : nLen : '$,.');

      return;
  /end-free
```

The %LEN built-in function is used to retrieve the declared length of the return variable named MYNUMVALUE. The %DECPOS built-in function is used to retrieve the decimal positions of that same field. Note that %DEC does not allow these built-in functions when converting from character to numeric—you must hard-code the length and decimals when using %DEC. This is another advantage of using _CVTEFN instead of %DEC. Then, %TRIM and %LEN are used to calculate the number of bytes in the text string and eliminate any trailing or leading blanks.

When _CVTEFN is called, %TRIM(szChar) is used to ensure that only the data is passed to the function.

67 Converting To and From Hexadecimal

The ability to convert from plain text characters to the 2-part hexadecimal representation of those characters has had numerous techniques applied over the years. Fortunately, an efficient and easy interface is provided on OS/400 to perform this type of conversion.

There are two MI instructions to convert between hexadecimal and character. They are

- cvthc — Converts from character to hexadecimal: 'ABC' -> 'C1C2C3'
- cvtch — Converts to hexadecimal from character: 'C1C2C3' -> 'ABC'

While the MI instruction names may seem backwards, they are actually following the order of their parameters. Conversion by these functions is always performed from the second parameter *into* the first parameter. The prototypes for cvthc() and cvtch() follow:

Prototypes for Converting To and From Hexadecimal

```
 **   The CVTHC MI (convert to hex) instruction
 **      '123' -> 'F1F2F3'
D ToHex           PR                        extProc('cvthc')
D  szHexVal                      65534A     OPTIONS(*VARSIZE)
D  szCharVal                     32766A     CONST OPTIONS(*VARSIZE)
D  nHexLen                         10I 0    Value

 **   The CVTCH MI (convert from hex) instruction
 **      'F1F2F3' -> '123'
D FromHex         PR                        extProc('cvtch')
D  szCharVal                     32766A     OPTIONS(*VARSIZE)
D  szHexVal                      65535A     CONST OPTIONS(*VARSIZE)
D  nHexLen                         10I 0    Value
```

To use these MI instructions in RPG IV, specify them with the length parameter (third parameter) containing the length of the hexadecimal data, because whether you are converting to or from hexadecimal, the length parameter is always the length of the hexadecimal data.

When using these instructions, be certain to specify the length of the data to be converted. Normally, this is the length of the variable that contains the data, but often it is the length of the data in that variable without trailing blanks. Specify the *correct* length—or else extra data may appear in the result.

The following example illustrates the use of the cvthc() and cvtch() MI instructions in RPG IV.

```
    H OPTION(*SRCSTMT) BNDDIR('QC2LE')          Note the binding directory
    H DFTACTGRP(*NO)                            QC2LE is required for
                                                MI instructions

       **   The CVTHC MI instruction
    D ToHex           PR                              extProc('cvthc')
    D  szHexVal                      65534A     OPTIONS(*VARSIZE)
    D  szCharVal                     32766A     Const OPTIONS(*VARSIZE)
    D  nHexLen                          10I 0 Value

       **   The CVTCH MI instruction
    D FromHex         PR                              extProc('cvtch')
    D  szCharVal                     32766A     OPTIONS(*VARSIZE)
    D  szHexVal                      65535A     Const OPTIONS(*VARSIZE)
    D  nHexLen                          10I 0 Value

    D name            S                10A     Inz('Bob Cozzi')
    D hexName         S                20A
    D nDataLen        S                10I 0
    D nHexLen         S                10I 0

    C                    eval        *INLR = *ON

    C                    eval        nDataLen = %Len(%TrimR(name))
    C                    callp       ToHex(hexName:name:nDataLen*2)

    C                    clear                   name

    C                    eval        nHexLen = %Len(%TrimR(hexName))
    C                    callp       FromHex(name:hexName:nHexLen)
    C                    return
```

The first EVAL calculates the length of the data in the NAME field. The length, 9, is stored in the nDataLen field. When TOHEX is called, this length is multiplied by 2 to represent the hexadecimal length of the data.

The call to TOHEX creates the hexadecimal version of 'Bob Cozzi'. The result is 'C2968240C396A9A989'. Note that since the %TRIMR() built-in function is used to calculate the length, only the actual 9 characters in the NAME field are converted to hexadecimal—the trailing blanks are not converted. Depending on the situation or application requirements, trailing blanks may or may not need to be converted.

If the trailing blanks were included, *hex forties* (X'40') would have followed the other hexadecimal character pairs.

To convert the data back to character, the length of the hexadecimal data is calculated, again stripping off all trailing blanks. That length, 18, is stored in the nHexLen field. The hexadecimal string 'C2968240C396A9A989' is converted back to a set of single characters. The result is that the string 'Bob Cozzi' is stored in the NAME field.

68 Using Decimal Fields as Real-Date Values

Since the beginning of OS/400, Date data-types have been available. It wasn't until the Y2K panic, however, that application developers started to include them in their programs and databases.

In DDS, a Date data-type is defined with an L (for *Lillian*). Date variables are stored in the database in an internal 4-byte integer (10u0) value, which is hidden from high-level interfaces. This integer contains the number of days since January 1, 0000. Many date-based interfaces, such as CEEDYWK (see Tip #59) don't use January 1, 0000 as their base date but instead use October 14, 1582. This date was the day before the adoption of the Gregorian calendar. October 15, 1582 is represented as day 1.

Date data-types are stored in an internal format and displayed in the external form. The external format is the date format specified on the DATFMT keyword associated with the date field. There is no way to view the internal form of the date variable. The external form is the only format you can view or manipulate.

To display the content of a date variable (in its external format), the system is constantly converting from the internal form to the external form. All this conversion uses processing power and, therefore, takes time. Consequently, many application programmers decided to avoid using date variables in their database designs, opting instead for 8-digit zoned or packed numeric fields.

Fortunately, RPG IV allows numeric fields that contain date information to be converted to a real-date data-type value. That value can be used as a real-date value with any of the opcodes or built-in functions that support date variables.

Simply wrapping an 8-digit zoned numeric variable in the %DATE built-in function allows the non-real-date value to be used as a real-date value.

The following database file's DDS includes two fields that contain date information: ORDDTE and SHIPDTE. These fields are not date fields but 8-digit zoned numeric fields with the date information stored in YYYYMMDD format.

```
 **   Order Record
A          R ORDREC
A            ORDNBR        7P 0
A            ORDDTE        8S 0
A            DUEDTE        8S 0
A            SHIPDTE       8S 0
A            INVNBR       11P 0
```

This technique allows dates that are stored in non-date fields to be sorted correctly when used as a key field of the file.

When records from the ORDERS file are created, the current system date is used as the order date, the due date is 30 days from the order date, and the ship date is normally set to zero until the order is shipped.

Since none of the fields are actually date data-types, opcodes or built-in functions need to be used to convert the numeric values to date values.

- Use the %DATE() built-in function to convert a numeric value into a real-date value.
- Use the %DEC() built-in function to convert real-date values to decimal.
- When converting numeric variables containing a date value in YYYYMMDD format, specify *ISO on the second parameter of the %DATE() built-in function, as follows:

Convert an 8-digit Numeric Value to a Real-Date Variable

```
D ORDDTE          S             8S 0 Inz(20061030)
D OrderDate       S             D

/free
     OrderDate = %date(ORDDTE:*ISO);
/end-free
```

The %DATE() built-in function converts numeric or character values to a real-date value that can be used in subsequent date arithmetic. The second parameter specifies the format of the nondate value being converted. Storing the new date value in a variable is not required, but it often helps simplify the coding when the value must be reused.

To convert the date value back to a numeric value, use the %DEC() built-in function. Specify the format for the numeric value in parameter two of the %DEC() built-in function.

Convert a Real-Date Value to an 8-digit Numeric Value

```
D ORDDTE          S             8S 0
D OrderDate       S             D    Inz(D'2006-10-30')

/free
   ORDDTE = %dec(OrderDate:*ISO);
/end-free
```

In this example, the date variable ORDERDATE is converted to numeric by the %DEC built-in function. The resulting date stored in the numeric variable is specified as being in YYYYMMDD (*ISO) format.

Convert a Real-Date Value to a 10-Position Character Value

```
D ORDDATE          S              10A
D OrderDate        S               D    Inz(D'2006-10-30')

 /free
    ORDDTE = %char(OrderDate:*ISO);
 /end-free
```

In the above example, the date variable ORDERDATE is converted to character by the %CHAR built-in function. The target date stored in the ORDDATE variable is stored as '2006-10-30', which is the *ISO date format.

It is relatively easy to read a database record with an 8-digit zoned numeric field that contains a date value. Simply use that date value in your code (adding 30 days to it, for example) and then update it back out to the database file without ever storing it in a work field. The %DATE() and %DEC() help accomplish this:

```
FORDERS     UF A E          K DISK

 /Free
    read OrdRec;
    if not %EOF();
                    // Initialize the ORDDTE to the job date
        ORDDTE = %dec(%date():*ISO);

            //  Add 1 day to ORDDTE to get INVDTE
        INVDTE = %dec(%date(ORDDTE)+%days(1):*ISO);

            // Add 30 days to INVDTE to get DUEDTE
        DUEDTE = %dec(%date(INVDTE)+%days(30):*ISO);

            //  If the product is being shipped today,
            //  set the ship date to the job date.
        if (bShipped);
            SHPDTE = %dec(%date():*ISO);
        else;
            SHPDTE = 0;
        endif;
            // Calc the difference between
            // the job date and the DUEDTE.
        if (%diff( %date():%date(DUEDTE):*days) > 0);
            callp latePayment(ORDNBR);
        endif;
    endif;

 /end-free
```

69 Check Object Existence

It is rather easy to check for an object's existence in a CL program: Simply use the CHKOBJ CL command and monitor for error message CPF9810. But how do you check for an object's existence in RPG IV?

There are two solutions: one requires the use of the RSLVSP MI instruction; the other uses the QUSROBJD API. However, in my opinion, the RSLVSP method is best suited for C or C++ as it is not easily implemented in RPG IV. The RSLVSP MI instruction method is several times faster than calling the API. However, it doesn't warrant the extra complexity.

The QUSROBJD (Retrieve Object Description) API attempts to retrieve information about a given object. The least amount of information QUSROBJD returns includes the object creation date/time and the last changed date/time. There are a number of other attributes returned, but none of them are helpful unless you're looking for the library name for an object on the library list. (For retrieving the library for an object from the library list, see Tip #71.)

When calling QUSROBJD, you can pass it the standard API error data structure. When the call to QUSROBJD is complete, then if there are no errors generated, the object exists. If there are errors, the object may not exist.

As with the CHKOBJ CL command, checking for CPF9810 can be accomplished after calling the QUSROBJD API. The CPF message, if generated, is returned to the CPFMSGID subfield of the QUSEC_T data structure.

QUSEC Data Structure Template

```
D QUSEC_T          DS                  Qualified Based(ptr_Nothing)
D  bytesProvided              10I 0
D  bytes_Provided...
D                             10I 0 Overlay(bytesProvided)
D  bytesProv                  10I 0 Overlay(bytesProvided)
D  bytesReturned              10I 0 Inz
D  bytes_Returned...
D                             10I 0 Overlay(bytesReturned)
D  bytesRtn                   10I 0 Overlay(bytesReturned)
D  cpfmsgID                    7A
D  reserved                    1A   Inz(X'00')
D  exceptionData              64A   Inz(*ALLX'00')
```

This version of QUSEC varies from the QUSEC in the QSYSINC library in two ways. First, the subfield names are different; second, the length of the exceptionData (exception error message data) subfield is specified as 64 bytes—long enough for most error conditions.

After calling QUSROBJD, test the bytesReturned subfield for non-zero. If it is greater than 0, an error has occurred. Further inspection of the CPFMSGID subfield will indicate the kind of error that occurred.

Check if Object Exists Subprocedure

```
H Copyright('(c) 2006 Robert Cozzi, Jr. All rights reserved.')
H NOMAIN OPTION(*NODEBUGIO:*SRCSTMT) BNDDIR('QC2LE')

/INCLUDE RPGTNT/QCPYSRC,rpgtnt

P ChkObj           B                    Export
D ChkObj           PI             1N
D  objName                       21A    Const
D  ObjType                       10A    Const
D  msgID                          7A    OPTIONS(*NOPASS)

D object           S             20A
D bNotFound        S              1N    Inz(*OFF)
D bFound           S              1N    Inz(*ON)
 **  See Appendix A item 2
D myObj            DS                    LikeDS(OBJD0100_T) INZ
 **  See Appendix A item 1
D apiError         DS                    LikeDS(QUSEC_T)

 /free
      clear    apiError;
      apiError.bytesProvided = %size(apiError);
      object = parseObject(objName);
      QusRtvObjd(myOBJ:%size(myOBJ):'OBJD0100'
        : object : objType : apiError);
      if  (apiError.bytesReturned > 0);  // Error
         if   (apiError.cpfmsgid<>*BLANKS);
            if (%parms() >= 3);
               msgID = apiError.cpfmsgID;
            endif;
            Select;
               When  (apiError.cpfmsgID='CPF9801' or
                      apiError.cpfmsgID='CPF9810' or
                      apiError.cpfmsgID='CPF9811' or
                      apiError.cpfmsgID='CPF9812' or
                      apiError.cpfmsgID='CPF9814');
                  return    bNotFound;
               other;
               //  QUSROBJD failed for another reason
            endSL;
         endIf;
      endif;
      return  bFound;
 /end-free

P ChkObj           E
```

parseObject() is featured in Tip #70

To call the CHKOBJ subprocedure, pass an object name and object type. If the object is found, CHKOBJ returns '1'—otherwise '0' is returned. The optional third parameter, MSGID, can be specified as a 7-position character variable that receives the CPF message ID that was generated by the call to QUSROBJD.

The returned value is an Indicator data-type that may be used on a conditional statement, as follows:

```
if  (chkobj('QGPL/QRPGLESRC':'*FILE' : msgid));
      joblog('QRPGLESRC exists in QGPL.');
else;
      joblog('Object not found. %s issued.':msgid);
endif;
```

The CHKOBJ subprocedure is called specifying 'QGPL/QRPGLESRC' as the object name and with '*FILE' specified as the object type. If the object is detected, the IF condition tests true, and the message *"QRPGLESRC exists in QGPL"* is written to the joblog. If the object is not found, the IF condition tests false, and *"Object not found"* is written to the joblog.

The Joblog() subprocedure, which provides an easy method for writing text strings out to the joblog, is featured in Tip #77.

70 Supporting Qualified Object Syntax

Some of the more contemporary features in RPG IV support a qualified object syntax that is similar to that supported by CL commands. For example, the CHKOBJ CL command and many others use 'library/object' qualified syntax:

```
CHKOBJ OBJ(QGPL/QRPGLESRC) OBJTYPE(*FILE)
```

Features recently added to RPG IV—such as the EXTFILE and EXTMBR keywords (see Tip #43) and the update to the DTAARA keyword—support this qualified syntax.

```
FCustmast  IF   E           K DISK    ExtFile('PRODLIB/CUSTMAST')
```

APIs, on the other hand, have traditionally supported a 20-byte object name where the first 10 positions are the object name and the final 10 positions are the library name. This is referred to as *fixed-position syntax*. In subprocedures, it is often more convenient to the caller of the subprocedure to specify an object name using CL-style qualified syntax rather than the 20-byte fixed-position syntax.

The CHKOBJ subprocedure (see Tip #69) allows the caller of the subprocedure to specify the object name in either traditional format or the new qualified syntax. It does this by calling a routine that converts object names from qualified syntax to the traditional format, which is required by the call to the QUSROBJD API.

The PARSEOBJECT subprocedure parses an object name and returns it in the traditional 20-byte format: the first 10 bytes with the object name and the second 10 bytes with the library name. The input to this subprocedure can be a qualified object name or the traditional 20-byte fixed-format object name.

PARSEOBJECT works by searching the input string for a forward slash (qualified syntax) or a blank (traditional format). When it detects either of these characters, it discerns which format was specified. It returns a 20-byte fixed-format object name as its return value. The prototype for the ParseObject subprocedure follows:

```
D ParseObject     PR              20A
D  objName                        21A    Const
```

The input parameter is 21 bytes long so that it can accept either a traditional 20-byte object and library name or the qualified-object name. The extra byte is to hold the forward slash qualifier:

```
'QGPL/QRPGLESRC      '
```

This is converted to a traditional 20-byte object name and returned to its caller:

```
'QRPGLESRC QGPL      '
```

ParseObject() also accepts traditional 20-byte object names, and round-trips them back to the caller.

The source for the parseObject() subprocedure, is as follows:

ParseObject() Subprocedure Source

```
P ParseObject     B                      Export
D ParseObject     PI            20A
D   objName                     21A       Const

D obj             DS                      Qualified
D   name                        10A
D   lib                         10A
D i               S             10I 0

 /free
    for i = 1 to %len(ObjName);
      if (%subst(objName:i:1)='/');
        if (i < %len(objName));
          obj.name = %subst(objName:i+1);
        endif;
        if (i > 1);
          obj.lib  = %subst(objName:1:i-1);
        endif;
        leave;  // finished, so leave.
      elseif (%subst(objName:i:1)=' ');
        if (i > 1);
          if ((i-1) <= %size(obj.name));
            obj.name = %subst(objName:1:i-1);
            if (i < %len(objName));
              obj.lib = %trim(%subst(objName:i+1));
            endif;
          else; // If mark is beyond object name maxlen...
                // assume value is traditional syntax.
            obj.name = %subst(objName:1:%size(obj.name));
            obj.lib  = %TrimL(%subst(objName:%size(obj.name)+1));
          endif;
        endif;
        leave; // finished, so leave.
      elseif (i >= %len(ObjName)); // No marks?
        obj.name = %subst(objName:1:%size(obj.name));
        obj.lib  = %TrimL(%subst(objName:%size(obj.name)+1));
```

Continued...

...continued

```
             leave;  // At end of name, so leave.
           endif;

       endfor;
       return obj;
    /end-free

    P ParseObject     E
```

Explained: Bytes Provided, Bytes Available, and Bytes Returned

API use requires API Data Structures or *formats*, as the API documentation calls them. These formats have a distinct structure for each API.

There are 4 "length" values associated with many API formats. One is the Receiver Variable Length, which is normally specified as a separate parameter. This value indicates the length of the data structure that you provide to receive the results of the API.

The other three values are somewhat ambiguous due to their naming conventions. They are

- Bytes Provided
- Bytes Returned
- Bytes Available

Bytes Provided—Length of the Data Structure

The Bytes Provided subfield is used to indicate the length of the data structure being provided to the API. This value is used with API parameters that do not include a format identifier or when a Receiver Variable Length parameter would make things too cluttered.

The Bytes Provided field is normally embedded as the first subfield of an API data structure. For example, the API Error Data Structure, QUSEC, can be defined as follows:

```
D QUSEC_T          DS                  QUALIFIED
D  bytesProvided              10I 0
D  bytesReturned              10I 0
D  cpfmsgID                    7A
D  reserved                    1A
D  exceptionData              64A
```

The bytesProvided subfield must be initialized before calling any API that uses its parent data structure:

```
D myUSEC          DS              LIkeDS(QUSEC_T)

 /free
      myUSEC.bytesProvided = %size(myUSEC);
 /end-free
```

This sets the bytes-provided subfield to the size of the data structure itself.

Some programmers prefer to initialize the Bytes Provided subfield (rather than set it at runtime):

```
D QUSEC_T         DS              QUALIFIED
D  bytesProvided              10I 0  Inz(%size(myUSEC))
D  bytesReturned              10I 0
D  cpfmsgID                    7A
D  reserved                    1A
D  exceptionData              64A
```
> Specify %SIZE(ds) as the initial value for the Bytes Provided subfield

This allows the data structure to be reset to its initial value while retraining the original Bytes Provided value; for example:

```
D myUSEC          DS              LIkeDS(QUSEC_T) Inz(*LIKEDS)

 /free
     QusRtvObjd(myOBJ:%size(myOBJ):'OBJD0100'
                : object : objType : myUSEC);
     reset myUSEC;
     QusRtvObjd(myOBJ2:%size(myOBJ2):'OBJD0100'
                : object : objType : myUSEC);
 /end-free
```

The bytesProvided subfield is initialized to the length of the parent data structure. An API is called using—and potentially changing the content of—MYUSEC. The RESET opcode is used to change the data structure back to its original value; clearing out the structure and setting bytesProvided back to its original value.

Bytes Returned

Many APIs require a format identifier. This format identifier is similar to a record format name—that is, it has a specific layout and typically has a fixed length. The formats are actually a way to inform an API as to what information it should return. For example, 'FMT0100' might return the minimum amount of information, whereas 'FMT0200' would return everything that 'FMT0100' returns plus addition information.

These Format Data Structures directly relate to data structure layouts used by the API.

The first subfield of many of these format data structures is *Bytes Returned*. The API sets the Bytes Returned subfield to the number of bytes it returned into the user-supplied return buffer (i.e., data structure).

The QUSROBJD (Retrieve Object Description) API, for example, returns data in several different formats. All these formats have the following subfields in common:

```
D OBJD0100        DS                 QUALIFIED Inz
D   bytesReturned            10I 0
D   bytesAvail               10I 0   ← Bytes Returned by the API
D   name                     10A
D   library                  10A
D   type                     10A
D   objtype                  10A   Overlay(type)
D   rtnLibrary               10A
D   rtnLib                   10A   Overlay(rtnLibrary)
D   ASP                      10I 0
D   domain                    2A
D   crtDate                  13A
D   chgDate                  13A
```

The Bytes Returned subfield is set to the number of bytes returned by the QUSROBJD API. If Bytes Returned is less than the Bytes Available subfield, the data structure may not have been long enough to receive all the data generated by the API.

There are two situations in which this can occur: either the API has been updated or altered by IBM, and the format of the returned data has changed; or the data structure being passed is defined incorrectly—that is, it is not large enough to handle all the data being returned.

Therefore, when processing data returned by an API, you should always check the Bytes Returned rather than assume that the data returned to the data structure is complete.

Bytes Available

When an API is called, it generates a known set of data. That data is referred to as the *available data;* the length of that available data is referred to as *bytes available*. The API returns the Bytes Available to the Bytes Available subfield of the return data structure. The Bytes Available subfield represents the *potential* number of bytes that may be returned by the API. It may not be the number of bytes *actually* returned.

The Bytes Available may be greater than or equal to the Bytes Returned. If Bytes Available is greater than Bytes Returned, the API could have returned more data if the programmer had provided a larger return data structure to the API.

The Bytes Available is normally specified as the second subfield of the API's returned data structure:

```
D OBJD0100         DS                    QUALIFIED Inz
D  bytesReturned                  10I 0
D  bytesAvail                     10I 0  ←  Bytes Available is the potential
D  name                           10A          byte count returned by an API
D  library                        10A
D  type                           10A
D  objtype                        10A   Overlay(type)
D  rtnLibrary                     10A
D  rtnLib                         10A   Overlay(rtnLibrary)
D  ASP                            10I 0
D  domain                          2A
D  crtDate                        13A
D  chgDate                        13A
```

72 Converting To or From ASCII and Other Character Sets

Reading files from the Integrated File System (IFS) requires the use of the so-called IFS APIs or the Unix®-type APIs. Both these APIs allow a file on the IFS to be read by RPG and other programming languages.

These APIs can be adjusted to automatically convert the data in the file from its native character set (typically ASCII) to the character set of the RPG program's job (typically EBCDIC). This conversion is performed automatically when a text file is read from the IFS and that text file was open with the O_TEXTDATA flag.

But what if you need to convert data between EBCDIC and ASCII within the RPG IV program itself? This is often necessary when sending it to a Web service, writing it to a Web browser, or writing out binary data to the IFS in the ASCII character set. The best choice for this type of conversion is the iconv() API.

The iconv() API converts a group of characters from one coded character set identifier (CCSID) to another. Using iconv() isn't very straightforward, and many programmers tend to use the less accurate and, in fact, deprecated QDCXLATE API to perform conversions.

The confusion may be that iconv() really consists of three different steps and requires the use of three out of four APIs:

- QtqIconvOpen() — Opens/Creates an iconv() "environment"
- iconv_open() — Opens/Creates an iconv() "environment" (old version)
- iconv() performs conversion of data using the iconv() environment handle
- iconv_close() destroys ("closes") the iconv() environment

There are three steps to performing a conversion with iconv() APIs:

- Create and Open an iconv environment
- Perform a conversion 1 or more time using the iconv environment
- Close/Destroy the conversion environment

This design allows a conversion to be performed more efficiently than other methods because the conversion environment is created once and then used as much as necessary by an application.

To create and open a Conversion Environment, the iconv_open() API may be used. However, the more contemporary QtqIconvOpen() API is preferred. These APIs create a conversion environment and return an identifier or *handle* to that environment. The handle is similar to using a file handle returned by the sockets or IFS I/O APIs.

The iconv() Conversion Environment handle provides a way to reference the conversion environment. It also allows the environment to be created once and used many times, *and* it allows multiple conversion environments to be created or open in the application at once. For example, conversion from CCSID(37) to CCSID(819) can be created along with another conversion environment for CCSID(37) to CCSID(1208).

Once a Conversion Environment has been created and the handle saved, one or more conversions may be performed with the iconv() API using the handle as a reference.

When finished converting, the conversion environment needs to be destroyed using the iconv_close() API.

The key to using these APIs together is the conversion environment handle that is returned by the QtqIconvOpen() API. The template for this handle is the iconv_T data structure as follows:

The iconv() Conversion Environment Handle

```
D iconv_T         DS              Qualified BASED(NULL)
D   rtn_value                10I 0
D   cd                       10I 0 Dim(12)
```

To create the conversion environment, a data structure containing the original data's CCSID and conversion options must be specified. In addition, the output data's CCSID and conversion options must also be specified. Fortunately, when using QtqIconvOpen(), these data structures are identical:

The iconv() Conversion Structure

```
D QtqCode_T       DS              Qualified Based(NULL)
D   CCSID                    10I 0
D   CvtAlt                   10I 0
D   SubstAlt                 10I 0
D   shiftState               10I 0
D   inLengthOpt              10I 0
D   errMixDataOpt            10I 0
D   reserved                  8A
```

To declare the conversion structures for from and to values, two data structure should be declared.

```
D fromConv        DS                     LikeDS(QtqCode_T) Inz
D toConv          DS                     LikeDS(QtqCode_T) Inz
```

The fromConv data structure contains the CCSID and conversion options for the original data. The toConv data structure contains the target CCSID and conversion options for the output data.

These values are initialized and passed to the QtqIconvOpen() API. The Prototype for QtqIconvOpen() is as follows:

Prototype for QtqIconvOpen — Open iconv() Environment

```
D QtqIConvOpen    PR                     extProc('QtqIconvOpen')
D                                        LikeDS(iconv_t)
D   toCCSID                              LikeDS(QtqCode_T)
D   fromCCSID                            LikeDS(QtqCode_T)
```

The return value for QtqIconvOpen() is an ICONV_T data structure. The two input parameters are TOCCSID and FROMCCSID, which are both QTQCODE_T data structures.

Be sure to specify the target CCSID structure in the *first* parameter and the original or from CCSID in the *second* parameter. It is a common error to inadvertently reverse these parameters.

Calling the QtqIconvOpen() API to create a conversion environment requires just a few lines of code:

```
D fromConv        DS                     LikeDS(QtqCode_T)
D toConv          DS                     LikeDS(QtqCode_T)
D hAscii          DS                     LikeDS(iconv_T)

 /free
     Clear fromConv;
     Clear toConv;
     Clear hASCII;

     fromConv.reserved = *ALLX'00';
     fromConv.CCSID    = 37;  // EBCDIC CCSID(37)

     toConv.reserved = *ALLX'00';
     toConv.CCSID    = 819; // IFS ASCII CCSID(819)

     hASCII = qtqIconOpen(toConv : fromConv );
     if   (hASCII.rtn_value < 0);  // Did it work?
       // Failed to open conversion environment
        return;
     endif;

     //  hASCII = The handle to conversion environment.
 /end-free
```

In this example, from and to conversion data structures are declared along with a handle to the conversion environment. The CCSID of the fromConv data structure is set to 37 (U.S. North America EBCDIC) and the toConv CCSID is set to 819 (IFS ASCII).

The QtqIconvOpen() API is called with the conversion handles toConv, and fromConv data structures as parameters. At this point, the conversion environment for EBCDIC to ASCII has been created. The environment handle is stored in the hASCII data structure. If the RTN_VALUE subfield of the handle is less than zero, an error occurred and the conversion environment was not created.

Once the conversion environment is created, it can be used to convert text from the original CCSID (specified in fromConv) to the target CCSID (specified in toConv). The iconv() API is used to do this. Calling this API is not as simple as most programs or subprocedures; the parameter list is a bit tricky with "pointer to pointer" data-types, as follows:

Prototype for iconv() API

```
D iconv           PR            10U 0 extProc('iconv')
D  hConv                               LikeDS(iconv_t) VALUE
D  pInBuff                        *
D  nInLen                        10U 0
D  pOutBuff                       *
D  nOutLen                       10U 0

D iconv_ERROR      C                   Const(X'FFFFFFFF')
```

The first parameter of iconv() is the conversion environment returned from a previous call to QtqIconvOpen() or iconv_open().

The second parameter is the address of a pointer variable. Because RPG passes parameters by reference, which also means *by address*, then all that is needed is a pointer variable passed by reference. The iconv() API modifies these pointers, so they must be pointer variables and not simply a %ADDR() built-in function.

The third parameter is the length of the data specified on the first parameter. The API may update this value so that it also needs to be passed in a variable rather than a built-in function or named constant.

The third and fourth parameters are the same as the second and third parameters, respectively, but apply to the output data.

When iconv() finishes performing the conversion, the nInLen and nOutLen parameters are modified. The nInLen parameter contains the number of characters that have not been converted. If everything ran correctly (which is typical), then nInLen is set to zero. The nOutLen parameter will contain the number of characters remaining in the output buffer. The difference between this value and the original value for this parameter is the length of the data written to the output buffer (parameter 4). This output length is helpful when converting between CCSIDs that represent different length character sets, such as when converting from CCSID(1200) (a multi-byte CCSID) to CCSID(37) (a single-byte CCSID)—where the output length is half the length of the input.

The named constant ICONV_ERROR is defined as a –1 (hence the X'FFFFFFFF') to compare with the value returned from iconv(). If iconv() returns a –1, it failed to perform a conversion. Unfortunately, iconv() designers chose an unsigned integer value (10u0) as the return value, which obviously cannot be compared against a negative value. Use the ICONV_ERROR named constant when testing for a failure condition on iconv().

Once a conversion environment is created, call iconv() to convert data between the two CCSIDs, as follows:

```
/free
     pFrom = %addr(myData);
     pTo   = %addr(myOutput);
     nLen  = %size(myData); // Entire field
 //    nLen  = %len(%TrimR(myData)); // Only non-blanks
     if (iconv(hASCII : pFrom : nLen : pTo : nLen) = ICONV_ERROR);
         //  An error occurred during conversion! :(
     else;
         // The data in myOutput is ASCII.
     endif;
/end-free
```

The field named MYDATA is declared as Char(50) (not shown). However, only 7 nonblank characters are stored in it. Blanks in EBCDIC(37) are X'40'. Specifying a length of 50 will convert not only the first 7 characters but also the trailing blank characters. Blanks in ASCII(819) are X'20'. If only the text up to the last nonblank character should be converted, consider using %LEN(%TRIMR(MYDATA)) to calculate the length of the data to be converted.

Destroy the conversion environment—a necessary step—after it is no longer needed by calling the iconv_close() API. Specify the conversion handle of the environment you want to close. The prototype for iconv_close() is as follows:

Prototype for the iconv_close() API

```
D iconv_close    PR              10I 0 extProc('iconv_close')
D   hConv                               LikeDS(iconv_t) VALUE
```

After calling iconv_close(), clear the handle variable so that it does not contain any of the old information from the previous conversion environment. This is done in case the variable is reused later in the same application for another conversion handle; for example:

```
/free
     if (iconv(hASCII : pFrom : nLen : pTo : nLen)=ICONV_ERROR);
         //  An error occurred during conversion! :(
     else;
         // The data in the OUTPUT variable is ASCII!
     endif;

     iconv_close(hASCII);  // Close the conversion handle

     clear hASCII;  // Clean up the handle
/end-free
```

The logic behind using iconv() and its related APIs isn't difficult. Its logic is similar to reading a file, processing it, and then closing the file. To help clarify any remaining obscurity, the following flowchart illustrates the workflow when using iconv().

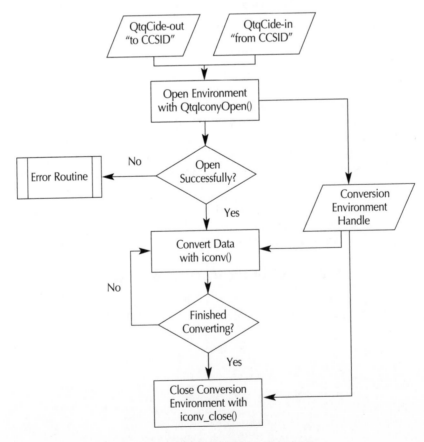

Flowchart of the iconv() Conversion Process

A complete program that illustrates the iconv() APIs to convert between EBCDIC and ASCII follows.

Using iconv() for CCSID/Character Conversion — Complete Example

```
H BNDDIR('QC2LE') DFTACTGRP(*NO)

 /COPY  RPGTNT/QCPYSRC,RPGTNT

D fromConv        DS                      LikeDS(QtqCode_T)
D toConv          DS                      LikeDS(QtqCode_T)
D hAscii          DS                      LikeDS(iconv_T)
D rtn             DS                      LikeDS(size_T)

D myData          S              50A      Inz('RPG TNT Book')
D output          S              50A
D nLen            S              10U 0
D pFrom           S               *
D pTo             S               *

C                   eval      *INLR = *ON
 /free
      // Clear the data structures used by the API.
    Clear fromConv;
    Clear toConv;
    Clear hASCII;

    fromConv.reserved = *ALLX'00';
    fromConv.CCSID = 0;  // Use the Job's CCSID

    toConv.reserved = *ALLX'00';
    toConv.CCSID   = 819; // ASCII CCSID(819)

      // Open the conversion environment
    hASCII = QtqIconvOpen(toConv : fromConv );
    if    (hASCII.rtn_value < 0);
      // Failed to open conversion environment.
      return;
    endif;

    pFrom = %addr(msg);
    pTo   = %addr(output);
    nLen  = %size(myData);

    if (iconv(hASCII : pFrom : nLen : pTo : nLen)=ICONV_ERROR);
       // An error occurred during conversion! :(
    else;
       // The data in the OUTPUT variable is ASCII!
    endif;

    iconv_close(hASCII);
    clear hASCII;  // Clean up the handle
    return;

 /end-free
```

73 Register an Exit Routine for a Program or Service Program

When a service program ends, it is often necessary to call a routine that will perform clean up tasks—delete objects, close files, or free up memory that was allocated during the life of the service program. Normally, when an activation group ends, the Integrated Language Environment (ILE) automatically cleans things like memory allocations and open files, but it does not clean up temporary objects such as those created in QTEMP or other libraries.

If the program or service program creates objects—such as work files, data areas, or IFS files—how do you ensure that these temporary objects are cleaned up?

In this situation, there are only three options: (1) Create everything in QTEMP and then clear QTEMP when the application finishes. (2) Require that the user of the program or service program call a generic clean up routine (e.g., call to a CL program or a subprocedure). And (3) register a subprocedure that performs the cleanup automatically before the destruction of the activation group in which the program or service program is running.

The first option is rather easy: issue a CLRLIB QTEMP CL command after the application has finished. This will delete all the objects in that library. The library is normally deleted when the job ends so this may be a nonissue.

The second option is rather simple as well: call a CL program that issues DLTF, DLT-DTAQ, or other CL commands to clean up the temporary objects no matter where they are located. This option is a bit more complex, but it certainly isn't rocket science.

Implement the third option by registering what's known as an Activation Group Exit Procedure. This exit procedure is automatically called when the activation group in which it is registered ends.

An API named CEE4RAGE is used to register an activation group exit procedure. The API is straightforward—it accepts a pointer to the exit procedure and an error/feedback parameter, which can be omitted.

The prototype for CEE4RAGE follows.

CEE4RAGE Prototype — Register Activation Group Exit Procedure

```
D cee4rage        PR                      extProc('CEE4RAGE')
D   myExitProcPtr                 *       PROCPTR CONST
D   fc                          12A       OPTIONS(*OMIT:*VARSIZE)
```

The first parameter is a procedure pointer to the Exit Procedure being specified. Use the %PADDR() built-in function to retrieve a procedure pointer to any RPG IV subprocedure. Pass that procedure pointer to the registration API as follows:

```
cee4rage(%pAddr(myExitProc): *OMIT);
```

There is a 64-bit version of CEE4RAGE named CEE4RAGE2 that is available on OS/400 V5R3 and later. This variation applies to the parameter passed to the user-written exit procedure—the parameters of CEE4RAGE and CEE4RAGE2 are identical. The prototype for CEE4RAGE2 follows.

CEE4RAGE2 Prototypes with Conditional Directives

```
/IF DEFINED(*V5R3M0)
**   64-bit Register A/G Exit Proc w/64-bit marker
D cee4rage2       PR                      extProc('CEE4RAGE2')
D   myExitProcPtr                 *       PROCPTR CONST
D   fc                          12A       OPTIONS(*OMIT:*VARSIZE)
/ENDIF
```

The subprocedure being registered must have a specific set of parameters. These parameters are the same for all Activation Group Exit Procedures registered with CEE4RAGE. The following is a sample prototype for a subprocedure called by CEE4RAGE.

Exit Subprocedure Prototype for CEE4RAGE

```
D myExitProc      PR
D   ag_mark                     10U 0 Const
D   reason                      10U 0 Const
D   result_code                 10U 0
D   user_rc                     10U 0
```

Four parameters are passed to the exit subprocedure by CEE4RAGE. Parameters 1 and 2 are not modifiable by the subprocedure, so the CONST keyword is added. Parameters 3 and 4 may be changed by the subprocedure.

1. ag_mark — A 32-bit activation group marker that uniquely identifies the activation group within the job. This is a sequential number assigned by the system to the activation group when the activation group is created.

2. reason — A 32-bit reason code that indicates why the activation group is being destroyed. The reason codes are assigned to specific bits in this 32-bit value. You will need to use the V5R3 built-in functions for bit processing—such as %BITAND and %BITXOR—to test the bits of the reason code.

3. result_code — A 32-bit response to the CEE4RAGE routine that indicates what it should do when this exit subprocedure is finished.

4. user_rc — A 32-bit value that was passed by the previous exit procedure (if any). This value is zero the first time the exit procedure is called.

An exit procedure registered with the CEE4RAGE2 API supports a 64-bit activation group mark and is prototyped as follows:

CEE4RAGE2 — Exit Subprocedure Prototype

```
D myExitProcs      PR
D   ag_mark                       20U 0 Const
D   reason                        10U 0 Const
D   result_code                   10U 0
D   user_rc                       10U 0
```

The activation group mark is a 64-bit unsigned integer that is passed to the user-written exit procedure. This is defined as a 20U0 value in RPG IV. The rest of the parameters are identical to those of the CEE4RAGE exit subprocedure.

The following subprocedure is a skeleton or *shell* of a subprocedure that may be registered as an exit procedure with CEE4RAGE.

User-Written Exit SubProcedure Skeleton

```
P myExitProc       B                        EXPORT
D myExitProc       PI
D   ag_mark                       10U 0 Const
D   reason                        10U 0 Const
D   result_code                   10U 0
D   user_rc                       10U 0

 /free
     // Activation Group Exit SubProcedure.
     // TODO: Insert clean-up routine here.

     // Set result_code = (if necessary)
     // Set user_rc = (if necessary)
    return;

 /end-free

P myExitProc       E
```

The following program registers a subprocedure with CEE4RAGE. It then performs normal programlike functions (which have been omitted due to space constraints).

```
 H BNDDIR('QC2LE')
  /IF DEFINED(*CRTBNDRPG)
 H DFTACTGRP(*NO) ACTGRP(*NEW)
  /ENDIF

  /INCLUDE RPGTNT/QCPYSRC,rpgtnt

  ** User-write Exit Subprocedure prototype
 D myExitProc       PR
 D   ag_mark                      10U 0 Const
 D   reason                       10U 0 Const
 D   result_code                  10U 0
 D   user_rc                      10U 0

 D pSomeData        S              *
 D szData           S              1A    Based(pSomeData)

 C                   eval      *INLR = *ON
  /free

      // Register my exit subprocedure.
      cee4Rage(%pAddr(myExitProc): *OMIT);

      // Do the rest of the program/application...

      // Create a work file in QGPL.
      system('CRTPF FILE(QGPL/JUNK) RCDLEN(92)');

      // Create a data area in QTEMP.
      system('CRTDTAARA DTAARA(QTEMP/WORKDA) +
              TYPE(*CHAR) LEN(128)');

      // Allocate 1/4 meg of storage
      pSomeData = %alloc(256000);

      /////////////////////////////////////
      // The rest of the program goes here.
      /////////////////////////////////////

    return;
  /end-free
    // This is the user-written Exit SubProcedure
 P myExitProc       B                  EXPORT
 D myExitProc       PI
 D   ag_mark                      10U 0 Const
 D   reason                       10U 0 Const
 D   result_code                  10U 0
 D   user_rc                      10U 0

 D reason_bits      S             33A
 D bits             DS                  Qualified Inz
 D   bit                           1A   Dim(32)
 D   nBitLen                      10I 0
 D nSize            S             10I 0
```

Continued...

...continued

```
/free
    //  Exit Procedure: Free up any unneeded objects

    // This routine converts the 10U0 value
    // in the reason parm to binary 1's & 0's
    ultoa(reason:%addr(reason_bits):2);

    bits.nBitLen = %scan(X'00':reason_bits)-1;

    %SUBST(bits:%size(bits.bit:*ALL)-(bits.nBitLen-1):bits.nBitLen)
            = %subst(reason_bits:1:bits.nBitLen);

    bits.bit = %xlate(' ':'0':bits.bit);

      // If you need to determine why the exit proc
      // was called, test the corresponding bit value.
    if (bits.bit(2)  = *ON); // Exception message detected
    endif;
    if (bits.bit(3)  = *ON); // Bits(3 to 16) reserved
    endif;
    if (bits.bit(17) = *ON); // '1'=abnormal end; '0'=Normal end
    endif;
    if (bits.bit(18) = *ON); // '1'=Activation Group is ending
    endif;
    if (bits.bit(19) = *ON); // '1'=RCLACTGRP command issued
    endif;
    if (bits.bit(20) = *ON); // '1'=EndJob command issued
    endif;
    if (bits.bit(21) = *ON); // '1'=CEETREC or C's exit() issued.
    endif;
    if (bits.bit(22) = *ON); // '1'=Unmonitored function check
    endif;
    if (bits.bit(23) = *ON); // '1'=LongJmp or out-of-scope jump
    endif;

      //  Clean up any objects or memory that needs it.
      system('DLTF FILE(QGPL/JUNK)');
      system('DLTDTAARA DTAARA(QTEMP/WORKDA)');
      dealloc pSomeData;
    return;
/end-free

P myExitProc      E
```

Here, a file is created in QGPL, and then a data area is created in QTEMP. Finally, a quarter of a megabyte (.25MB) of storage is allocated. When the program ends and the activation group is cleaned up, the registered exit subprocedure is called, and the user-written cleanup tasks are performed.

74 Specifying IFS File Names Correctly

If you don't know this trick, specifying the name of a file that is stored on the Integrated File System (IFS) can be problematic.

When a function calls for the name of a file on the IFS, it wants the name in the C language's *null-terminated string* format. This means that trailing blanks cannot be specified. Why? Unlike RPG IV, when a null-terminated string is compared with another null-terminated string, trailing blanks *are* considered in the comparison. Consequently, the name *'/home/cozzi/sales.csv'* (with no trailing blanks) is different from *'/home/cozzi/sales.csv '* (with trailing blanks).

When specifying an IFS file name—with or without a path—be sure to trim off the trailing blanks or else IFS interfaces will generate an error (such as "File not found") even if the file exists.

For this reason, it's a good practice to always use VARYING fields to hold IFS file and/ or path names. For example, the following routine always fails, even when the SALES.CSV file exists in the /home/cozzi directory.

```
 D myPath            S              256A
 D hFile             S               10I 0

  /free
      myPath = '/home/cozzi/sales.xls';
      hFile = open(myPath : O_TEXTDATA+O_APPEND);
      if (hFile < 0);
          joblog('Failed to open %s':myPath);
      else;
          joblog('%s open successfully.' : myPath);
      endif;
  /end-free
```

The open() function fails because the string '/home/cozzi/sales.csv' is copied to a fixed-length character field whose length is 256 bytes. This leaves 235 blanks following the file name! These blanks are included in the search for the SALES.CSV file; consequently, open() fails.

To resolve this issue, you have to trim off all trailing blanks. There are three common methods to accomplish this:

- Use %TRIMR(ifsFileName) when calling the open() API
- Use a VARYING field and truncate trailing blanks in that field
- Use the V5.3 OPTIONS(*STRING:*TRIM) feature

To eliminate the trailing blanks using the %TRIMR built-in function, simply pass %trimR(myPath) to the open() API:

Open an IFS File Name Trimmed with %TRIMR

```
hFile = open(%trimR(myPath) : O_TEXTDATA+O_CREAT);
```

Another solution is to declare the MYPATH field as a VARYING field. Then when data is assigned to it, it is implicitly or explicitly trimmed of trailing blanks.

Properly Specifying IFS File Names and Paths

```
D myIFSFile       S           256A  Inz('home/cozzi/sales.xls')
D myPath          S           640A  VARYING

 /free
        // Implicit trailing blanks are trimmed
      myPath = '/home/cozzi/sales.xls';

        // Or explicitly trim trailing blanks.
      myPath = %TrimR(myIFSFile);

      if (access(myPath : F_OK) = 0);
          joblog('Opening %s':myPath);
      else;
          joblog('%s not found.':myPath);
      endif;
 /end-free
```

The final method requires redefinition of the IFS APIs so that all file/path parameters include the OPTIONS(*STRING:*TRIM) feature introduced in V5.3:

IFS open(), access(), and stat() Prototypes with *TRIM

```
D ifsAccess        PR              10I 0 extProc('access')
D  szIFSFile                        *    Value options(*string:*TRIM)
D  nAccessMode                     10I 0 Value

D ifsStat          PR              10I 0 ExtProc('stat64')
D  ifsFile                          *    Value options(*string:*TRIM)
D  pStat                            *    Value

D ifsOpen          PR              10I 0 extProc('open64')
D  szIFSFile                        *    Value options(*string:*TRIM)
D  openFlags                       10I 0 Value
D  fMod                            10U 0 Value options(*nopass)
D  CCSID                           10U 0 Value options(*nopass)
```

When OPTIONS(*STRING:*TRIM) is specified, the compiler trims off trailing blanks from the value before converting it to a C-style null-terminated string.

75 Checking if IFS Files Exist

The native object system includes the CHKOBJ command. This CL command can be used to verify whether or not an object exists on the system. The CHKOBJ command, however, does not support the IFS naming convention and therefore cannot be used to check whether or not a file exists on the IFS.

Since RPG IV can call any runtime function of the C language (see Tip #28) and because C has the ability to check for an IFS file, we can use that ability to check whether or not an IFS file exists.

Two C functions are commonly used to check for a file's existence:

- stat — Get File Statistics/Information
- access — Get File Accessibility

The stat() function returns a data structure of information on the file and also returns a negative or non-zero value when it fails. However, failure does not necessarily mean that the file does not exist. Since stat() returns a data structure of information, it takes longer to run (compared to the access() function) when the file exists.

The access() function checks for access permissions for a file. If the file exists, access() returns a zero. If it does not exist, a negative or non-zero value is returned. To further determine whether the file truly does not exist, the C runtime error number (errno) may be retrieved.

The prototype for the access() function follows.

Prototype for the C Runtime access() Function

```
D access           PR            10I 0 extProc('access')
D  ifsFile                         *    Value OPTIONS(*STRING)
D  nAccessMode                   10I 0 Value
```

The access() function accepts two parameters. The first is the name of the file; the second parameter must be one of the valid access modes:

Symbolic ID	Numeric Representation	Description
F_OK	0	Checks if the file exists.
R_OK	4	Checks whether the file has read access.
W_OK	2	Checks whether the file has write access.
X_OK	1	Checks whether the file can be accessed for execution (a program or ".exe" file).

In RPG IV, these symbols may be declared as follows:

```
        // access() modes
  D R_OK           C                       Const(4)
  D W_OK           C                       Const(2)
  D X_OK           C                       Const(1)
  D F_OK           C                       Const(0)
```

Assuming the file named qtrsales.xls does not exist in the '/home/acctfiles' directory, the following would return –1.

Check for IFS File Existence

```
D acctFile       S              640A    Varying

/free
    acctFile = '/home/acctfiles/qtrsales.xls';
    if (access(acctFile : F_OK)=0);
        joblog('File %s exists.':acctFile);
    else;
        joblog('File not found %s': acctFile);
    endif;
/end-free
```

76 RC4 Encryption Using Encryption APIs

The ability to encrypt data has been available for years. The MI CIPHER instruction has been available to perform T-DES (triple DES), RC4, AES, and other encryption schemes for many years. The problem, however, is that the CIPHER instruction is complex.

In V5R1, Encryption APIs were introduced to the operating system. These APIs provide a way to perform encryption without using the CIPHER instruction. The only problem with the APIs is that they are not specific enough (attempting to handle too many encryption algorithms) and are often thought of as being more complex than the original CIPHER instruction.

The proof for this view can be found in the Qc3EncryptData API prototype, as follows:

Qc3EncryptData API Prototype

```
D Qc3EncryptData  PR                         extProc('Qc3EncryptData')
D  clearData                      1A         OPTIONS(*VARSIZE)
D  nLenClearData                 10I 0 Const
D  clearDataFmt                   8A         Const

D  algorithmDescription...
D                                64A         Const OPTIONS(*VARSIZE)
D  algorithmFormatName....
D                                 8A         Const

D  keyDescription...
D                               512A         Const OPTIONS(*VARSIZE)
D  keyDescFormatName...
D                                 8A         Const

   ** '0'=Best choice, '1'=Software, '2'=Hardware
D  CryptoService                  1A         Const
   **   Hardware Cryptography device name or blanks
D  CryptoDevName                 10A         Const OPTION(*OMIT)

D  encryptedDataRtnVar...
D                                 1A         OPTIONS(*VARSIZE)
D  nEncryptedDataRtnVarLen...
D                                10I 0 Const
D  nLenOfEncryptedDataReturned...
D                                10I 0
D  api_ErrorDS                               LikeDS(QUSEC_EX)
D                                            OPTIONS(*VARSIZE)
```

The first parameter is the unencrypted or *clear* text that is to be encrypted.

The second parameter is the length of the data being encrypted (i.e., the length of the first parameter).

The third parameter may be the literal 'DATA0100' or 'DATA0200'. For one-time encryption routines, this parameter should be 'DATA0100'. If the data is too large to encrypt with one call to the Qc3EncryptData API, specify 'DATA0200', which indicates that encryption is continuing from a previous call to Qc3EncryptData.

The fourth parameter is a data structure that contains control fields for the specify type of encryption algorithm being requested. For example, if RC4 encryption is requested, a data structure with the ALGD0300 format is passed, and the literal 'ALGD0300' should be specified on the fifth parameter. The ALGD0300 data structure is defined as follows:

```
D ALGD0300_T      DS                       Qualified
D   Algorithm                        10I 0 Inz(30)
```

The Algorithm subfield should be initialized to 30 to indicate that RC4 encryption is being requested. When the ALGD0300_T data structure template is used, the Algorithm subfield can be initialized as follows:

```
D myRC4Algo       DS                       LikeDS(ALGD0300_T) Inz

C                 eval       myRC4algo.Algorithm = 30
```

The sixth and seventh parameters are used to identify the encryption key format. The sixth parameter accepts a data structure that contains the key to be used to perform the encryption. The seventh parameter is a literal that identifies the key description.

For RC4 encryption, specify a data structure with a format of KEYD0200 for the sixth parameter and the literal 'KEYD0200' for the seventh parameter. The format of the KEYD0200 data structure is as follows:

```
D KEYD0200_T      DS                       Qualified
D   type                             10I 0
D   length                           10I 0
D   format                            1A
D   keyValue                        256A
```

The eighth parameter is the type of cryptography service to be used. The choices for this parameter are '0'=Any, '1'=Software only, '2'=Hardware only. Unless you are certain that a hardware encryption feature is installed on the system, specify a value of '0', which uses the best available service.

The ninth parameter is the cryptography device name. If no device is being used, pass a null pointer or—even better—all blanks.

The tenth parameter is a variable that receives the encrypted data. This field should be large enough to receive all the encrypted data.

The eleventh parameter is the length of the variable specified for the tenth parameter.

The twelfth parameter is a variable that receives the number of bytes returned (encrypted) by the API.

The thirteenth and final parameter is the extended API error data structure.

Data can be encrypted with the RC4 algorithm using the Qc3EncryptData API as follows:

```
 D ALGO_RC4        C              Const(30)
 D ANY_CRYPTO_SRV  C              Const('0')
 D CRYPTO_SRV      S         10A  Inz(*BLANKS)
 D myAlgo          DS             LikeDS(ALGD0300_T)
 D myKey           DS             LikeDS(KEYD0200_T)
 D apiError        DS             LikeDS(qusec_ex)

 D nRtnLen         S         10I 0

   /free
     myAlgo.Algorithm = ALGO_RC4;

     myKey.type    = ALGO_RC4;
     myKey.length  = %Len(%TrimR(pwd));
     myKey.Format  = '0';
     myKey.KeyValue = %TrimR(pwd);

     apiError = *ALLX'00';
     apiError.bytesProvided=%size(apiError);

     Qc3EncryptData(szInData:nInLen:'DATA0100':
                    myAlgo  : 'ALGD0300' :
                    myKey   : 'KEYD0200' :
                    ANY_CRYPTO_SRV : CRYPTO_SRV :
                    szOutData : %size(szOutData) :
                    nRtnLen   : apiError );
   /end-free
```

Since this API can be complex, here is a simplified subprocedure wrapper that encrypts data using RC4 encryption:

rc4Encrypt() — Subprocedure to Encrypt Data Using RC4

```
H NOMAIN OPTION(*NODEBUGIO:*SRCSTMT) BNDDIR('QC2LE')
H Copyright('(c) 2006 Robert Cozzi, Jr. All rights reserved.')

 /INCLUDE rpgtnt/QCPYSRC,rpgtnt

D ALGO_DES         C                         Const(20)
D ALGO_TDES        C                         Const(21)
D ALGO_AES         C                         Const(22)
D ALGO_RC4         C                         Const(30)
D ALGO_RSA_PUB     C                         Const(50)
D ALGO_RSA_PRIV    C                         Const(51)
D ANY_CRYPTO_SRV   C                         Const('0')
D SWF_CRYPTO_SRV   C                         Const('1')
D HWD_CRYPTO_SRV   C                         Const('2')

D CRYPTO_SRV       S              10A    Inz(*BLANKS)

P rc4Encrypt       B                         Export
D rc4Encrypt       PI             10I 0
D  pwd                            64A    Const VARYING
D  szInData                        1A    OPTIONS(*VARSIZE)
D  nInLen                        10I 0 Const
D  szOutData                      1A    OPTIONS(*VARSIZE)
D  nOutLen                       10I 0 Const

D myAlgo           DS                      LikeDS(ALGD0300_T)
D myKey            DS                      LikeDS(KEYD0200_T)
D apiError         DS                      LikeDS(qusec_ex)

D nRtnLen          S              10I 0

 /free
   myAlgo.Algorithm = ALGO_RC4;

   myKey.type   = ALGO_RC4;
   myKey.length = %Len(%TrimR(pwd));
   myKey.Format = '0';
   myKey.value  = %TrimR(pwd);
   apiError = *ALLX'00';
   apiError.bytesProvided=%size(apiError);

   Qc3EncryptData(szInData:nInLen:'DATA0100':
                  myAlgo : 'ALGD0300' :
                  myKey  : 'KEYD0200' :
                  ANY_CRYPTO_SRV      : CRYPTO_SRV :
                  szOutData : nOutLen : nRtnLen  :
                  apiError );

   return nRtnLen;
 /end-free
P rc4Encrypt       E
```

To use the rc4Encrypt() subprocedure, pass it the data to be encrypted, the length of the data to be encrypted, and the return variable and length. In addition, specify the password or Cipher Key to use when performing the encryption; for example:

```
/free
     pwd = 'Rosebud';
     car = 'Corvette';
     nLen = %Len(%TrimR(car));

     rc4Encrypt(pwd : car : nLen :
                encData : %size(encData));
/end-free
```

RC4 is an interesting encryption algorithm. By simply running the encrypted data through the RC4 encryption routine a second time (assuming the same key is specified), the data will be decrypted. You can also call the decryption API to perform decryption.

77 Writing Text to the Joblog

Programmers have long used the system debugging tools to display the content of program variables at runtime. In addition, the DSPLY opcode is often used to display field values at runtime. Neither of these methods, however, provides a convenient or easy-to-use user interface.

The Unix® environment on the system includes a set of "UNIX-type" APIs. These APIs provide a way for IBM to interface with the operating system from within C and PASE environment programs. These UNIX-type APIs are also available to RPG IV programs written for the ILE environment.

Qp0zLprintf() is one such API. This API writes a line of text to the joblog. For example, the following writes "Hello World!" to the joblog:

```
callp qp0zlprintf('Hello World!');
```

Simple enough—but it doesn't stop there. This API accepts substitution variables. The API automatically inserts a substitution value into the output text in place of substitution identifiers.

The RPG IV prototype for the Qp0zLprintf() can be debated since the API itself has a variable parameter list, and those parameters may be character, numeric, or some other type of data. The substitution identifiers are used to indicate the type of parameter data being passed. For example, if the identifier %s is embedded, a character string is expected, whereas if %d is embedded, a numeric integer is expected.

Unfortunately, RPG doesn't support varying data-types for parameters. Therefore, it's easier to assume all substitution values will be one type or another. For example, the following prototype for Qp0zLprintf() accepts up to seven substitution variables:

QpOzLprintf API Prototype

```
D QpØzLprintf      PR              1ØI Ø extProc('QpØzLprintf')
D  szFormattedOutputString...
D                                   *    Value OPTIONS(*STRING)
D                                   *    Value OPTIONS(*STRING:*NOPASS)
D                                   *    Value OPTIONS(*STRING:*NOPASS)
D                                   *    Value OPTIONS(*STRING:*NOPASS)
D                                   *    Value OPTIONS(*STRING:*NOPASS)
D                                   *    Value OPTIONS(*STRING:*NOPASS)
D                                   *    Value OPTIONS(*STRING:*NOPASS)
D                                   *    Value OPTIONS(*STRING:*NOPASS)
```

This version of the prototype for QpOzLprintf() accepts up to 7 substitution parameters; all the parameters must be character variables or literals.

Substitution parameters are optional. They are required when the first parameter contains substitution identifiers that correspond to the parameter count. There must be one substitution parameter for each substitution identifier; for example:

```
D szName           S             2ØA
D szTitle          S             2ØA    Varying
 /free
     szName = 'Bob';
     szTitle= 'President';
     qpØzlprintf('%s is %s of the company.'+X'25':
                 szName : szTitle);
 /end-free
```

In the example above, two substitution identifiers are specified along with two substitution parameters. The message appears in the joblog as follows:

```
"Bob                is President of the company."
```

The values of the two variables are inserted into the output string in chronological order. The szName field is a 20-position character field. The szTitle field is a 20-position variable-length character field. Since the fixed-length field (szName) is fixed, the trailing blanks are also embedded into the output text. The szTitle field, however, is varying length, and, therefore, the assignment statement implicitly sets the length to the exact length of the literal on the assignment—that is, the trailing blanks in the field are omitted.

The workaround to exclude trailing blanks from the szName field is to use the %TRIMR built-in function:

```
qpØzlprintf('%s is %s of the company.'+X'25':
            %TrimR(szName) : szTitle);
```

This causes the following message to be written to the joblog:

```
"Bob is President of the company."
```

Note the X'25' at the end of the first line in the following example.

```
qp0zlprintf('%s is %s of the company.'+X'25':
            %TrimR(szName):szTitle);
```

This is a linefeed symbol and is required to force-write the data written to the joblog. Without it, successive calls to Qp0zLprintf() will be cached until a X'25' is sent or until the buffer is filled with about 4k of data. Then the entire buffer is flushed at once to the joblog.

Certainly Qp0zLprintf() can be called directly from RPG IV. However, to ensure that each message line is sent, you must send a linefeed symbol (X'25') at the end of each line.

To provide an easier interface, a wrapper subprocedure for Qp0zLprintf() would be beneficial. This wrapper subprocedure would reroute the input parameters to Qp0zLprintf() and then write out a X'25'. The source code for the Joblog() subprocedure is as follows:

Joblog Subprocedure

```
P Joblog          B                EXPORT
**********************************************************
 **    Write a text message with substitution values
 **    to the joblog.
**********************************************************
D Joblog          PI
D  pMsg                        *   Value OPTIONS(*STRING)
D  pS1                         *   Value OPTIONS(*STRING : *NOPASS)
D  pS2                         *   Value OPTIONS(*STRING : *NOPASS)
D  pS3                         *   Value OPTIONS(*STRING : *NOPASS)
D  pS4                         *   Value OPTIONS(*STRING : *NOPASS)
D  pS5                         *   Value OPTIONS(*STRING : *NOPASS)
D  pS6                         *   Value OPTIONS(*STRING : *NOPASS)
D  pS7                         *   Value OPTIONS(*STRING : *NOPASS)

 /free
         // Pass parms thru to API
         Qp0Lprintf(pMsg:pS1:pS2:pS3:pS4:pS5:pS6:p7);

         // Force it out to the joblog
         Qp0zlprintf(X'25');

         Return;
 /end-free

P Joblog          E
```

This JOBLOG subprocedure may be called from RPG IV to write a text string to the joblog. It provides an interface that can be easier to use than sending a program message to the joblog using message APIs. The resulting message in the joblog does not have a message ID associated with it.

Writing to the Joblog with the Joblog Subprocedure

```
H BNDDIR('RPGTNT/RPGTNT')

/include rpgtnt/qcpysrc,rpgtnt

/free
   joblog('%s parms passed to this program.':%char(%parms()));
   chain custno custmast;
   if not %Found();
     joblog('Customer %s not found.':%char(custno));
   endif;
/end-free
```

In this example, the BNDDIR keyword on the Header specification uses the RPGTNT binding directory to link this program to the RPGTNT service program. This service program is created from the subprocedure included in this book. The JOBLOG subprocedure is exported from a service program that is included in the RPGTNT binding directory. This service program must be created by you from the code in this book in order to use it.

The /INCLUDE statement indicates that the prototypes for the RPGTNT service program should be included into this source member. Once the prototypes are included, the compiler can syntax-check calls made to the subprocedures using the prototypes from the /INCLUDE member. The Joblog subprocedure's prototype is included in the RPGTNT source member, featured in the Appendix.

78 Reading Save Files with RPG IV

A save file or "savf" is simply an online version of a backup. Objects are saved to a save file instead of to tape or other offline media.

RPG has the ability to read, write, and update save files. But save files have a Message Digest (shelf-check number) to verify that the data in the file has not been modified. This means that altering the data in a save file will cause it to become corrupt, and the system will not allow its objects to be restored.

Save files can be read by RPG just like a sequential database file. They are declared in RPG IV as 528-byte program-described file. There is no other special declarative or handling necessary for save files versus other files.

Often a database file contains an image of a save file. This often occurs when a save file has been FTP'd to the system or when a save file has been encrypted. The encrypted save file is stored in a database file, and that file (and its encrypted data) is subsequently saved off line.

A simple RPG program can be used to copy data between a real save file and a database file. To do this, create an RPG program that includes two 528-byte program-described files, as follows:

```
Finput     IF   F   528        DISK
Foutput    O    F   528        DISK
```

Data being written to a save file must have originated in a save file itself—that is, it must have been previously read from a save file and written to a database file.

A save file must be created before it is processed with RPG. To do this, the CRTSAVF command is used:

```
CRTSAVF FILE(mylib/mysavf) TEXT('Bob''s save file')
```

where MYLIB is the library name and MYSAVF is the name of the save file being created.

To create a database file that can contain a save file, create a 528-byte program described file as follows:

```
CRTPF FILE(mylib/mydbf) RCDLEN(528)
```

where MYLIB is the library name and MYDBF is the name of the database file being created.

To save object to a save file, use the SAVOBJ or SAVLIB command:

```
SAVLIB LIB(RPGTNT) DEV(*SAVF) SAVF(mylib/mysavf)
```

This saves the library named RPGTNT to the save file named MYSAVF in the MYLIB library. The save file must exist before running the SAVLIB command.

An example program that copies between a database file and a save file follows:

Copy Save File — Example Program

```
 H OPTION(*NODEBUGIO: *SRCSTMT)
 H DFTACTGRP(*NO) ACTGRP(*NEW)

 Finput     IF   F   528        DISK
 Foutput    O    F   528        DISK

 Iinput     NS
 I                              A   1   528  szData

 C                      eval    *INLR = *ON
   /free
      // Read the input data
       read input;
       dow not %eof(input);
        except update;
        read input;
       enddo;
   /end-free

 Ooutput    E              Update
 O                         szData            528
```

This is a simple "read/write" program. It reads a record then writes a record. To copy from a save file to a database file, override the INPUT file to the save file name, and override the OUTPUT file to the database file name. Then call the program as follows:

```
OVRDBF FILE(input)  TOFILE(MYLIB/mysavf) LVLCHK(*NO)
OVRDBF FILE(output) TOFILE(MYLIB/mydbf)  LVLCHK(*NO)
call   cpysavfile
```

To copy back to a save file from a database file, override the INPUT file to the database file name, and override the OUTPUT file to the save file name. Then call the program as follows:

```
OVRDBF FILE(input)  TOFILE(MYLIB/mydbf) LVLCHK(*NO)
OVRDBF FILE(output) TOFILE(MYLIB/mysavf) LVLCHK(*NO)
call   cpysavfile
```

Once a save file is stored in a database file, it can be processed just like any other database file and can be copied, renamed, deleted, saved, and restored.

79 Encrypting Save Files in RPG IV

The requirement to encrypt and decrypt the data in save files is growing. With several Federal laws in the U.S. (as well as credit card licensing that requires personal information to be encrypted), the need to encrypt data, particularly when it is offline, is something every RPG shop needs to consider.

Unfortunately, IBM does not currently offer an encrypted backup command. When a save file is created using the SAVLIB or SAVOBJ commands, the data is compressed but not encrypted. Virtually anyone can read and restore the data using an OS/400 or i5/OS system or a PC tape drive with EBCDIC-to-ASCII conversion capabilities.

To encrypt a backup, the data must be saved to a save file, and then that save file must be copied to a database file. The data can be encrypted as it is written to the database file. That database file can be subsequently saved offline to tape or other backup medium.

The save file cannot be directly encrypted because of the nature of its object structure. Therefore, reading its data, encrypting it, and copying the encrypted data to a database file is the only solution. The save file should be cleared (using the CLRSAVF command) once the data has been successfully encrypted.

When the database file is restored back onto the system, it can be decrypted as it is being copied back to the save file.

Encrypting the data is simply a matter of reading the data from the save file, encrypting it using the rc4Encrypt() subprocedure illustrated in Tip #76. The encrypted data is then written to a database file. Encryption routines other than RC4 may be used.

To add encryption capabilities to the CPYSAVF program from Tip #78, the following lines would be added:

Copy Save File with Encryption

```
/free
   // Read the input data
   read input;          ◄——— rc4Encrypt() is featured in Tip #76
   dow not %eof(input);

      // Encrypt/Decrypt the input data
      if (szPwd <> '*NONE'and szPwd <> *BLANKS);
         rc4Encrypt(%TrimR(szPwd):szInData:inInfDS.nRecLen:
                                   szOutData:%size(szOutData));
      endif;

      // Write the new data to the output file
      except update;

      // Read the next record from the input
      read input;
   enddo;

/end-free
```

To simplify this capability, a user-written CPYSAVF command can be created. This command allows the input and output file and member names to be specified along with the encryption password.

The Command Definition source and RPG IV program that accomplishes this encryption follows:

Copy and Encrypt Save File Command Definition

```
CPYSAVF:    CMD          PROMPT('Copy Save File to/from DB File')
                         /* Command processing program is: CPYSAVF   */
FROMFILE:   PARM         KWD(FROMFILE) TYPE(QUAL1) MIN(1) +
                            PROMPT('From file')
            PARM         KWD(FROMMBR) TYPE(*NAME) DFT(*FIRST) +
                            SPCVAL((*FIRST) (*LAST) (*ALL)) +
                            PROMPT('From member')
TOFILE:     PARM         KWD(TOFILE) TYPE(QUAL1) MIN(1) +
                            PROMPT('To file')
            PARM         KWD(TOMBR) TYPE(*NAME) DFT(*FROMMBR) +
                            SPCVAL((*FROMMBR)) PROMPT('To member')
            PARM         KWD(PWD) TYPE(*CHAR) LEN(32) EXPR(*YES) +
                            DFT(*NONE) SPCVAL((*NONE)) +
                            PROMPT('Encryption password')
QUAL1:      QUAL         TYPE(*NAME) MIN(1) EXPR(*YES)
            QUAL         TYPE(*NAME) DFT(*LIBL) EXPR(*YES) +
                            PROMPT('Library')
```

The source code listed above can be compiled using the CRTCMD command as follows:

```
CRTCMD CMD(CPYSAVF) PGM(mylib/CPYSAVF)
```

where MYLIB/CPYSAVF is the name of the RPG IV program that follows.

The following is the complete RPG IV source member that, when compiled, may be used as the command processing program for the CPYSAVF command.

Encrypt a Save File

```
H OPTION(*NODEBUGIO: *SRCSTMT)
H BNDDIR('QC2LE':'RPGTNT/RPGTNT')

 /IF DEFINED(*CRTBNDRPG)
H DFTACTGRP(*NO) ACTGRP(*NEW)
 /ELSE
H NOMAIN
 /ENDIF

Finput     IF  F 528      DISK    EXTFILE(inFile) EXTMBR(inMbr)
F                                 USROPN          Infds(inINFDS)

Foutput    O   F 528      DISK    EXTFILE(outFile) EXTMBR(outMbr)
F                                 USROPN           Infds(outINFDS)

D qualfile        DS              Qualified based(nothing)
D  file                   10A
D  name                   10A     overlay(file)
D  library                10A
D  lib                    10A     overlay(library)

D infds_T         DS              Qualified based(nothing)
D  szFileName             10A     Overlay(infDS_T:83)
D  szFileLib              10A     Overlay(infDS_T:93)
D  szFileMbr              10A     Overlay(infDS_T:129)
D  nRecLen                 5I 0   Overlay(infDS_T:125)
D  nRecCount              10I 0   Overlay(infDS_T:156)

D inFile          S       21A
D inMbr           S       10A
D outFile         S       21A
D outMbr          S       10A

D inInfDS         DS              LikeDS(infds_T)
D outInfDS        DS              LikeDS(infds_T)

D szOutData       S               Like(szInData)

  // Prototype for the CPYSAVF routine.
D cpySavf         PR
D  Fromfile                       Const LikeDS(qualFile)
D  FromMbr                10A     Const
D  ToFile                         Const LikeDS(qualFile)
D  ToMbr                  10A     Const
D  szPwd                  32A     Const

  // Our *INZSR simulation routine.
D inzsrProc       PR      10I 0
D  Fromfile                       Const LikeDS(qualFile)
D  FromMbr                10A     Const
D  ToFile                         Const LikeDS(qualFile)
D  ToMbr                  10A     Const
 /include rpgtnt/qcpysrc,rpgtnt
```

Continued…

…continued

```
  /IF NOT DEFINED(*CRTBNDRPG)
 Iinput      NS
 I                               A   1  528  szInData
 Ooutput     E            Update
 O                        szOutData        528

 P cpysavf        B                    Export
  /ENDIF

 D cpySavf        PI
 D  Fromfile                           Const LikeDS(qualFile)
 D  FromMbr                    10A     Const
 D  ToFile                             Const LikeDS(qualFile)
 D  ToMbr                      10A     Const
 D  szPwd                      32A     Const

  /IF DEFINED(*CRTBNDRPG)
 Iinput      NS
 I                               A   1  528  szInData

 C                  eval     *INLR = *ON
  /ENDIF

  /free
        if (inzsrProc(fromFile:fromMbr:toFile:toMbr)<0);
           return;   // We failed to launch!
        endif;

     // Read the input data
       read input;
       dow not %eof(input);
       // Encrypt/Decrypt the input data
       if (szPwd <> '*NONE');
          rc4Encrypt(%TrimR(szPwd):szInData:inInfDS.nRecLen:
                              szOutData:%size(szOutData));
       endif;

       // Write the new data to the output file
       except update;

       // Read the next record from the input
       read input;
      enddo;
  /end-free

  /IF NOT DEFINED(*CRTBNDRPG)
 P cpysavf        E
  /ELSE
 Ooutput     E            Update
 O                        szOutData        528
  /ENDIF

 P inzsrProc       B
 D inzsrProc       PI         10I 0
 D  Fromfile                           Const LikeDS(qualFile)
 D  FromMbr                    10A     Const
 D  ToFile                             Const LikeDS(qualFile)
 D  ToMbr                      10A     Const
```

Continued…

…continued

```
/free
    //  INPUT File
        inFile  = %TrimR(fromFile.lib) + '/' + fromFile.name;
        inMbr   = fromMbr;
        if  (inMbr = *BLANKS
              or inMbr = '*'
              or inMbr = '*NONE'
              or inMbr = '*BLANKS');
            inMbr = '*FIRST';
        endif;

    //  OUTPUT File
        outFile = %TrimR(toFile.lib) + '/' + toFile.name;
        outMbr = toMbr;
        if (outMbr='*FROMMBR');
            outMbr = inMbr;
        endif;
        if  (outMbr = *BLANKS
              or outMbr = '*'
              or outMbr = '*NONE'
              or outMbr = '*BLANKS');
            outMbr = '*FIRST';
        endif;

        open   input;
        if   NOT %OPEN(input);
            Joblog('Input file %s in %s did not open.':
                    %trimR(fromFile.file):%trimR(fromFile.lib));
            return -1;
        endif;

        open  output;
        if   NOT %OPEN(output);
            Joblog('Output file %s in %s did not open.':
                    %trimR(toFile.file):%trimR(toFile.lib));
            return -2 ;
        endif;
        return 0;
    /end-free

  P inzsrproc        E
```

This command and program can be used to encrypt backups and can help ensure that data is protected when it is being backed up. In addition, the nature of the RC4 encryption algorithm is such that data that has already been encrypted will be decrypted if processed by the RC4 algorithm—provided the identical cipher key or *password* is supplied.

This means that the CPYSAVF command and program may be used to encrypt and copy a save file to a database file. Then the encrypted database file can be saved offline. Later, if it needs to be restored, the encrypted database file is restored using RSTOBJ. Then CPYSAVF is used to copy the decrypted data back to a save file. The RC4 encryption routine reverses the previous encryption (assuming the password is correct) and decrypts the data.

The original data can then be restored from the save file.

80 Global and Local Variables

Every field or data structure declared in an RPG III program (yes, that's "RPG III") is considered a *global variable*. Every field or data structure declared in every RPG IV program that does not contain subprocedures is also considered global variables.

With the introduction of subprocedures, the term *local scope* was introduced. Local Scope refers to fields, arrays, data structures, prototypes, named constants, and anything else that is *declared inside a subprocedure*. The term *local variable* is normally used when referring to fields, arrays, and data structures, whereas the term *local scope* is used when generically referring to anything declared in a subprocedure.

As the name implies, global variables are available *globally* throughout the entire source member. Local variables are available only in the subprocedure in which they are declared.

In RPG IV, indicators and the indicator array are scoped globally. All files (including input and output fields) are also scoped globally.

If a program branches into a subprocedure, the subprocedure has access to all of its locally declared variables as well as all global variables.

A conflict may occur in this scenario when a local variable in a subprocedure has the same name as a global variable. When this happens, access to the like-named global variable is blocked while the subprocedure is running—that is, only the local variable is available while running the subprocedure that has the name conflict.

While in a subprocedure, if that subprocedure includes a local variable that has the same name as a global variable, the subprocedure is prevented from accessing the global variable. For example, a global variable named CUSTNO is declared at the top of a source member. A subprocedure named GETCUST is included in that same source member and has a locally declared variable named CUSTNO.

In this situation, when the GETCUST subprocedure is called, access to the local variable named CUSTNO is available; however, access to the global variable named CUSTNO is prohibited.

Global and Local Variable Name Conflict

```
FCustMast   IF    E              K DISK ◄-------------------
                                                   Global Variable

D custNo            S                    7P 0

C                         callp    GetCust()

P GetCust           B
D GetCust           PI
D  nOption                          10I 0 Options(*NOPASS)
D
D custNo            S               10I 0 ◄-------------
  /free                                     Local Variable
      chain custNo CustMast;
      if    NOT %found();
         joblog('Customer %s not found.':%char(custNo));
      endif;
      return;
  /end-free
P GetCust           E
```

The field CUSTNO—declared in the Global Definition specifications—is only available
while the Mainline Calcs are running. When GETCUST is called, the local variable named
CUSTNO is available to the Calculation specifications running in the subprocedure; the
global variable named CUSTNO is not available.

81 Create Source Members Used to Create Service Programs

Service programs are simply a collection of subprocedures. One or more *MODULE objects were created from individual source members are combined into one *SRVPGM object.

To create a service program, you really only need one source member—but, typically, more than one is used. In that source member, at least one subprocedure should exist. I say "should exist" because technically speaking a service program can contain no subprocedures—but how useful would that be?

A source member can contain only exported variables—variables that are shared with other modules.

A source member that will be used in a service program should contain two things:

- The NOMAIN keyword on the Header specification
- At least one subprocedure, preferably with the EXPORT keyword

The NOMAIN keyword is used on the Header specification to control the way the RPG IV compiler generates the object code (i.e., the *MODULE object). When NOMAIN is specified, most of the RPG Logic Cycle is not inserted into the object. Instead, a slimmed down version of the Logic Cycle is included; just enough to automatically open and close files, initialize the traditional RPG "things" (such as the indicators, PSDS and INFDS) and a few other features.

The word *NOMAIN* literally means that the source member does not contain the traditional Mainline Calculations section. Instead, it contains only subprocedures.

To illustrate, review the GetDayOfWeek subprocedure featured in Tip #59 and the GetDayName subprocedure featured in Tip #18. If we want to create a module named DATERTN (Date Routines) that contains these two subprocedures, the source member would need to include the NOMAIN keyword on its Header specification as follows:

Source Code for the DATERTN Module

```
H NOMAIN ◄──────
```

> The NOMAIN keyword means a "Lite" version of the RPG Cycle is used. This also enables the module to be used in a *SRVPGM.

```
/INCLUDE RPGTNT/QCPYSRC,datertn

P GetDayOfWeek      B                        EXPORT
```

> Prototypes are required even for the subproc's implementation module. Prototypes are inserted via the /INCLUDE directive.

```
     //   2001 by Robert Cozzi, Jr. All Rights reserved.
     //   Permission to use is hereby granted provided this
     //   notice is included in its entirety.

D GetDayOfWeek      PI               10I 0
D  InputDate                          D    CONST DATFMT(*ISO)

     // Base date is based on date the calendar changed
D BaseDate          S                 D    INZ(D'1582-10-14')
D nDayOfWeek        S               10I 0
D nDays             S               10I 0

C                   TEST(E)                    InputDate
C                   if        %ERROR
C                   Return    -1
C                   endif

C       InputDate   SubDur    BaseDate         nDays:*DAYS

C                   CALLB     'CEEDYWK'
C                   Parm                        nDays
C                   Parm                        nDayofWeek
C                   return    nDayOfWeek
P GetDayOfWeek      E

P GetDayName        B                        EXPORT
D GetDayName        PI               10A
D  inputDate                          D    Const DATFMT(*ISO)
D  szDay                            10A

D BaseDate          S                 D    INZ(D'1582-10-14')
D nDayOfWeek        S               10I 0
D nDays             S               10I 0
C                   TEST(E)                    inputDate
C                   if        %ERROR
C                   return    'Invalid'
C                   endif
C       inputDate   SubDur    baseDate         nDays:*DAYS
C                   CallB(DE) 'CEEDATE'
C                   Parm                        nDays
C                   Parm      'Wwwwwwwwwz'      szFmt
C                   Parm                        szDayName
C                   return    szDayName
P GetDayName        E
```

To create a module named DATERTN from the source member, compile the source member using PDM option 15 (CRTRPGMOD):

```
CRTRPGMOD MODULE(RPGTNT/DATERTN) SRCFILE(RPGTNT/QRPGLESRC) +
          DBGVIEW(*SOURCE) TGTRLS(V5R2M0)
```

Once the module named DATERTN is created, a service program may be created. A service program only *requires* one module, but normally it is made up of several modules. To create the service program named DATERTN, use the CRTSRVPGM command:

```
CRTSRVPGM SRVPGM(RPGTNT/DATERTN) +
          MODULE(*SRVPGM) EXPORT(*ALL)
```

This creates a service program named DATERTN. The EXPORT(*ALL) parameter allows all the subprocedures that have the EXPORT keyword on their Procedure specification to be called from other programs. Subprocedures that do not have EXPORT on their Procedure specification cannot be called from other programs.

EXPORT(*ALL) is a cheap way to create a service program and should only be used for small service programs like the one in the example. For a more robust service program, binder source should be used (see Tip #82).

82 Binder Source for a Service Program

When a service program is created with the CRTSRVPGM, the EXPORT keyword defaults to EXPORT(*SRCFILE). With simple service programs, changing this parameter to EXPORT(*ALL) may be practical (see Tip #81) but isnormally frowned upon.

If the service program is not so simple, or it has several exported subprocedures, or you simply want more control over how the service program is used, then using the default value for the EXPORT parameter is recommended.

When a service program is created and the default for the EXPORT parameter is specified as EXPORT(*SRCFILE), the command would appear as follows:

```
CRTSRVPGM SRVPGM(RPGTNT/DATERTN) MODULE(*SRVPGM) +
          EXPORT(*SRCFILE) SRCFILE(QSRVSRC) SRCMBR(*SRVPGM)
```

If the EXPORT source file exists, the following error message is issued:

```
File QSRVSRC in library *LIBL with member DATERTN not found.
```

If source file QSRVSRC exists but the member does not, the same message is generated. In this situation, if the message were a bit more accurate, it might read

```
Member DATERTN not found in QSRVSRC
```

What does EXPORT(*SRCFILE) mean? It means that the source file named QSRVSRC contains a source member that includes EXPORT statements. These EXPORT statements identify the names of subprocedures that are exported from the service program. This lets the programmer control the subprocedures that are exported, whereas EXPORT(*ALL) simply exports everything.

Why do you need this level of control? Why not just export everything? Because you need continuity in the export list so that applications will continue to function without a massive rebind or recompile.

The service program's signature will be different (1) if the number of subprocedures in the service program is altered (such as when a new subprocedure is added), or (2) if the order of the existing subprocedures is altered (such as when rebinding the service program) and (3) if specifying the modules in an order that is different from the original service program.

A service program's Signature is similar to a level-check ID for a database file. It is based on the order and number of subprocedures and other exports in the service program.

Binder source allows the programmer to control the order and number of subprocedures being exported. Without this, the order of the modules specified on the MODULE parameter of the CRTSRVPGM command and the order of the subprocedures in those modules are used to build a signature. Binder source is used to force the export of subprocedures in a specific sequence. This ensures future program compatibility with the service program. In addition, the signature can be hard coded or *user specified* to avoid level-check issues entirely.

The following is an excerpt of the binder source for the RPGTNT service program.

Binder Source with Hard-Coded Signature

```
          STRPGMEXP   PGMLVL(*CURRENT) LVLCHK(*YES) +
                      SIGNATURE('RPGTNT')
/**********************************************************/
/***  Begin EXPORTED items                          **/
/**********************************************************/
          EXPORT      SYMBOL("sndmsg")        /* Send impromptu msg  */
          EXPORT      SYMBOL("GetDayName")     * Get Day Name         */
          EXPORT      SYMBOL("joblog")        /* Write to joblog      */
          EXPORT      SYMBOL("GetDayOfWeek")  /* Get day of week      */
          EXPORT      SYMBOL("rc4Encrypt")    /* Encrypt data         */
          EXPORT      SYMBOL("rc4Decrypt")    /* Decrypt data         */
          EXPORT      SYMBOL("cvtCCSID")      /* Convert between CCSIDs */
          EXPORT      SYMBOL("GetUserInfo")   /* Get User Profile Info. */
          ENDPGMEXP
```

The STRPGMEXP statement is used to control the service program signature. The SIGNATURE parameter in the example above is 'RPGTNT'.

Here is the benefit of a hard-coded signature: Programs that use the service program *do not* need to be recompiled when the service program is updated. However, hard-coded signatures mean that the programmer has more responsibility: They need to ensure that any new exports are added to the bottom of the list of EXPORT statements. For example, to add the GetPtnInfo subprocedure to this export list, the following EXPORT statement would be added just after the one for GetUserInfo.

```
          EXPORT      SYMBOL("GetPtnInfo") /* Get Partition Info */
```

When the service program is recreated, the signature remains the same even with the new subprocedure exports. The new binder source would be as follows:

Binder Source with New Export

```
STRPGMEXP  PGMLVL(*CURRENT) LVLCHK(*YES) +
                SIGNATURE('RPGTNT')
   EXPORT  SYMBOL("sndmsg")
   EXPORT  SYMBOL("GetDayName")
   EXPORT  SYMBOL("joblog")
   EXPORT  SYMBOL("GetDayOfWeek")
   EXPORT  SYMBOL("rc4Encrypt")
   EXPORT  SYMBOL("rc4Decrypt")
   EXPORT  SYMBOL("cvtCCSID")
   EXPORT  SYMBOL("GetUserInfo")  ◄─── New EXPORTs are added here
   EXPORT  SYMBOL("GetPtnInfo")
ENDPGMEXP
```

Note that the names being exported (those specified on the SYMBOL parameter of the EXPORT keyword) are enclosed in double quotes. This allows them to be specified in the same upper- or lowercase letters specified on the EXTPROC keyword in the RPG IV source. They must match the upper- or lowercase export keyword. Normally subprocedure names in RPG IV are exported as all uppercase, even so, they still need to be enclosed in quotes.

83 Creating Binder Language the Easy Way

One way to create the initial binder source for a service program is to compile the source members as usual and then run the RTVBNDSRC command.

The RTVBNDSRC command allows you to create the binder source for a list of modules or an individual service program. That binder source can then be modified and used when the service program is recreated.

To retrieve the binder source for the RPGTNT service program, the following CL command could be used:

```
RTVBNDSRC SRVPGM(RPGTNT/RPGTNT) +
          SRCFILE(RPGTNT/QSRVSRC)
```

The results from this RTVBNDSRC command produce a source member named RPGTNT in the QSRVSRC source file in the RPGTNT library. The source would look similar to the following:

Results of a RTVBNDSRC Command

```
STRPGMEXP PGMLVL(*CURRENT) SIGNATURE(X'D9D7C7E3D5E34040404040404040404040')
/***********************************************************/
/*    *SRVPGM      RPGTNT       RPGTNT      10/27/06  11:51:14      */
/***********************************************************/
   EXPORT    SYMBOL("sndmsg")
   EXPORT    SYMBOL("GetDayName")
   EXPORT    SYMBOL("joblog")
   EXPORT    SYMBOL("GetDayOfWeek")
   EXPORT    SYMBOL("rc4Encrypt")
   EXPORT    SYMBOL("rc4Decrypt")
   EXPORT    SYMBOL("cvtCCSID")
   EXPORT    SYMBOL("GetUserInfo")
ENDPGMEXP
```

From this point you can modify the binder source and use it for all future binds of the service program. Remember, as new subprocedures are added to the service program, their EXPORTed names should appear at the bottom of the binder source member just above the ENDPGMEXP statement.

Binder Source — A Closer Look

Note the SIGNATURE parameter of the STRPGMEXP statement. It is always returned by RTVBNDSRC in hexadecimal notation. A quick conversion from hex to character indicates that the signature for this service program is 'RPGTNT' followed by 10 blanks. Signatures need to be 16 bytes long, so the compiler extends the signature to the full 16 characters by padding it with blanks. In this case, the signature can be modified once the source is retrieved to one that's more human friendly. For example

```
STRPGMEXP PGMLVL(*CURRENT) SIGNATURE('RPGTNT')
```

The other statements are EXPORT identifiers. These statements identify the subprocedures that you want to export from the service program. Normally, all subprocedures would be exported. The order in which they are exported is usually not important; what is important is that the *order* does not change. If the order does change, existing programs will begin to fail. Why? Because programs that are bound to a service program are linked to its subprocedures by ordinal number, not a subprocedure name. Translation from procedure name to ordinal occurs when the CRTPGM command is called directly or when it is implicitly called (behind the scenes) by the CRTBNDRPG command.

For example, a program uses the JOBLOG subprocedure, accessing it as ordinal 3 in the service program. Two new subprocedure exports are added to the binder source above the first export (SNDMSG in our example). The JOBLOG subprocedure is now in position 5 of the export list. When the service program recreates, the programs using JOBLOG will begin to fail because they will not be calling JOBLOG any longer but instead calling the SNDMSG subprocedure (formerly in position 1, now in position 3). The parameter definitions for SNDMSG are different than for JOBLOG, consequently all kinds of interesting situations will come up.

Here is the bottom line: When you use a static signature, make sure the sequence of existing subprocedures never changes by adding all new subprocedure exports to the bottom of the export list.

84 Linking to a Service Program from an RPG IV Program

Service programs are simply a collection of module objects. One or more *MODULE objects created from source members are combined into one *SRVPGM object. The modules in the service programs have subprocedures in them. To call these subprocedures requires very little additional work on the part of the programmer.

In the RPG IV source member that needs to call the subprocedure of a service program call the subprocedure. Next, compile the source member using PDM option 14 (CRTRPGMOD). Once that's done, bind the module into a *PGM object with the CRTPGM command and specify the name of the service program on the BNDSRVPGM parameter.

Note that the CRTBNDRPG command does not include a BNDSRVPGM parameter, so CRTBNDRPG and CRTPGM are necessary.

That's it!

Most programmers, however, prefer to use a Binding Directory instead of the BND-SRVPGM parameter. There are two useful advantages to using binding directories:

- The CRTBNDRPG (PDM option 14) does not have a BNDSRVPGM keyword, but it does support the BNDDIR keyword.
- The BNDDIR parameter may be embedded in the RPG source member.

The CRTBNDRPG, which is PDM option 14, does not support the BNDSRVPGM parameter. CRTBNDRPG does, however, support the BNDDIR (binding directory) parameter. This parameter allows you to specify the name of a binding directory that is used in addition to any MODULE and BNDSRVPGM parameters.

What Is a Binding Directory?

Binding directories are, as the name implies, a directory of object names that are used during the *bind* phase the compile process. The bind phase is performed when the CRTPGM command is run—either implicitly (via CRTBNDRPG) or explicitly (via the CRTPGM) command from Command Entry.

Most first-time users of binding directories think they contain a copy of the service programs or modules whose names have been added to them. They do not. They contain *only the names* of the modules or service programs. This allows the modules and service programs whose names appear in a binding directory to be recreated as needed. Then the next time their dependent programs are compiled, they use the latest version.

The three primary commands to build and maintain binding directories are

```
CRTBNDDIR  BNDDIR( bnddir-name )
ADDBNDDIRE OBJ(( obj1  obj-type1 ) (obj2 obj-type2) ...)
WRKBNDDIRE BNDDIR( bnddir-name )
```

The CRTBNDDIR command creates the binding directory. There's no size or any attribute other than the customary text-description parameter.

The ADDBNDDIRE adds module or service program names to an existing binding directory.

The WRKBNDDIRE command allows you to add and remove module or service program names from a binding directory using a limited "work-with" style application.

Once a binding directory is created, any program or service program can leverage it by specifying its name on the BNDDIR keyword of the CRTBNDRPG or CRTPGM commands.

A more practical and common method is to include a reference to the binding directory in the RPG IV source member by adding a BNDDIR('MYBND') keyword to the Header specification (where 'MYBND' is the name of a binding directory that should be used), as follows:

Specifying a Binding Directory

```
H  BNDDIR('RPGTNT')
```

The names of the service program(s) that the source member needs to successfully compile must appear in the binding directory.

To create a binding directory named RPGTNT, the following CL command can be used:

```
CRTBNDDIR  BNDDIR(RPGTNT/RPGTNT)
ADDBNDDIRE BNDDIR(RPGTNT/RPGTNT) +
           OBJ((CIPHER *MODULE) (ICONV *MODULE) +
           (MESSAGES *MODULE) (OBJECTS *MODULE) +
           (USERINFO *MODULE))
```

Once created, this binding directory can be used on the BNDDIR parameter of the CRT-BNDRPG or CRTPGM commands. It can also be used with the BNDDIR keyword on the Header specification of an RPG IV source member along with other binding directory names:

```
H   BNDDIR('QC2LE'  :  'RPGTNT/RPGTNT')
```

Note that the binding directory name specified on the BNDDIR keyword must be enclosed in single quotes and specified in *all uppercase letters*. If specified in lower case or mixed case, the compiler will not be able to locate the binding directory. Binding directory names specified on the BNDDIR keyword on the Header specification are objects, and object names are case sensitive—and virtually all objects have all-uppercase names.

85 Swap Bytes — Big Endian to Little Endian in RPG IV

IBM PowerPC-based systems process data in what's called *big endian*[1] format. An Intel *x*86-based system processes data in what's called Little Endian format.

The origin of the word *endian*—like most contemporary computer science terms—is a result of non sequitur associations. A loose example of this is in the movie "Dances with Wolves." In there, the protagonist is given the name "Dances with Wolves" by a Native American who first sees him as he apparently is "dancing" with a wolf.

The person who came up with *endian* had enjoyed Jonathan Swift's tale *Gulliver's Travels*. In that story, there was controversy over the proper way to open soft-boiled eggs: big end first or little end first. They referred to this as a *Big Endian* or a *Little Endian*.

The endian of a system is normally unimportant to the RPG programmer. But with more and more non-EBCDIC data being stored on the system as ASCII data (on the IFS, for example), being aware of big and little endian may become important.

Most endian conversion routines use bit-shifting operations to move data around. RPG does not have bit-shifting operations, so traditional data-manipulation methods need to be employed.

So what is endian? On the iSeries, it is the manner in which numeric data is stored. The most significant digits are on the right side of the integer, and they increase as you move to the left. With little endian, the most significant digits are on the left side of the integer and increase as you move right.

The basic premise in converting between big endian and little endian is a simple byte-flipping algorithm. This comes into play primarily with integers. Typically 2-byte or 4-byte integers (5i0 and 10i0 in RPG IV) are the type of integer that needs to be flipped; however, so-called long long integers (20i0 in RPG IV) are also supported.

Let's look at a typical 32-bit (4-byte) integer and convert its endian.

Original Big Endian 32-Bit Data

Byte ⟶	1	2	3	4
Data ⟶	X'00'	X'22'	X'33'	X'44'

To convert this data into little endian format, the bytes in each 16-bit "word" need to be flipped, and then the 32-bit word needs to be flipped.

The first step is to flip the two 8-bit bytes in each 16-bit word. This results in the following:

First Step — Swap Byte 1 with 2 and 3 with 4

Byte ⟶	1	2	3	4
Data ⟶	X'22'	X'00'	X'44'	X'33'

The second step is to flip the two 16-bit words. This means we now must treat bytes 1 and 2 as a single entity and swap them with bytes 3 and 4, as follows:

Second Step — Swap 2-Byte Words

Byte ⟶	1	2	3	4
Data ⟶	X'44'	X'33'	X'22'	X'00'

It doesn't matter if you're going from big endian to little endian or from little endian to big endian—the routine is the same.

To perform the byte swapping in RPG IV, support for 2-, 4-, and 8-byte integers should be provided. Certainly using another language (such as C with its bit-shifting abilities) would perform better if you need to convert large volumes of data.

Specifying the length of the integer and then writing a generalized routine to handle the byte swapping should provide support for any size integer. To achieve this, the Swap-Bytes subprocedure is provided. It accepts the address of the data whose bytes need to be swapped and the number of bytes to swap. SwapBytes performs the swap using as few RPG IV instructions as possible.

SwapByte Subprocedure — Convert Big Endian to Little Endian

```
P SwapBytes       B                     Export
D SwapBytes       PI
D  pBytes                         *      Value
D  nInLen                       10I 0 Const OPTIONS(*NOPASS)

D nWordLen        S             10I 0 Inz(2)
D szFirst         S              1A    Based(pFirst)
D szSecond        S              1A    Based(pSecond)
D szReg           S              1A

 /free
    if (%parms() >= 2);
        nWordLen = nInLen;
    endif;
      pFirst  = pBytes;
      pSecond = pBytes + (nWordLen - 1);
      dow (pSecond > pFirst);
        szReg    = szFirst;
        szFirst  = szSecond;
        szSecond = szReg;
        pFirst   += 1;   // V5.2
        pSecond  -= 1;   // V5.2
      enddo;
    return;
 /end-free

P SwapBytes       E
```

To call the subprocedure in the example above, specify the address of the integer whose bytes should be swapped as parameter 1. Use the %ADDR built-in function to pass the address of the variable. For the second parameter, specify the length of the data passed on the first parameter. Use the %SIZE built-in function to calculate the length; do not use %LEN, as the value must equal the number of bytes being swapped, *not* the field's length; for example:

```
D nTiffWidth      S              5I 0
D nTiffDepth      S              5I 0
D nTiffSize       S             10I 0
 /free
    SwapBytes(%addr(nTIFFWidth) : %size(nTIFFWidth));
    SwapBytes(%addr(nTIFFDepth) : %size(nTIFFDepth));
    SwapBytes(%addr(nTIFFSize ) : %size(nTIFFSize));
 /end-free
```

86 Dumping the Call Stack with Qp0zDumpStack

It is often necessary to view the program call stack for a job running on the system. The DSPJOB CL command can be used to easily accomplish this task:

```
DSPJOB OUTPUT(*PRINT) OPTION(*PGMSTK)
```

The output from DSPJOB can be directed to the display or to a print file.

But what about situations where it is necessary to process the output? In that case, an API can be called to dump the call stack. At any given point, the Qp0zDumpStack API can be called to generate an unformatted dump of the call stack. The Qp0zDumpStack API writes the call stack for the job to a User Space in QUSRSYS. The name of the user space is the same as the job number plus has a prefixed of QP0Z. The API automatically creates the user space—for example, if the job number is 030836, the user space is named QP0Z030836 in QUSRSYS.

Qp0zDumpStack accepts one parameter: a Dump Label. This label is written with the call stack to help identify the context of the call stack dump. The prototype for Qp0zDump-Stack is as follows:

Prototype for the Qp0zDumpStack API

```
D dumpCallStack   PR                    extProc('Qp0zDumpStack')
D  label                           *    Value OPTIONS(*STRING)
```

Calling Qp0zDumpStack from RPG IV is easy. Using the prototype provided above, specify the prototype name along with a custom label for the dump:

Dumping the Call Stack from within a Program

```
/free
   dumpCallStack('Payroll System Inquiry');
/end-free
```

The text string 'Payroll System Inquiry' is used as the label for the formatted dump. Labels are included in the output so that multiple calls to Qp0zDumpStack can be isolated from one another.

Once the dump is created, you can copy the output to a database file using the DMPUS-RTRC (dump user trace) CL command:

```
DMPUSRTRC OUTPUT(*FILE)
```

DMPUSRTRC creates a so-called flat file in QTEMP named QAP0ZDMP. To view the contents of the call stack data after copying it to a database file, use the DSPPFM command or any third-party database utility or a query tool. DSPPFM can be used to display the call stack:

```
DSPPFM FILE(QTEMP/QAPØZDMP)
```

The output should appear similar to the following.

Formatted Call Stack Dump Output

```
00000028:112872 Stack Dump for Current Thread
00000028:112896 Stack:  Payroll System Inquiry
00000028:138416 Stack:  Library    / Program    Module      Stmt      Procedure
00000028:138448 Stack:  QSYS       / QCMD                    1298    :
00000028:138472 Stack:  QSYS       / QUICMENU                193     :
00000028:138504 Stack:  QSYS       / QUIMNDRV                1439    :
00000028:138536 Stack:  QSYS       / QUIMGFLW                1224    :
00000028:138568 Stack:  QSYS       / QUICMD                  1165    :
00000028:138600 Stack:  QPDA       / QUOCPP                  1960    :
00000028:138632 Stack:  QPDA       / QUOMAIN                 1457    :
00000028:138664 Stack:  QSYS       / QUOCMD                  301     :
00000028:144168 Stack:  QBPAYROLL  / PAY719     PAY719      0       : _QRNP_PEP_PAY719
00000028:144184 Stack:  QBPAYROLL  / PAY719     PAY719      1018    : PAY719
00000028:149872 Stack:  QSYS       / QPØZCPA    QPØZUDBG    3       : QpØzDumpStack
00000028:167760 Stack:  QSYS       / QPØZSCPA   QPØZSDBG    2       : QpØzSUDumpStack
```

Use Qp0zDumpStack any time you need to record the current call stack list, but the API is not meant to beused in a performance-critical situation.

To retrieve the call stack into a program at runtime, the QWVRCSTK API can be used. This API dumps the call stack into a return variable passed to the API. The QWVRCSTK API has a complex return value that includes nested lists within lists, whereas Qp0zDump-Stack has a simple, raw structure that can be easily processed.

Using Subprocedure Return Values

When a subprocedure accepts parameters, any of those parameters may be modified just like the parameters on a program-to-program call. Subprocedures, however, have additional controls—such as the CONST and VALUE keywords—that allow parameters to be more flexible or more restrictive. For example, when CONST is used on a parameter, no changes to that parameter are allowed.

Often a subprocedure needs to return a value to the caller in a functionlike manner. This means the value returned to the caller is specified on the RETURN opcode and not through a parameter:

```
balanceDue = GetCustBal(custno);
```

The subprocedure named GETCUSTBAL accepts a Customer Number as its parameter. To simplify its interface, a return value is used instead of a second parameter. This allows the subprocedure to be used as a function.

A *function* can return a single value to its caller using the return operation. Multiple return opcodes may be conditioned in a subprocedure, but only one will return the value to the caller.

A value specified for the return variable does not need to be stored in a variable; instead, the attributes of the return value are specified on the PI line (procedure interface) of the subprocedure; for example:

Define a Subprocedure Return Value

```
P GetCustBal      B                    Export
D GetCustBal      PI          7P 2
D   custnbr                   5P 0 Const
```
The Return Value Definition is Packed(7.2)
```
  /free
      chain custnbr custrec;
      if %found();
         return balDue;
      else;
         return -1;
      endif;
  /end-free

p GetCustBal      E
```
The value returned to the caller is either BALDUE or –1 depending on the condition.

In this example, the return value for a subprocedure is specified on the RETURN opcode. Two RETURN opcodes are specified: one is a field, and one is a literal. Both are converted to Packed(7,2) and returned to the caller.

The data-type of the value being returned must match the basic data-type of the return value definition. That is, if the return value is defined as packed, zoned, integer, or float, then Factor 2 of the RETURN opcode must be numeric. Factor 2 of the RETURN opcode is automatically converted to the specific data-type and length defined on the procedure interface.

One benefit of using a return value is that the subprocedure can be called as a function—that is, it can be used either on the right side of the assignment operator (equals sign) or as a parameter of another subprocedure or built-in function; for example:

Using a Returned Value

```
FCUSTMAST  IF   E          K DISK

D GetCustBal     PR            7P 2
D   custnbr                    5P 0 Const

D balance        S            11P 2
D custno         S                 Like(cstnbr)

 /free
        dou  (FKey = F3);
        exfmt  GetCustNo;
        select;
          when  fKey = F3;
            *inlr = *ON;
            return;
          when  FKey = Enter;
            msg = 'Customer ' + %char(custno) +
                  ' owes us ' +
                  %editc(GetCustBal(CUSTNO):'J':*CURSYM);
        endsl;
        enddo
 /end-free
```

> The Returned Value is embedded in the %EDITC built-in function.

In this example, when customer 128 has a balance due of 12500.00, the message created is as follows:

```
'Customer 128 owes us $12,500.00 '
```

88 How Does the %EDITC (Edit Code) Built-in Function Work?

%CHAR is one of the easiest methods for converting packed or zoned numeric values to text. It is safe, efficient, and returns the data in a format that is highly effective when creating formatted text messages or copying numeric data to character variables.

Another way to convert numeric data to character is with the %EDITC (edit code) built-in function. This built-in function works similar to %CHAR; however, %EDITC has two major differences compared with %CHAR:

- %EDITC supports applying an edit code to the value.
- %EDITC returns a fixed-length value that is based on the length of the variable.

For example, if a field is defined as Packed(7,2), then %CHAR returns a value with decimal positions and, if applicable, a negative sign. Leading zeros are truncated, and no thousands notation (i.e., commas in North America) or currency symbols are inserted. This causes a value with a variable length to be returned based on the value stored in the variable being processed by %CHAR.

%EDITC returns a value with a fixed length based on the declared length of the variable and the edit code being applied. This length is consistent regardless of the numeric value stored in the variable being processed by %EDITC.

Because %CHAR truncates leading zeros, the resulting value is considered to be a variable-length value. This makes it relatively easy to use when creating a message such as 'Customer 128 not found'. Using %CHAR, this message could be generated as follows:

```
/free
                    msg = 'Customer ' + %char(custno) ' not found.'
    /end-free
```

But what about more complex situations, such as embedding a currency symbol or requesting leading asterisks to be embedded—or even thousands separators? Answer: The %EDITC built-in function can be used. %EDITC returns a numeric value as character text after applying the requested edit code. For example, to apply the 'J' edit code to the AMTDUE field and include it with our previous text message, the following could be used:

```
/free
        msg = 'Customer ' + %char(custno) ' owes '
              + %editc(amtdue : 'J');
/end-free
```

If the amount due variable is defined as a Packed(7,2), and customer 128 owes $1,040.50, the resulting text message created by the above statement would be

```
'Customer 128 owes   1,040.50 '
```

Note the extra space between the text and the value returned from %EDITC. This is a characteristic of %EDITC—it always returns the same number of characters for a variable. Because a Packed(7,2) value has 7 digits, a decimal point, a thousands separator, and a sign, this particular %EDIT(amtdue:'J') always returns 10 characters regardless of the value of AMTDUE. A field that is Packed(9,2), for example, will return a value that is always 13 bytes long. Of course if the editcode is something other than 'J', the length of the returned values may not be 10 and 13, respectively.

To remove leading blanks, %EDITC can be wrapped in the %TRIML built-in function:

```
/free
        msg = 'Customer ' + %char(custno) ' owes '
              + %trimL(%editc(amtdue : 'J'));
/end-free
```

Given the same set of data, the resulting output would be as follows:

```
'Customer 128 owes 1,040.50 '
```

At this point, there is only a marginal difference between what is produced by %CHAR and %EDITC wrapped in %TRIML. To further illustrate the additional features of %EDITC, consider that the AMTDUE variable is set to 1200.50, and a currency symbol is needed.

A third parameter of %EDITC allows you to indicate that a floating currency symbol should be inserted in front of the value, as follows:

```
%editc(amtdue:'J':*CURSYM) returns: ' $1,200.00 '
```

The addition of the *CURSYM parameter causes a floating currency symbol to be included in the result. The currency symbol is based on the locale for the job running the program and changes with the various regions and country codes.

89 Solid Parameter Testing

One of the biggest challenges in writing a good subprocedure is verifying that which parameters are passed to it. Testing can be relatively easy or can be slightly complex. Choosing to test parameters depends on whether a subprocedure is allowed to blow up occasionally or run smoothly.

The most common method to test if a parameter has been passed to a subprocedure is the %PARMS built-in function. %PARMS returns the number of parameters passed to a subprocedure (or program); for example:

Testing Parameter Count with %PARMS()

```
FCUSTMAST  IF   E           K DISK     PREFIX('CUST.')
D CUST                 DS                LikeRec(CUSTREC:*INPUT)

D balance              S             7P 2

 /free
    *inlr = *ON;

    balance = GetBalDue(3741);    ◄──  Call the subprocedure
 /end-free                              with 1 parameter

P GetBalDue            B                 Export
D GetBalDue            PI           11P 2
D   custNo                           7P 0 Const
D   rtnBal                          11P 2 OPTIONS(*NOPASS)

 /free
      chain (custno) custmast;
      if (NOT %FOUND());
         clear cust;
      endif;
      if (%parms() >= 2);   ◄──  Use %PARMS to test for number of
         rtnBal = cust.balance;        parms passed to GetBalDue.
      endif;

      return cust.balance;
 /end-free
P GetBalDue
```

In the example above, the %PARMS built-in function is used to check the number of parameters passed to the GetBalDue() subprocedure. If two parameters are passed, the second parameter is assigned the current customer balance. If fewer than two parameters are passed, accessing the second parameter is avoided.

But what happens in a situation where the subprocedure is modified to accept another parameter, as follows:

```
D GetBalDue      PI            11P 2
D    custNo                     7P 0 Const
D    rtnBal                    11P 2 OPTIONS(*NOPASS)
D    payDate                    L   OPTIONS(*NOPASS)
```

A third parameter has been added to the subprocedure definition. The implementation of the subprocedure still works as is, because it tests for 2 or more parameters being passed. However, the code to assign a value to the new PAYDATE parameter needs to be added, as follows:

```
P GetBalDue      B             Export
D GetBalDue      PI            11P 2
D    custNo                     7P 0 Const
D    rtnBal                    11P 2 OPTIONS(*NOPASS)
D    payDate                    L   OPTIONS(*NOPASS)

 /free
      chain (custno) custmast;
      if (NOT %FOUND());
         clear cust;
      endif;
      if (%parms() >= 2);
         rtnBal = cust.balance;
      endif;
      if (%parms() >= 3);
         payDate = %date(cust.lstpaydte:*ISO);
      endif;

      return cust.balance;
 /end-free
P GetBalDue
```

%PARMS checks for 2 or 3 parameters and then populates the return values

In the example above, the LSTPAYDTE (last payment date) subfield is copied to the PAYDATE parameter when a value for PAYDATE is passed to the subprocedure. But what's wrong with this picture?

The problem with this is that now whenever the programmer wants to use the PAYDATE parameter, they must also pass a variable on the second parameter even when RTNBAL (return balance) isn't needed.

Another setting for the OPTIONS keyword, *OMIT can be used to resolve this problem. By specifying both *NOPASS and *OMIT for parameter 2, it can be omitted or "skipped" when it isn't wanted. For more details on skipping parameters with *OMIT see Tip #48.

Testing for Skipped Parameters

```
FCUSTMAST  IF   E            K DISK     PREFIX('CUST.')
D CUST                DS                LikeRec(CUSTREC:*INPUT)

D balance             S              7P 2

 /free        ←─────── Call the subprocedure without a 2nd
    *inlr = *ON;       parameter but with a 3rd parameter.

    balance = GetBalDue(3741:*OMIT: prePayDate);
 /end-free

P GetBalDue           B                Export
D GetBalDue           PI             11P 2
D    custNo                           7P 0 Const
D    rtnBal                          11P 2 OPTIONS(*NOPASS:*OMIT)
D    payDate                           L  OPTIONS(*NOPASS:*OMIT)

 /free
        chain (custno) custmast;
        if (NOT %FOUND());
           clear cust;
        endif;
        if (%parms() >= 2 and %addr(rtnBal)<>*NULL)    %PARMS checks for
           rtnBal = cust.balance;                      2 or 3 parameters
        endif;                                         and then the address
        if (%parms() >= 3 and %addr(payDate)<>*NULL);  of the parameter is
           payDate = %date(cust.lstpaydte:*ISO);       compared to *NULL
        endif;

        return cust.balance;
 /end-free
P GetBalDue
```

In the example above, the number of parameters is tested and if correct, the parameter's address is compared to *NULL. When a subprocedure is called and passed *OMIT in place of a parameter value, the address of that parameter is set to null. To allow a parameter to be unspecified, include OPTIONS(*OMIT) or OPTIONS(*NOPASS:*OMIT). To pass no value for the parameter, specify *OMIT in place of a real value.

90 Create ASCII Text Files on the IFS

The Integrated File System (IFS) supports PC-style files. Often integration between RPG IV applications and PC applications requires that data be stored on the IFS instead of in traditional database files.

One of the confusing aspects of the IFS is creating a new file. To create a new file the IFS open() or open64() API is used. These APIs open an IFS file and optionally create it. That is, if the file does not exit, it is created and then the newly created file is opened. If it already exists, the existing file is open.

This causes a lot of confusion because when creating the file, the character set assigned to the file (i.e., the file's CCSID) does not get translated in an expected fashion until after the file has been closed and then reopened.

Files created on the IFS are normally created with a PC ASCII character set, which is CCSID(819). For example, to create file named NOTES.TXT on the IFS, the open64() API would be used as follows:

Creating an ASCII Text IFS File

```
/free
    szFile = 'NOTES.TXT';
    nCCSID = 819;
    nFlags = O_CODEPAGE + O_RDWR + O_CREATE;
    nFlags2 = S_IRWXU + S_IRWXO + S_IRWXG;
    hFile = open64(%trimR(szFile) : nFlags : nFlags2 : nCCSID);
    ifsClose(hFile);
/end-free
```

In the example above, the open64() API is called. It creates the new file named NOTES.TXT in the home directory (probably '/home/user' where 'user' is the user profile of the user running the program) and then opens it for read/write operations.

The data written to the NOTES.TXT file is not automatically converted between the program's CCSID (probably CCSID(37) in North America) and the file's CCSID of 819. This is because CCSID conversion applies when the file is open with the O_TEXTDATA flag. If the file is not yet created, that flag does not apply.

Therefore, the IFS file is closed by calling the close() API and then reopened.

To reopen the file different flags are needed to indicate that the file should be open as a text file. This causes the file file's CCSID to be translated to that of the job's CCSID automatically. To reopen the file with implicit CCSID conversion, specify the O_TEXTDATA and O_APPEND flags, as follows:

Reopening an IFS File as Text

```
/free
    szFile = 'NOTES.TXT';
    nFlags = O_TEXTDATA + O_APPEND + O_RDWR;
    hFile = open64(%trimR(szFile) : nFlags);
/end-free
```

In the example above, the IFS file is opened as a text file; the O_TEXTDATA and O_APPEND flags included to ensure the file is open as text and its existing data is not deleted.

The O_TEXTDATA flag causes the file to be open as a text file. As data is read from the file it is automatically converted from the CCSID of the file to the CCSID of the job. When data is written to the file, it is converted to the CCSID of the file from the CCSID of the job. Normally IFS files that are open in RPG IV do not perform this task, but plain ASCII text file have this capability though the O_TEXTDATA flag.

The O_APPEND flag causes the file to be opened and positioned after the last character in the file; that is at end-of-file. Any write operations to the file are added after the existing data.

Once the file is open with O_TEXTDATA, the IFS read() and write() APIs can be used to read or write data to the file. When you are finished, close the file with the IFS close() API is used to close the file.

When the IFS file needs to be read from the beginning, avoid using the O_APPEND flag. When O_APPEND is not specified, the file is open and positioned to byte 1. Any input or output operation begin with that position and move the file cursor forward. Subsequent I/O operations begin at the current file cursor position and adjust it accordingly.

If the IFS file already exists, (does not need to be created) the file only needs to be open once; it does not need to be created, closed an then reopen. You can check if an IFS file exists using the access() API. (See Tip #75.)

IFS API Prototypes

To summarize the APIs needed to create, open, read, write and close an IFS file, the following prototypes and named constants are provided.

Figurative Constants used by IFS APIs

```
D O_RDONLY        C                    Const(1)
D O_WRONLY        C                    Const(2)
D O_RDWR          C                    Const(4)
D O_CREAT         C                    Const(8)
D O_CREATE        C                    Const(8)
D O_EXCL          C                    Const(16)
D O_TRUNC         C                    Const(64)
D O_APPEND        C                    Const(256)
D O_CODEPAGE      C                    Const(8388608)
D O_TEXTDATA      C                    Const(16777216)
```

IFS API Prototypes for RPG IV

```
D ifsOpen         PR            10I 0 extProc('open64')
D  szIFSFileName                    * Value options(*string)
D  openFlags                    10I 0 Value
D  fMod                         10U 0 Value options(*nopass)
D  CCSID                        10U 0 Value options(*nopass)

D ifsRead         PR            10I 0 extProc('read')
D  hFile                        10I 0 Value
D  szBuffer                         * Value
D  nBufLen                      10U 0 Value

D ifsWrite        PR            10I 0 extProc('write')
D   hFile                       10I 0 Value
D   pBuffer                         * Value
D   nBufferLen                  10U 0 Value

D ifsClose        PR            10I 0 extProc('close')
D  hFile                        10I 0 Value

D ifsAccess       PR            10I 0 extProc('access')
D  szIFSFile                        * Value options(*string)
D  nAccessMode                  10I 0 Value

D ifsStat         PR            10I 0 ExtProc('stat64')
D  ifsFile                          * Value options(*string)
D  pStat                            * Value

D ifsStat_T       DS                  Qualified based(null_Template)
D  fileMode                     10U 0
D  srlNbr                       10U 0
D  userID                       10U 0
D  groupID                      10U 0
D  nFileSize                    20I 0
D  lastFileAccess...
D                               10I 0
D  lastModTime                  10I 0
D  lastStsChgTime...
D                               10I 0
D  devID                        10U 0
D  blockSize                    10U 0
```

Continued...

…continued

```
D   symbLinkCount                5U 0
D   codePage                     5U 0
D   allocSize                   20U 0
D   genID                       10U 0
D   objectType                  11A
D   reserved1                   57A
```

CrtASCIIFile (Create ASCII File) Subprocedure

```
H NOMAIN OPTION(*NODEBUGIO:*SRCSTMT) BNDDIR('QC2LE')
H Copyright('(c) 2007 Robert Cozzi, Jr. All rights reserved.')

 /include rpgtnt/qcpysrc,rpgtnt

P crtAsciiFile    B                        Export
D crtAsciiFile    PI              10I 0
D   szFile                       640A      Const VARYING
D   bKeepOpen                      1N      Const OPTIONS(*NOPASS)

D dftCCSID        C                        Const(819)
D nCCSID          S               10I 0    Inz(dftCCSID)
D nFlags          S               10I 0
D nFlags2         S               10I 0
D hFile           S               10I 0

C                 eval      nFlags = O_CODEPAGE + O_RDWR

   // Does the file already exist?
   // if not, add the O_CREAT flag.
C                 if        ifsAccess(%trimR(szFile) : F_OK) < 0
C                 eval      nFlags = nFlags + O_CREAT
C                 else
C                 eval      nFlags = nFlags + O_APPEND
C                 endif

 **   Add User, Other, and Group authorities to the created IFS file.
C                 eval      nFlags2 = S_IRWXU + S_IRWXO + S_IRWXG

 **   First create the file as ASCII., then close it., then
 **   Then close the file.
 **   Then open the file as an ASCII Text file.
 **     That way OS/400 automatically converts
 **       the data to the ASCII codepage.
C                 eval      hFile=ifsOpen(%trimR(szFile) :
C                                   nFlags : nFlags2 : nCCSID)
C                 if        hFile < 0
C                 callp     logErrNo()
C                 return    hFile
C                 endif

C                 callp     ifsClose(hFile)
C                 eval      hFile = 0

C                 if        %Parms()>= 2
C                             and bKeepOpen=*ON
```

Continued…

…continued

```
        ** Reopen the file for RDWR processing (Rarely used)
  C                        eval      hFile=ifsOpen(%trimR(szFile) :
  C                                          O_TEXTDATA + O_RDWR + O_APPEND)
  C                        endif
  C                        return    hFile
  P CrtAsciiFile    E

        ***********************************************************
        **  ifsGetSize - Get the size of a file on the IFS.     **
        ***********************************************************
  P GetIFSSize       B                      Export
  D GetIFSSize       PI            20I 0
  D   pFileName                      *     Value OPTIONS(*STRING)

  D myStatus         DS                   LikeDS(ifsStat_T) Inz

        **  If the file exists return the size, else return -1
  C                        if        ifsStat(pFIleName :
  C                                          %addr(myStatus) ) < 0
  C                        callp     logErrNo()
  C                        return    -1
  C                        endif
  C                        return    myStatus.nFileSize
  P GetIFSSize       E
```

In the example above, the CRTASCIIFILE subprocedure uses the access() API to determine if the IFS file already exists. If the file already exists, the O_APPEND flag is added to the open files. The file is then opened using the open64() API. If the file already exists, it is open with the O_TEXTDATA flag so that the CCSID of the file is automatically converted to the CCSID of the program. If this is not desired, then you should not use this subprocedure.

If the file does not exist, the O_CREAT flag is added to the open flags. This causes open64() to create the file if it doesn't exist, and replace it if it does exist.

Another subprocedure, GetIFSSize, returns the current file size, in bytes for an IFS file.

91 High-level Math in RPG IV

RPG IV includes several mathematical opcodes, but does not include integrated support for high-level match functions. To perform trigonometric functions, such as sine, cosine, arctangent, two options are available. One involves using the C runtime library (C includes support for high-level math functions) the other involves using the CEExxxx math APIs. The CEExxxx API may be slightly faster, but the C functions are easier to implement in RPG IV.

The complexity in the CEExxxx match APIs stems from a multitude of parameter options. Many have 2, 3, 4 or as many as 6 different versions of the same API—each with a subtle name variation. Each API supports a different data-type for their input and output parameters. Most allow floating point only, but others allowing integer and floating point as well as several size variations of each.

Most of the CEExxxx built-in math APIs are restricted to floating point values. By utilizing the CONST keyword for these parameters on the API prototype, non-float numeric fields and literals may also be specified. The output however is still going to be floating point and a floating point variable must be specified.

To declare a floating point variable in RPG IV, the "F" data-type is specified, as follows:

```
D   term            S              8F
D   rate            S              4F
```

The size of a floating point may be specified as 8 (double precision) or 4 (single precision) depending on which API is called (there are versions for both sizes). It is most effective to use double precision since RPG tends to convert 4F to 8F, performs the operations using 8F and then converts it back to 4F. By using 8F this extra conversion can be avoided, as follows:

```
D   cos             PR                    extProc('CEESDCOS')
D    fInput                        8F     Const
D    fOutput                       8F
D    apiErrorDS                           LikeDS(QUSEC_T)
D                                         OPTIONS(*OMIT)
D   cos_of_x        S              8F
D   x               S              9P 7 Inz(3.1415926)

C                   callp         cos(x : cos_of_x : *OMIT)
```

In the preceeding example, the input value is 8F and is CONST. The return value (parameter 2) is 8F but it is not const. This means that the value specified on parameter 1 (the input value) may be any type of numeric format and the compiler converts it to 8F automatically. The second parameter, however is returned as a floating-point value and therefore must be specified as an 8F variable.

The CEE math API prototypes are as follows:

CEE Math API Prototypes

```
D acos           PR                        extProc('CEESDACS')
D  fInput                       8F         Const
D  fOutput                      8F
D  apiErrorDS                   12A         OPTIONS(*OMIT)

D aTan            PR                        extProc('CEESDATN')
D  fInput                       8F         Const
D  fOutput                      8F
D  apiErrorDS                   12A         OPTIONS(*OMIT)

D sin             PR                        extProc('CEESDSIN')
D  fInput                       8F         Const
D  fOutput                      8F
D  apiErrorDS                   12A         OPTIONS(*OMIT)

D cos             PR                        extProc('CEESDCOS')
D  fInput                       8F         Const
D  fOutput                      8F
D  apiErrorDS                   12A         OPTIONS(*OMIT)

D tan             PR                        extProc('CEESDTAN')
D  fInput                       8F         Const
D  fOutput                      8F
D  apiErrorDS                   12A         OPTIONS(*OMIT)

D coTan           PR                        extProc('CEESDCTN')
D  fInput                       8F         Const
D  fOutput                      8F
D  apiErrorDS                   12A         OPTIONS(*OMIT)

D exp             PR                        extProc('CEESDEXP')
D  fInput                       8F         Const
D  fOutput                      8F
D  apiErrorDS                   12A         OPTIONS(*OMIT)

D exp2            PR                        extProc('CEESJXPJ')
D  fInput1                      20I 0      Const
D  fInput2                      20I 0      Const
D  fOutput                      20I 0
D  apiErrorDS                   12A         OPTIONS(*OMIT)

D Factorial       PR                        extProc('CEESJFAC')
D**  fInput must be <= 20 or a runtime error is issued.
D  fInput                       20I 0      Const
D  fOutput                      20I 0
D  apiErrorDS                   12A         OPTIONS(*OMIT)
```

C Math Library — An Alternative to CEE Math APIs

The C runtime library also supports a full set of math functions. To improve the performance of a function when performing mathematical operations, IBM moved the C math functions down into the MI layer. This means that the C functions are converted directly into MI instructions for the best available performance. This means their performance is similar to the CEExxxx APIs, but they have the advantage of a much cleaner syntax.

The C runtime math functions have a more programming-friendly parameter list than the CEExxxx math APIs. For example, the cosine function may be called as follows:

```
 H BNDDIR('QC2LE')

 D cos             PR            8F   extProc('cos')
 D   radians                     8F   Const
 D cos_of_x        S            11P 9
 D x               S             7P 6 Inz(3.14159)

 C                 eval         cos_of_x = cos(x)

       // Or in free format, as follows:
   /free
         cos_of_x = cos(x);
   /end-free
```

The C runtime library uses double precision floating point parameters and return values. The use of CONST for the parameters and the implicit conversion when assigning one numeric value to another allows floating point variables to be avoided. The following are the prototypes for most C runtime math library functions.

C Runtime Math Function Prototypes in RPG IV

```
   /IF NOT DEFINED(C_MATH_PROTOS)
   /DEFINE C_MATH_PROTOS
 D acos            PR            8F   extProc('acos')
 D   radians                     8F   Const

 D asin            PR            8F   extProc('asin')
 D   radians                     8F   Const

 D atan            PR            8F   extProc('atan')
 D   radians                     8F   Const

 D atan2           PR            8F   extProc('atan2')
 D   radians1                    8F   Const
 D   radians2                    8F   Const

 D ceil            PR            8F   extProc('ceil')
 D   radians                     8F   Const

 D cos             PR            8F   extProc('cos')
 D   radians                     8F   Const
```

Continued...

...continued

```
D cosh            PR              8F   extProc('cosh')
D   radians                       8F   Const

D exp             PR              8F   extProc('exp')
D   radians                       8F   Const

D floor           PR              8F   extProc('floor')
D   radians                       8F   Const

D fmod            PR              8F   extProc('fmod')
D   arg1                          8F   Const
D   arg2                          8F   Const

D log             PR              8F   extProc('log')
D   radians                       8F   Const

D log10           PR              8F   extProc('log10')
D   radians                       8F   Const

D pow             PR              8F   extProc('pow')
D**  pow(x:y) = x**Y
D   x                             8F   Const
D   y                             8F   Const

D sin             PR              8F   extProc('sin')
D   radians                       8F   Const

D sinh            PR              8F   extProc('sinh')
D   radians                       8F   Const

D sqrt            PR              8F   extProc('sqrt')
D   radians                       8F   Const

D tan             PR              8F   extProc('tan')
D   radians                       8F   Const

D tanh            PR              8F   extProc('tanh')
D   radians                       8F   Const

D erf             PR              8F   extProc('erf')
D   radians                       8F   Const

D erfc            PR              8F   extProc('erfc')
D   radians                       8F   Const

D gamma           PR              8F   extProc('gamma')
D   radians                       8F   Const

D hypot           PR              8F   extProc('hypot')
D   side1                         8F   Const
D   side2                         8F   Const
```

Continued...

…continued

```
      /IF DEFINED(BESSEL_FUNC)
      /IF NOT DEFINED(BESSEL_MATH)
      /DEFINE BESSEL_MATH
       **   Bessel functions, first order
     D j0              PR              8F    extProc('j0')
     D   x                             8F    Const
     D j1              PR              8F    extProc('j1')
     D   x                             8F    Const
     D jn              PR              8F    extProc('jn')
     D   n                           10I 0  Const
     D   x                             8F    Const

       **   Bessel functions, second order
     D y0              PR              8F    extProc('y0')
     D   x                             8F    Const
     D y1              PR              8F    extProc('y1')
     D   x                             8F    Const
     D yn              PR              8F    extProc('yn')
     D   n                           10I 0  Const
     D   x                             8F    Const
      /ENDIF
      /ENDIF

      /ENDIF
```

92 Program Described Print File with Dynamic Spacing

In RPG III, IBM introduced the ability to vary the number of lines skipped or spaced when printing. This is accomplished through the Print Control Data Structure in RPG III and RPG IV.

RPG IV has greater printer spacing capabilities than RPG III, consequently the data structure used for print control was changed when RPG IV was introduced.

This Print Control Data Structure is specified on the PRTCTL keyword on the printer file's File Description specification, as follows:

PRTCTL Printer File Keyword and Data Structure

```
FQPRINT     O   F   132      PRINTER OFLIND(*INOF)
F                                    PRTCTL(myPrtCtrl)

D myPrtCtrl         DS                    Qualified
D  SpaceB                        3A
D  SpaceA                        3A
D  SkipB                         3A
D  SkipA                         3A
D  CurLine                       3S 0
```

When an EXCEPT opcode is used to write to the QPRINT print file, the values stored in the SPACEB subfield controls the number of lines to space before printing the line, SPACEA controls the number of lines to space after printing the line, and SKIPB and SKIPA control the line number to skip to before or after printing the line, respectively.

The CURLINE subfield reports the current print line of the print file, it should not be changed by the programmer.

A traditional, program-described output specification would appear as follows:

```
FQPRINT    O   F   132        PRINTER OFLIND(*INOF)

C                    Except    Output

.....OFormat++++DAddn01n02n03Except++++SpbSpaSkbSka...
   OQPRINT    E              OUTPUT         2
.....O................n01n02n03Field++++++++YB?End++PConstant++++++++++
   O                                         +1 'Hello World!'
```

In the example above, the first output line controls the Space After setting. The line "Hello World!" is printed and then the printer spacing two lines.

```
Line *...v....1.........2.........3
  1    Hello World!
  2
  3 ◄─────────────  Printer is positioned to line 3 after printing.
```

Now, let's look at the same functionality using the PRTCTL feature, as follows:

Using PRTCTL to Control Printed Output

```
FQPRINT    O   F   132        PRINTER OFLIND(*INOF)
F                                     PRTCTL(myPrtCtrl)

D myPrtCtrl        DS                 Qualified
D   SpaceB                    3A
D   SpaceA                    3A
D   SkipB                     3A
D   SkipA                     3A
D   CurLine                   3S 0
 /free
       evalR myPrtCtrl.spaceAfter = '3';
       except output;

       evalR myPrtCtrl.spaceAfter = '1';
       except output;

       evalR myPrtCtrl.spaceAfter = '0';
       except output;
 /end-free
```

*Using PRTCTL means Spacing/Skipping controls should **not** be specified on Output specifications.*

```
.....OFormat++++DAddn01n02n03Except++++SpbSpaSkbSka...
   OQPRINT    E              OUTPUT
.....O*............n01n02n03Field++++++++YB?End++PConstant/Editword++++++
   O                                         +1 'Hello World!'
```

In the example above, the output line "Hello World!" is written 3 times. The first time it is printed, the space after control is set to 3 lines, then it is printed again after changing the space after control to 1 line, then it is printed a third time after setting the space after control to zero lines.

When the output is finished, the printer is positioned on line 5 of the printed page. This line number is relative to where printing began.

```
Line *...v....1.........2.........3
   1   Hello World!
   2
   3
   4   Hello World!
   5   Hello World!  ◄─────────────────  Printer is positioned to line 5 after printing.
```

The reason SPACEA, SPACEB, SKIPA, and SKIPB are character fields is because when they are blank, they are treated just like blank entries on an Output specification. To assign a value to one of these fields, the data must be right justified, as follows:

```
myPrtCtrl.SpaceA = '002';
```

or

```
EVALR myPrtCtrl.SpaceA = '3'
```

The entry needs to be right-justified, so either the full 3 positions need to be specified, or the EVALR (eval right-justified) opcode must be used.

A cautious programmer could modify the printer control data structure to include numeric subfields that overlay the original subfields, as follows:

Enhanced PRTCTL Data Structure

```
D myPrtCtrl         DS                    Qualified
D   SpaceB                        3A
D   SpaceA                        3A
D   SkipB                         3A
D   SkipA                         3A
D   CurLine                       3S 0
D   SpaceBefore                   3S 0 Overlay(spaceB)
D   SpaceAfter                    3S 0 Overlay(spaceA)
D   SkipBefore                    3S 0 Overlay(skipB)
D   SkipAfter                     3S 0 Overlay(skipA)
```

In the preceeding example, additional zoned numeric subfields have been added to the MYPRTCTRL data structure. This allows the spacing and skipping controls to be assigned using simple assignment operations rather than EVALR opcodes; for example:

```
myPrtCtrl.SpaceAfter = 3;
```

To reset the space after control to blanks, however, the original subfield should be cleared, as follows:

```
clear myPrtCtrl.SpaceA;
```

Blanks are required since setting *space after* to zero is not the same as setting it to blanks. For example, the following two statements do *not* result in the same *space after* control.

```
myPrtCtrl.SpaceA = *BLANKS;
myPrtCtrl.SpaceAfter = 0;
```

Blanks in the space after control cause the default space after behavior to occur; which is: space 1 line after printing the current line. Whereas assigning a value of 0 to space after (as in the second line, above) results in spacing zero lines after printing. That is, the printer does not advance to the next line.

Use PRTCTL whenever dynamic spacing or skipping is required for program described print files.

93 Aligning or Centering Text in a Character Field

Routines to shift text within a field have been around for decades. Right-justification, left-justification, centered, and paginated are the most often created text manipulation routines.

RPG IV makes two of these routines incredibly easy. Left and right justification can be accomplished in just one statement with RPG IV, as follows:

Left- or Right-Justifying Text

```
C                   EVAL      left  = %trimL(text)
C                   EVALR     right = %trimR(text)
```

In the example above, the EVAL opcode is used in conjunction with the %TRIML built-in function. This deletes leading blanks from the TEXT field and copies its content left justified to the target field.

The EVALR (eval right-justified) opcode is used in conjunction with the %TRIMR built-in function. This deletes trailing blanks from the TEXT field, and copies it right justified to the target field.

This illustrates two extremely easy methods for right and left-justifying text.

Centering text is more complex, however. No built-in function exists to do this, so a routine needs to be created. One centering routine that I like to use involves a subprocedure that does all the work, as follows:

Centering Text

```
P center           B                    EXPORT
D center           PI        2048A      OPDESC
D  inText                    2048A      Const OPTIONS(*VARSIZE)

D nType            S          10I 0
D nCurLen          S          10I 0
D nMaxLen          S          10I 0
D nDataLen         S          10I 0
D nStart           S          10I 0
D nPad             S          10I 0
D rtnText          S                    Like(inText)

 /free
        ceegsi(1 : nType:nCurLen:nMaxLen:*OMIT);
        if (nCurLen > 0);
            if %subst(inText:1:nCurLen)=' ';
                return ' ';
            endif;
        endif;
        nDataLen = %Len(%Trim(%subst(inText:1:nCurLen)));
        nStart = %check(' ':inText);
        if (nDataLen < nCurLen);
          nPad  = %DIV((nCurLen - nDataLen):2);
          nPad += %REM((nCurLen - nDataLen):2);
          %subst(rtnText:nPad+1) =
%subst(inText:nStart:nDataLen);
        endif;
        return rtnText;
 /end-free
p center            E
```

> The prototype for CEEGSI is listed in the Appendix

In the example above, the CEEGSI API is used to retrieve the length of a variable or value passed on the first parameter of this subprocedure. This length is important for calculating the center of the value being processed.

Next, the length of the data from the input parameter and the starting location of the data in the input parameter are calculated.

Next, the length of the data in the input variable is subtracted from the length of the input variable itself. That figure yields the number of blanks we have in the field verses real data. Since we want to center the text in this field the number of blanks is divided by 2. If there are 8 blanks, we want 4 on each side of the data, if there are 10 blanks, then 5 go on each side. If an odd number of blanks are detected, the additional blank goes in front of the text.

The CENTER subprocedure centers text based on the length of the variable passed to the subprocedure verses the length of the data in that variable.

To use the CENTER subprocedure, call it implicitly via an EVAL opcode, as follows:

Using the CENTER Text Subprocedure

```
H   BNDDIR('RPGTNT/RPGTNT') DFTACTGRP(*NO)

    /copy rpgtnt/qcpysrc,rpgtnt

D centered       S               50A
D right          S               50A
D left           S               50A

D text           S               50A   Inz('   Please show me how!   ')

C                   EVAL      *INLR = *ON

C                   EVALR     right = %trimR(text)
C                   EVAL      left  = %trimL(text)

C                   EVAL      centered = center(text)
```

In the example above, the %TRIMR and %TRIML built-in functions are used to illustrate how to right and left-justify text. The CENTER subprocedure is called to center the text. A more appropriate name for the CENTER subprocedure might be %TRIMC (Trim and Center).

94 Debug a Batch Job

Everyone knows that the STRDBG command is used to debug programs, as follows:

```
STRDBG  PGM(MYPGM) UPDPROD(*NO | *YES)
```

But how do you debug a program running in a batch job? The answer is also STRDBG. However before issuing STRDBG, the STRSRVJOB (Start Service Job) command must be issued identifying the job to be debugged.

The Start Service Job command starts a remote service operation for another job. This allows dump, debug, and trace commands to be run in the other job until an END-SRVJOB (end Service Job) command is issued.

For example, if a batch job is running and an RPG IV program named AR0100 is going to run in that job, the program can be debugged from another interactive job.

The best way to do this is to place the batch job on hold. To hold a job that is already running, issue a HLDJOB command, as follows:

```
HLDJOB JOB(123456/COZZI/AGING)
```

Another approach is to specify HOLD(*YES) parameter when a program is submitted to batch via the SBMJOB command, as follows:

```
SBMJOB CMD(CALL PGM(AR0100)) JOB(AGING) HOLD(*YES)
```

This ensures that the job doesn't start running the program you want to debug before you have control over the job.

Next, issue the STRSRVJOB command, as follows:

```
STRSRVJOB JOB(123456/COZZI/AGING)
```

To begin a debug session for the AR0100 program in the batch job you just placed into service mode, run the STRDBG command as you normally would, for example

```
STRDBG  PGM(AR0100) UPDPROD(*YES)
```

At this point, the source-level debugger is loaded and you can set breakpoints anywhere they are needed. Note that the UPDPROD(*YES) parameter is specified. Typically this is required for batch job debugging since it is often being performed on production applications. But use caution when UPDPROD(*YES) is specified.

Set the breakpoints you want for the debugging session. Once the breakpoints have been set, press F12 to return to Command Entry. Then release the job that was previously held, using the RLSJOB command, as follows:

```
RLSJOB JOB(123456/COZZI/AGING)
```

As soon as the batch job loads the program placed in debug and reaches one of the breakpoints, the source level debugger will break into the interactive screen. At this point you can debug the program just like any other program.

When you've finished debugging, press F12 to allow the program to continue running, or press F3 to cancel the program. You'll be brought back to the interactive job's Command Entry display. At this point, if you are finished debugging the batch job, issue the ENDDBG command, as follows:

```
ENDDBG
```

If you have finished completely and no longer need the service job, issue the END-SRVJOB command to disconnect the batch job from the interactive job, as follows:

```
ENDSRVJOB
```

A Faster Way to Enter the Job Number

Want a faster way to start debugging a batch job? Using WRKACTJOB, you can display the job you want to debug. Then select option 5 (WRKJOB) on the WRKACTJOB display, as follows:

```
                        Work with Active Jobs
                                                07/23/06  12:12:58
     CPU %:      .0    Elapsed time:  00:00:00    Active jobs:   662

     Type options, press Enter.
       2=Change    3=Hold    4=End    5=Work with   6=Release   7=Display message
       8=Work with spooled files      13=Disconnect ...
                          Current
     Opt  Subsystem/Job   User        Type  CPU %   Function       Status
            COZZI         QTMHHTTP     BCH    .0    PGM-QZHBMAIN    SIGW
       _    COZZI         QTMHHTTP     BCI    .0    PGM-QZSRLOG     SIGW
       _    COZZI         QTMHHTTP     BCI    .0    PGM-QZSRLOG     SIGW
       _    COZZI         QTMHHTTP     BCI    .0    PGM-QZSRHTTP    SIGW
       5    COZZI         QTMHHTP1     BCI    .0    PGM-QZSRCGI     TIMW
       _    COZZI         QTMHHTP1     BCI    .0    PGM-QZSRCGI     TIMW
       _    COZZI         QTMHHTP1     BCI    .0    PGM-QZSRCGI     TIMW
       _    COZZI         QTMHHTP1     BCI    .0    PGM-QZSRCGI     TIMW
                                                                   Bottom
     Parameters or command
     ===>
     F3=Exit   F5=Refresh        F7=Find      F10=Restart statistics
     F11=Display elapsed data    F12=Cancel   F23=More options  F24=More keys
```

Work with Job

The WRKJOB menu will appear. From this menu, select option 10 (Display Joblog), as follows:

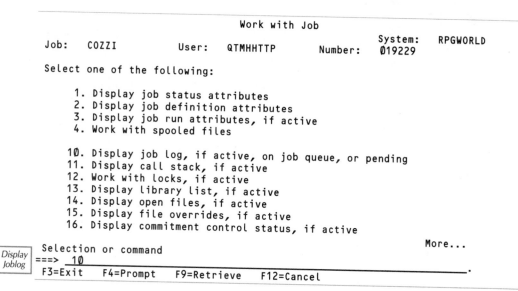

```
                            Work with Job
                                                  System:   RPGWORLD
   Job:   COZZI          User:   QTMHHTTP      Number:   019229

   Select one of the following:

       1. Display job status attributes
       2. Display job definition attributes
       3. Display job run attributes, if active
       4. Work with spooled files

      10. Display job log, if active, on job queue, or pending
      11. Display call stack, if active
      12. Work with locks, if active
      13. Display library list, if active
      14. Display open files, if active
      15. Display file overrides, if active
      16. Display commitment control status, if active
                                                          More...
   Selection or command
   ===>  10

   F3=Exit    F4=Prompt    F9=Retrieve    F12=Cancel
```

Display Joblog

When the joblog is displayed, it will contain message CPF1124 on the first line. This message is the "job started on..." message, it appears similar to the following:

Cut/Paste the fully qualified job number

```
                            Display Job Log
                                                  System:   RPGWORLD
   Job . . :   COZZI      User . . :   QTMHHTTP   Number . . . :   019229

   Job 019229/QTMHHTTP/COZZI started on 07/23/06 at 04:45:26 in subsystem
      QHTTPSVR in QHTTPSVR. Job entered system on 07/23/06 at 04:45:26.
      This is a CGI job for IBM HTTP Server instance COZZI.
```

If you are using a 5250 emulator, such as Client Access or MochaSoft's TN5250, you can simply cut and paste the job identification into the STRSRVJOB, HLDJOB, and other commands that have a JOB parameter. For example, type in STRSRVJOB, then press Ctrl+V under Windows or Apple+V in Mac OS X to insert the fully qualified job name.

95 Find and Replace with Regular Expressions

Most applications have a search or find option built into them. Most PC-based applications have a Find and Replace option built into them. Why not provide a Find and Replace capability in RPG IV applications.

One shortcoming with the %SCAN built-in function is that it is case sensitive. Most searches performed by programmers are usually case sensitive, but nearly all searches performed by end-users are case insensitive. This makes %SCAN challenging when trying to do a case insensitive search. (See Tip #100 for information on a case-insensitive scan using the %SCAN built-in function.)

There are two ways to do case insensitive searches in RPG IV. One is to convert the search pattern and the search data to all uppercase or all lowercase and then perform the search. The other is to use an API with case insensitive search capabilities. Two APIs provide case insensitive scanning options, and they are

- The QCLSCAN API
- The Regular Expression (regex) APIs

The QCLSCAN approach is obsolete. It has a decades-old interface that doesn't support contemporary data lengths. For example, it can scan up to 999 bytes at a time, and defines its parameters as Packed(3,0).

The regular expression APIs provide the kind of search capabilities found in most modern environments and languages. Regular Expressions or "regex" are the backbone of the search and match capability of PHP, Perl, Python, Grep, SED, and so on.

The downside to regular expression APIs is that they are (A) lot more complex than %SCAN or QCLSCAN and (B) overkill for simple searches.

However, once you set up regular expressions, they can be nearly as easy, if not easier than using QCLSCAN, and they have a lot more power.

With Regular Expressions, you can search for

- Plain text strings
- Generic text patterns
- Ignore upper/lowercase

- Find "not" conditions
- Find a list of characters
- Find more than one thing at a time

There are many more features of regular expressions, however a full discussion would be beyond the scope of this book. For our purposes, I will illustrate how to replace %SCAN with regular expressions so that it supports both generic and case insensitive searches as well as any other regular expression.

The first thing we need to do with Regular Expressions is prototype the APIs. There are a few reference variables that these APIs use, as follows:

```
D size_T          S              10U 0
D off_T           S              10I 0
D LC_COLVAL_T     S              10I 0
D mbState_T       S               5I 0
D regMatch_t      DS                       Qualified
D  rm_so                                   Like(off_T)
D  rm_ss                                   Like(mbState_T)
D  rm_eo                                   Like(off_T)
D  rm_es                                   Like(mbState_T)
```

Another reference variable, REGEX_T, which is actually a data structure. This data structure is a handle to the regular expression being processed. It is simply passed between the regular expression APIs and not modified by the programmer. REGEX_T is listed in the Appendix.

The prototypes for the six regular expression APIs are as follows:

REGCOMP — Compile a Regular Expression String

```
D regcomp          PR             10I 0 extProc('regcomp')
D  regex_t                              LikeDS(regex_T)
D  pattern                        *     Value OPTIONS(*STRING)
D  cflags                         10I 0 Value
```

The key to regular expression searching is the CFLAGS parameter of the regcomp() API. It is where you specify a basic search, extended search, ignore case and other options. This flags, as needed for RPG IV, are as follows:

REGCOMP Control Flags

```
D REG_BASIC       C                     Const(X'00')
D REG_EXTENDED    C                     Const(X'01')
D REG_ICASE       C                     Const(X'02')
D REG_NEWLINE     C                     Const(X'04')
D REG_NOSUB       C                     Const(X'08')
D REG_ALT_NL      C                     Const(X'10')
```

REGCOMP Return Values

```
       //  Return values
D REG_NOMATCH      C              Const(1)
D REG_BADPAT       C              Const(2)
D REG_ECOLLATE     C              Const(3)
D REG_ECTYPE       C              Const(4)
D REG_EESCAPE      C              Const(5)
D REG_ESUBREG      C              Const(6)
D REG_EBRACK       C              Const(7)
D REG_EPAREN       C              Const(8)
D REG_EBRACE       C              Const(9)
D REG_BADBR        C              Const(10)
D REG_ERANGE       C              Const(11)
D REG_ESPACE       C              Const(12)
D REG_BADRPT       C              Const(13)
D REG_ECHAR        C              Const(14)
D REG_EBOL         C              Const(15)
D REG_EEOL         C              Const(16)
D REG_ECOMP        C              Const(17)
D REG_EEXEC        C              Const(18)
D REG_LAST         C              Const(18)
```

REGEXEC — Search Using Regular Expression

```
D regexec        PR        10I 0 extProc('regexec')
D regex_t                        LikeDS(regex_T) Const
D string                      *  Value OPTIONS(*STRING)
D nMaxMatches                    Value Like(size_T)
D regMatch                       LikeDS(regMatch_T) Dim(40)
D                                OPTIONS(*VARSIZE)
D eflags                   10I 0 Value
```

REGFREE — Release the Regular Expression Work Buffer

```
D regfree        PR              extProc('regfree')
D regex_t                        LikeDS(regex_T)
```

REGERROR — Retrieve Regular Expression Errors

```
D regerror       PR              extProc('regerror')
D                                Like(size_T)
D errcode                  10I 0 Value
D regex_t                        LikeDS(regex_T) Const
D errBuffer                   *  Value
D errBuf_size                    Value Like(size_T)
```

In general, searching requires at least two pieces of information: (1) The Search Pattern and (2) The Search Data.

Search Pattern is the text string being searched for in the Search Data.

Normally, searching with RPG IV involves the %SCAN built-in function or SCAN opcode, as follows:

```
D myData           S              500A    Inz('My name is Bob Cozzi')
D pos              S               10I 0
 /free
       pos = %scan('Bob' : myData);
 /end-free
```

In the example above, the %SCAN built-in function returns 12, which is assigned to the POS field. The Search Pattern is the literal 'Bob', and the Search Data is contained in field named MYDATA. 'Bob" is location in position 12 of the MYDATA variable, so %SCAN returns 12.

Searching can't get much easier than this. If simple scanning is all that is required, the %SCAN built-in function or SCAN opcode are good choices.

To accomplish the same search using Regular Expressions, a more complex set of code is required, as follows:

```
 /include rpgtnt/qcpysrc,regex
D myMatch          DS                      LikeDS(regMatch_T) Dim(2) Inz
D myREG            DS                      LikeDS(regEx_T) Inz
D myData           S              500A     Inz('My name is Bob Cozzi')
D rc               S               10I 0

 /free
       rc = regcomp(myREG : 'Bob' : 0);   [1]
       if (rc = 0);
           rc = regexec(myREG : myData : 1: myMatch: 0);   [2]
           if (rc = 0);   // Found!
               pos = myMatch(1).rm_so+1;   [3]
           endif;
       endif;
       regfree(myREG);   [4]

 /end-free
```

The recomp() API is called (1) to compile the search pattern 'Bob.' No control flags are specified. If the compile is successful, the MYDATA field is searched (2) for the search pattern, specifying that up to 1 result is returned. After the search (3) the first element of MYMATCH is retrieved and the value of the RM_SO subfield is incremented from offset notation to position notion. Once searching is completed, the regular express handle is released (4).

The regcomp() API compiles the search pattern ('Bob' in this example) and returns a handle to the regular expression environment. MYREG is a data structure whose format is based on REGEX_T illustrated in the appendix. Compiling the search pattern allows it to be used more efficiently for multiple searches. For example, to read a source file member, one record at a time, the data being searched for is compiled with regcomp() and then after a record is read it is searched using the compiled version of the search pattern.

Using the flags parameter, we can easily turn this search into a case-insensitive search by modifying CFLAGS parameter of recomp(), as follows:

```
rc = regcomp(myREG : 'Bob' : REG_ICASE);
```

When the search is performed, upper/lowercase differences are ignored.

The MYREG data structure is passed from the recomp() API to the regexec() API along with the search data. The regexec() function searches MYDATA for 'Bob', using the compiled search pattern stored in MYREG. It locates 'Bob' in position 12. The position is reported using offset notation, so 11 is actually returned in the MYMATCH data structure array.

The MYMATCH data structure is based on REGMACTH_T and must be a data structure array of 1 or more elements. That is, the DIM keyword must be specified on the data structures derived from REGMATCH_T. The location where the search pattern is found is reported in element 1. The line from the example above that extracts the found location is as follows:

```
pos = myMatch(1).rm_so+1;
```

This statement converts from offset notation to absolute position by adding 1 to the found offset. That is, in our example it turns 11 into 12 by adding 1 to the first element's RM_SO subfield. This location is copied to the POS variable.

Remember regular expressions can search for more than one pattern at a time and for more than one occurrence of the pattern in the search data. To control the number of results returned, specify a maximum matches on the third parameter of the regexec() function. This is similar to specifying an array of integers for the Result field when searching with the SCAN opcode. In our example, we've specified that 1 response may be returned.

If the return code from regcomp() is 0, everything worked and the pattern was found. A return value of REG_NOMATCH indicates that no matches were found. Any other non-zero value indicates an error occurred. If an error occurs, the regerror() API can be called to retrieve the text of the error message.

Let's look at each of the regular expression APIs in a little more detail.

RegComp() Parameters

When the search pattern is compiled with regcomp(), the data structure passed as the first parameter is updated. It receives the compiled search pattern and flag settings. The search pattern is specified on the second parameter, and the flag settings are specified on the third parameter. The regcomp() function's prototype is as follows:

```
D regcomp         PR              10I 0 extProc('regcomp')
D  regex_t                              LikeDS(regex_T)
D  pattern                        *     Value OPTIONS(*STRING)
D  cflags                         10I 0 Value
```

The first parameter is a data structure. This data structure must be of the REGEX_T format. The data structure is the identifier or handle that identifies the compiled regular expression. It is passed between the various regular expression APIs. While the regular expression APIs may modify this data structure, the programmer does not do anything to it except pass it between the APIs.

The second parameter is the search pattern. This is the text you want to locate. You may specify a plain text string, a generic-style text string, or a complex regular expression—it's up to you.

The third parameter may be one of the Control Flags (see "REGCOMP Control Flags") or it must be zero. Specify a control flag to evoke extended expression searches, convert '\n' symbols into true line feeds and ignore upper/lowercase.

RegExec() Parameters

Once the regcomp() function is creates a REGEX_T structure, the regexec() function can be called. While the data being searched can change and regexec() can be called with new search data over and over, the search pattern often remains the same. For example, search a source file for the phrase "CUSTMAST." The pattern is consistent for each source record read from the file, but the data being searched changes with each call to regexec(). By first compiling the pattern with regcomp(), the search performance can be improved. When the pattern needs to change, delete (or save) the old identifier and compile the new search pattern.

The search pattern used by regexec() is created by a call to regcomp(). The regexec() API is passed a search pattern identifier and the data to be searched. The regexec() function's prototype is as follows:

```
D regexec         PR              10I 0 extProc('regexec')
D  regex_t                              Const LikeDS(regex_T)
D  string                         *     Value OPTIONS(*STRING)
D  nMaxMatches                          Value Like(size_T)
D  regMatch                             LikeDS(regMatch_T) Dim(40)
D                                       OPTIONS(*VARSIZE)
D  eflags                         10I 0 Value
```

The first parameter must be a data structure that was previously returned by a call to regcomp().

The second parameter is a character variable or literal that is searched using the original pattern passed to regcomp().

The third parameter is the maximum number of matches to be returned simultaneously. If you only want to verify that the search pattern exists in the search data, and do not need its location returned, then specify 0 for this parameter and interpret the return code. A return code of 0 means reexec() found the pattern, a return code of 1 means it did not find the pattern.

To return the location where the search pattern is detected, specify 1 for the third parameter.

A value greater than 1 may be specified for the third parameter to force regexec() to search for multiple occurrences of the search pattern in the search data.

The fourth parameter receives the location of the search pattern in the search data. It receives two values. Subfield RM_SO contains the starting offset to where the search pattern has been located. Add 1 to this value to calculate the real position. Subfield RM_EO contains the position following the end of the search pattern.

This parameter is a data structure array that is defined using the REGMATCH_T data structure template, as follows:

```
D regMatch_t      DS                  Qualified
D   rm_so                             Like(off_T)
D   rm_ss                             Like(mbState_T)
D   rm_eo                             Like(off_T)
D   rm_es                             Like(mbState_T)
```

To create a data structure array that uses this data structure as a template, use the LIKEDS keyword, as follows:

```
D matches          DS                  LikeDS(regMatch_t) Dim(6)
```

The number of elements specified for the array is arbitrary. I used DIM(40) on the prototype but the actual data structure array passed to the API may contain fewer elements. As illustrated above, DIM(6) is used. The number of element of the array must be one greater than the number specified on the MaxMatches (third) parameter.

96 Use DLTOVR when Using OVRDBF OVRSCOPE(*JOB)

With OS/400 V2R3, a new parameter was added to the OVRDBF command. This parameter provides the ability to control how long the override remains for the job. The default is to work like it has always worked; at the call-level. But two additional options were added.

OVRSCOPE(*ACTGRPDFN)—If the program applying the override is running in the *DFTACTGRP, the override is set to *CALLVL ("call-level"). This is the same way legacy overrides have been applied for decades. If the program is running in a named or *NEW activation group, then the override applies for the lifetime of the activation group. That is, the override is deleted when the activation group is destroyed or when a CALL transfers outside of the activation group.

OVRSCOPE(*JOB)—The override is permanently applied and applies to any program until the job ends or the override is explicitly deleted. This means regardless of where the program runs (in the default activation group, named activation group, *NEW activation group or anywhere in between) the override applies.

To ensure that a rogue override doesn't ruin your day, whenever OVRSCOPE(*JOB) is issued, make sure a corresponding DLTOVR is also run when the override is no longer needed.

OVRDBF OVRSCOPE(*JOB) Corresponds to DLTOVR LVL(*JOB)

```
OVRDBF   FILE(CUSTMAST) TOFILE(APLIB/CUSTOMER) OVRSCOPE(*JOB)
CALL     PGM(MYILEPGM)
DLTOVR   FILE(CUSTMAST) LVL(*JOB)
MONMSG   MSGID(CPF9841) /* Override not found? */
```

You might notice that the DLTOVR command has a LVL parameter, whereas the OVRDBF command has the OVRSCOPE parameter. These parameters correspond to one another. Why they have different name, only IBM knows.

It is critical when using OVRDBF OVRSCOPE(*JOB) to issue a corresponding DLTOVR LVL(*JOB) command, otherwise the job-level override is not deleted.

97

Use a FOR Loop to Allow Multiple Exit Points

Most programmers practice a programming methodology that every module should have one entry and one exit point. With this style of programming, deeply nested conditional statements can make the code less readable; for example:

Traditional Nested Logic

```
/free
    chain custno Custmast;
    if (NOT %Found());
        if (condition-A);

            if (condition-B);

                if (condition-C);

                    if (condition-D);

                        if (condition-E);

                        endif;
                    endif;
                endif;
            endif;
        endif;
    endif;
/end-free
```

Of course it is more confusing as additional conditional statements are inserted within those already illustrated.

To avoid nesting too deeply and therefore avoid maintaining seemingly endless IF/ENDIF control blocks, wrap the entire block of code in a FOR loop. Then use the LEAVE opcode to exit to the bottom of the block of code whenever an error or other condition occurs; for example:

Using a FOR Loop with LEAVE

```
/free
   for i = 1 to 1;
      chain custno Custmast;
      if (NOT %Found());
         LEAVE;
      Endif
         // Other code goes here
      if (error-condition-b);
         LEAVE;
      endif;

      //  etc.

   endfor;

/end-free
```

Anytime a LEAVE operation is detected, it branch to the ENDFOR statement of the closest FOR loop. Since this loop is being performed once, not calling a LEAVE opcode will allow it to complete normally. The FOR...ENDFOR loop is really just a cheat. It allows you to abnormally branch to the end of a block of code without coding GOTO/TAG, or deeply nested conditional logic.

Many programmers do not favor using LEAVE operations to exit a routine. Instead, they favor nesting conditional statements. It is really a matter of taste, but if this technique is used, be prepared for potentially unfavorable comments.

About the FOR OpCode

The FOR operation replaces the traditional "DO" opcode in fixed and free format. The "DO" opcode is not supported in free format and therefore, FOR must be used.

The FOR opcode has a slightly different syntax than the IF, DOW, and DOU opcodes as well as the DO opcode. In addition you cannot enclose a FOR statement's condition within parentheses. The syntax of the FOR opcode follows:

```
FOR  var = start TO limit [ BY increment];

endfor;
```

VAR is a numeric field with zero decimal positions; an integer variable (5i0 or 10i0) works best. The FOR loop is entered, VAR is set to the *START* value and is automatically incremented by *INCREMENT* amount each time the ENDFOR statement is encountered.

The TO or DOWNTO keyword (one of them must be specified) is used to specify the LIMIT of the loop. The LIMIT indicates the limit of the VAR field before the FOR loop exits.

If TO is specified, then when VAR exceeds LIMIT, the next encounter with the ENDFOR statement causes the loop to terminate.

If DOWNTO is specified, then when VAR drops below LIMIT, the next encounter with the ENDFOR statement causes the loop to terminate.

The BY keyword is optional and indicates the INCREMENT value. The values added to VAR (when TO is specified) or subtracted from VAR (when DOWNTO is specified) each time the ENDFOR statement encountered. The BY parameter and INCREMENT value are optional, and if unspecified, they default to 1.

Upon existing a FOR...ENDFOR loop normally, the value of the VAR variable is set to LIMIT+INCREMENT (for TO operations) and LIMIT-INCREMENT (for DOWNTO operations); for example:

```
/free
   for i = 1 to 100;
     // do something fun.
   endfor;

     //  i = 101 upon exit
/end-free
```

98 Source-level Debugger for Legacy RPG III

Most people know how to use the source-level debugger that was introduced for ILE programming languages such as RPG IV. It provides a level a debug capability previously unavailable to RPG.

But when using the ILE source-level Debugger to debug an RPG IV program that subsequently calls a legacy RPG III program, how do you debug the legacy program?

While debugging the original RPG IV program, set a breakpoint on the CALL opcode used to load the legacy RPG III program. When the debugger breaks on that statement, press Shift+F10 (command key F22). This is known as "Step Into." If the program was compiled correctly, the debugger will load a legacy source-level debugger for the RPG III program.

To make sure your RPG III programs support the Step Into option, two setup steps are required:

1. When the program is compiled, specify OPTION(*SRCDBG) or OPTION (*LSTDBG) on the CRTRPGPGM command (PDM option 14); for example:

```
CRTRPGPGM PGM(AGING)  OPTION(*SRCDBG)
```

2. Specify OPMSRC(*YES) on the STRDBG command; for example:

```
STRDBG PGM(AGING) OPMSRC(*YES)
```

Specify OPMSRC(*YES) when any program that may be debugged is an RPG III program (even when the main program is an RPG IV program). This ensures that the Debugger is ready to load the legacy source-level debugger when needed.

99 Set and Get Environment Variables from within RPG IV

Many "billions" of lines of code exist in the market today that uses either the Local Data Area or a named Data Area to store bits and pieces of information.

Data Areas are certainly a legacy object and have a very ridged and unforgiving structure.

There are also "billions" of lines of code in existence today in the non-RPG market that use the Environment. The Environment is used extensively on the PC, Unix/Linux/AIX/FreeBSD and Mac OS X (which is a FreeBSD-based operating system).

The major difference between a data area and the Environment is that data areas are objects, whereas the Environment is a text-only storage area.

The advantages of using a Data Areas have over the Environment are that Data Areas can store numeric information in packed decimal format and the data area object can be locked.

The advantages of the Environment over Data Areas are that the Environment allows you to store and retrieve information based on a symbolic name, the length of the information can be changed at any time without impacting the rest of the data in the Environment, and the Environment is dynamic in size (up to 15MB).

The two fundamental interfaces for accessing the Environment are the putenv() and getenv() APIs, and through the ADDENVVAR, CHGENVVAR, WRKENVVAR and RMVENVVAR CL commands. The prototypes for the Environment APIs are as follows:

Prototypes for PUTENV and GETENV APIs

```
D getenv          PR              *    extProc('getenv')
D  envVarName                     *    VALUE OPTIONS(*STRING)

D putenv          PR           10I 0 extProc('putenv')
D  envVar                         *    VALUE OPTIONS(*STRING)
```

To create or change an Environment variable within RPG IV, use the putenv() API. This API accepts one parameter, which must contain both the Environment variable name and its value. The syntax is simple:

```
varname=value
```

The variable name followed by an equals sign, followed by the value, as follows:

```
/free
      putenv('COMPNAME=The Lunar Spacecraft Company');
/end-free
```

You have to build the 'VARNAME=VALUE' string yourself in RPG IV. If a numeric value needs to be stored in the Environment, it must be converted to text. The %CHAR built-in function can be used to convert numeric values to text, as follows:

```
D orderQty        S              7P 0
 /free
      putenv('CART_TOTAL=' + %char(orderQty));
 /end-free
```

Retrieving an environment variable's value is only slightly more complex than creating one. The getenv() API is used to retrieve an environment variable's value. Specify the Environment variable whose value you want to retrieve, the API returns a pointer to that value, as follows:

```
    pCompID = getenv('COMPNAME');
```

Specify only the Environment variable's name. A pointer is returned if the variable is found, otherwise *NULL is returned.

```
D pCompID        S              *   Inz(*NULL)
D company        S            35A   Based(pCompID)

 /free
      pCompID = getenv('COMPNAME');
      if (pCompID = *NULL);
         // Can't find company name!
      else;
         // Got it!
      endif;
 /end-free
```

In the example above, the COMPNAME environment variable is retrieved. A pointer to its value is returned by the getenv() API. That pointer is copied to the pCOMPID field. Since the COMPANY field is based on the pCOMPID field, the contents of the COMPNAME environment variable are now available in the COMPANY field.

Retrieve numeric values requires one or two addition steps, but it isn't very difficult, as follows:

```
D pOrderTot      S                     *   Inz(*NULL)
D orderTot       S                   10A   Varying
D orderQty       S                   7P 0

 /free
       pOrderTot = getenv('CART_TOTAL');
       if (pOrderTot <> *NULL);
           orderTot = %str(pOrderTot);
           if (orderTot <> '');
               QtyOrder = %Dec(orderTot : 7 : 0);
           endif;
       endif;
 /end-free
```

In the example above, there is no based-on variable so %STR is used to convert the returned pointer to a character value. Then, if that value is not blank, the quantity field is assigned the value of ORDERTOT after converting it with %DEC. %INT could have been used in this example as well.

Item 10 in the appendix contains the following additional subprocedures that simply access to Environment variables:

- RtvEnvVar — Retrieve Environment Variable Value
- RtvEnvInt — Retrieve Environment Variable Value as an Integer
- RtvEnvDec — Retrieve Environment Variable Value as Packed Decimal

Whether you need a place to store a piece of information for a few minutes or pass it between applications, the Environment can save a lot of work.

One more benefit of the Environment is that it is a great place to store data that needs to be retrieved by a Java class. Rather than pass complicated parameters, store the data in an Environment variable, and then in the Java class, retrieve the data from the Environment.

Two Environments

There are two Environments. The *Job-level Environment* that is created when a job starts and deleted when the job ends—similar to the life cycle of the Local Data Area. And the *System-level Environment* that is persistent between each IPL of the system; that is, it retains its value even when the system is IPL'd.

Job-level environment variables can be accessed using the getenv(), putenv() APIs as described above, as well as the Qp0zDltEnv(), Qp0zGetEnv(), and Qp0zPutEnv() APIs.

In addition, several CL commands, including: ADDENVVAR, CHGENVVAR, RMVENVVAR, and WRKENVVAR can access Job-level environment variable by specifying the

LEVEL(*JOB) parameter. Job-level environment variables exist until they are deleted with the RMVENVVAR command, the Qp0zDltEnv() API, or the job ends. Up to 4095 Job-level environment variables may exist in each job at any given time.

System-level environment variables can be accessed using the Qp0zDltSysEnv(), Qp0zGetAllSysEnv(), Qp0zGetSysEnv(), and Qp0zPutSysEnv() APIs.

In addition, several CL commands, including: ADDENVVAR, CHGENVVAR, RMVENVVAR, and WRKENVVAR can access System-level environment variable by specifying the LEVEL(*SYS) parameter. System-level environment variables exist until they are deleted with RMVENVVAR or Qp0zDltSysEnv(). Up to 4095 System-level environment variables may exist at any given time.

The obvious benefit of using the system-wide environment is that information can be shared between jobs.

CL Access to the Environment

In addition to the Environment APIs, four CL commands can be used to access the Job-level or System-level Environment from within CL, as follows:

- ADDENVVAR—Create Environment Variable
- CHGENVVAR—Change Environment Variable
- RMVENVVAR—Remove (delete) Environment Variable
- WRKENVVAR—Work with All Environment Variables

The **ADDENVVAR** command allows you to, from CL or Command Entry, create an environment variable. You specify the environment variable name, its associated value and the optional LEVEL parameter.

The level parameter allows you to specify which Environment you want to impact; the Job's Environment or the System-wide Environment.

The LEVEL(*JOB) parameter adds the environment variable to the job-level environment, whereas LEVEL(*SYS) adds it to the system level environment. ADDENVVAR also supports a REPLACE(*YES | *NO) option, making it effectively the same as the CHGENVVAR command.

The **CHGENVVAR** command allows you to modify an existing environment variable's value. If the variable doesn't exist, message CPFA981 is issued.

The **RMVENVVAR** command allows you to delete an environment variable. Normally, you delete an environment variable by setting its value to an empty string ("), but the CL command works just as well.

The **WRKENVVAR** command allows you to display a traditional Work With panel of all the environment variables for the job or system. From that panel, you can run the other environment variable commands (ADD, CHG, and RMV) as well as display and print.

Additional Environment API Prototypes

In addition to the traditional putenv() and getenv() APIs, IBM provides other Environment-oriented APIs. These APIs allow access to either the Job-level environment or the System-level Environment. The prototypes for these additional APIs are as follows:

Environment APIs

```
D getenv          PR              *     extProc('getenv')
D  envVarName                     *     VALUE OPTIONS(*STRING)

D putenv          PR            10I 0 extProc('putenv')
D  envVar                         *     VALUE OPTIONS(*STRING)

D Qp0zGetEnv      PR              *     extProc('Qp0zGetEnv')
D  envVarName                     *     VALUE OPTIONS(*STRING)
D  CCSID                        10I 0

D Qp0zPutEnv      PR            10I 0 extProc('Qp0zPutEnv')
D  envVar                         *     VALUE OPTIONS(*STRING)
D  CCSID                        10I 0 VALUE

D Qp0zDltEnv      PR            10I 0 extProc('Qp0zDltEnv')
D  envVarName                     *     VALUE OPTIONS(*STRING)

D Qp0zPutSysEnv   PR            10I 0 extProc('Qp0zPutSysEnv')
D  envVar                         *     VALUE OPTIONS(*STRING)
D  CCSID                        10I 0 Const
D  reserved                       *     VALUE OPTIONS(*NOPASS)

D Qp0zGetSysEnv   PR            10I 0 extProc('Qp0zGetSysEnv')
D  envVarName                     *     VALUE OPTIONS(*STRING)
D  rtnBuffer                  65535A   OPTIONS(*VARSIZE)
D  bufLen                       10I 0 Const
D  CCSID                        10I 0
D  reserved                       *     VALUE OPTIONS(*NOPASS)

D Qp0zDltSysEnv   PR                    extProc('Qp0zDltSysEnv')
D  envVarName                     *     VALUE OPTIONS(*STRING)
D  reserved                       *     VALUE OPTIONS(*NOPASS)
```

Continued...

…continued

```
D QzsrGetEnvCCSID...
D                 PR                        extProc('QzsrGetEnvCCSID')
D  rtnBuff                      65535A      OPTIONS(*VARSIZE)
D  nLenRtnBuff                    10I 0     Const
D  nRtnValueLen                   10I 0
D  varName                       256A       Const OPTIONS(*VARSIZE)
D  nLenVarName                    10I 0     Const
D  nVarNameCCSID                  10I 0     Const
D  nRtnBuffCCSID                  10I 0     Const
D  apiError                                 LikeDS(QUSEC_T)
D                                           OPTIONS(*VARSIZE)

D QtmhGetEnv      PR                        extProc('QtmhGetEnv')
D  rtnBuff                      65535A      OPTIONS(*VARSIZE)
D  nLenRtnBuff                    10I 0     Const
D  nRtnValueLen                   10I 0
D  varName                       256A       Const OPTIONS(*VARSIZE)
D  nLenVarName                    10I 0     Const
D  apiError                                 LikeDS(QUSEC_T)
D                                           OPTIONS(*VARSIZE)
```

100 Simple Scan with Ignore Upper/Lowercase

Unfortunately the %SCAN built-in function and SCAN opcode are case-sensitive. That is, they only allow scanning for an exact match of the search data.

A quick way to get around these limitations is to use the power of the %XLATE built-in function to convert the searched data to uppercase and then perform the scan. When the data being searched and the search pattern are converted to all upper or all lowercase, you simulate a case insensitive search.

To perform a case-insensitive scan with %SCAN, no work fields are required, the built-in functions %SCAN and %XLATE do the work for you, as follows:

Use Nested %XLATE Inside %SCAN

```
D UP              C                       'ABCDEFGHIJKLMNOPQRSTUVWXYZ'
D low             C                       'abcdefghijklmnopqrstuvwxyz'
D desc            S              4096A    Varying Inz('john q public')
D nPos            S              10I 0

 /free
       nPos = %scan('Q' : %xlate(low:up:DESC));
 /end-free
```

By nesting %XLATE within %SCAN the compiler performs the translation and returns an internal variable that is subsequently scanned. The search pattern (the letter 'Q' in our example) must be in all uppercase to match the results of %XLATE. If the search pattern is also a variable, then both the search pattern and search data could be wrapped in nested %XLATE built-in functions, as follows:

```
/free
    nPos = %scan(%xlate(low:up:FINDME) : %xlate(low:up:DESC));
/end-free
```

In the example above, the field named FINDME contains the data to be searched for and DESC contains the data being searched. Both are converted by %XLATE to uppercase before the search is performed.

If the FINDME variable is a fixed-length field, consider wrapping it in a %TRIMR built-in function. This allows the data in FINDME to be used as the search pattern without its trailing blanks.

101

Set the CLASSPATH for Java within RPG IV

While I am not a fan of using Java in production applications, I do see the benefit of some of the Java packages that are available. The Java SendMail API is one, but there are others.

Calling a Java routine from RPG IV can be a challenge. Setting up the Java prototypes, declaring the CLASS Objects (data-type O in RPG IV), and setting up the CLASSPATH properly always seem like trial and error. Another major issue is the lack of RPG IV integration for accessing Environment Variables. (For information on Environment variable APIs see Tip #99.)

The putenv() and getenv() C runtime APIs (again, see Tip #99) can be used to read and modify the Java CLASSPATH environment variable, as follows:

```
/free
    putenv('CLASSPATH=/java/mailapi/mail.jar:' +
           '/java/jaf/activation.jar');

/end-free
```

Often Java routines need directory/folder names added to the existing CLASSPATH environment variable. The traditional way to indicate this, is to include the %CLASSPATH% symbolic name within the new CLASSPATH, as follows:

```
/free
    putenv('CLASSPATH=%classpath%/java/mailapi/mail.jar:' +
           '/java/jaf/activation.jar');

/end-free
```

The %CLASSPATH% symbolic name (upper/lowercase is ignored) is supposed to be replaced with the existing CLASSPATH value. This does not happen with putenv() API, so we have to write our own subprocedure to do this for us.

The SetClassPath() subprocedure allows you to add, change, or remove the Java CLASS-PATH environmental variable. For example, to add to the existing CLASSPATH environment variable, specify the new class path as the parameter of SetClassPath(), as follows:

```
/free
    SetClassPath('%classpath%/java/mailapi/mail.jar:' +
                 '/java/jaf/activation.jar');

/end-free
```

If SetClassPath() detects a %CLASSPATH% symbolic name, it replaces it in the new class path with the current CLASSPATH environment variable's value. To use the SetClassPath() subprocedure, specify the class path only, do not include the environment variable name (i.e., 'CLASSPATH=') when calling this subprocedure.

The SetClasspath() subprocedure, needs to perform four tasks to implement this capability:

- The existing classpath needs to be retrieved.
- The new classpath needs to be scanned for %classpath%.
- Replace %CLASSPATH% with the existing classpath.
- Set the CLASSPATH environment variable to the new value.

Retrieve the Existing CLASSPATH

To retrieve the existing classpath, the getenv() API is used. This API was selected over the others due to the simple interface. The down side to getenv() is that is returns a pointer to the existing CLASSPATH data, or *NULL if no existing data is detected, for example

```
D oldCP            S              4096A   Varying
D pOldCP           S                  *   Inz(*NULL)
 /free
        pOldCP = getenv('CLASSPATH');
        if (pOldCP <> *NULL);
            oldCP = %str(pOldCP);
        endif;
 /end-free
```

If the CLASSPATH contains a value, a pointer to it is returned and then the data is copied to the OLDCP (old classpath) variable. The %STR() built-in function is used to automatically convert the data at the pointer location to a real RPG IV field. %STR() makes this very easy.

Scan the New CLASSPATH for %CLASSPATH%

The new CLASSPATH (the one specify when calling the SetClasspath() subprocedure) needs to be scanned for %CLASSPATH% without regard for upper/lowercase. This means %classpath%, %ClassPath%, %CLASSPATH% or anything in between may be specified.

The easiest way to scan a variable in RPG IV is to use the %SCAN built-in function. But %SCAN is case-sensitive, so we have to cheat.

First we need to set up two named constants: one for uppercase letters; one for lowercase letters. Then using a nested %XLATE built-in function, we can perform an case-insensitive scan (see Tip #100) as follows:

```
 D UP             C                       'ABCDEFGHIJKLMNOPQRSTUVWXYZ'
 D low            C                       'abcdefghijklmnopqrstuvwxyz'
 D cpConst        C                       '%CLASSPATH%'

 /free
      nPos = %scan(cpConst : %xlate(low:up:newPath));
 /end-free
```

In the example above, UP and LOW are two named constants representing upper and lowercase character sets. The %XLATE built-in function is used to convert the new CLASS-PATH (stored in the NEWPATH variable) to all uppercase. The named constant CPCONST contains an uppercase version of %CLASSPATH%. %SCAN is used to scan for %CLASS-PATH% inside of NEWPATH.

If the %CLASSPATH% symbolic literal is found, its location within the string is returned. That location is subsequently use to insert the old classpath into the new classpath string.

Replace %CLASSPATH% with the Old CLASSPATH

If %CLASSPATH% is detected in the new path string, it needs to be replaced with the old classpath that was previously retrieved using getenv(). The %REPLACE built-in function makes this task easy, as follows:

```
 /free
      nPos = %scan(cpCONST: %xlate(low:up:newCP));

      if (nPos > 0);  // Replace '%classpath%' with old CP
         cPath = %Replace(oldCP+':' : newCP : nPos : %Len(cpCONST));
      endif;
 /end-free
```

In example above, the location of %CLASSPATH% is returned and used as the starting location for the %REPLACE built-in function. The number of bytes replaced in the original string is specified on the fourth parameter of %REPLACE. The length of '%CLASSPATH%' is used as the length to be replaced.

Set the CLASSPATH Environment Variable

Changing the classpath requires that the putenv() API be used. To set an environment variable with putenv() the environment variable name is concatenated with the value being assigned to it with an equals sign, as follows:

```
putenv('CLASSPATH=' + cPath);
```

In example above, the string 'CLASSPATH=' is concatenated to the complete classpath (stored in the CPATH variable). This is passed as one parameter to the putenv() API.

To verify that the classpath has been changed, use the WRKENVVAR CL command, and select option 5 for the CLASSPATH variable name. Remember, when using the SetClass-Path() subprocedure, specify the path only, not the environment variable name.

This is correct:

```
SetClasspath('/home/java/javamail:/java/jaf');
```

or

```
SetClassPath('%classpath%/java/activation.jar:/java/mail.jar');
```

This is not valid:

```
SetClasspath('CLASSPATH=/home/java/javamail:/java/jaf');
```

Nor is this:

```
SetClassPath('CLASSPATH=%classpath%/java/activation.jar:/java/mail.jar');
```

SetClasspath() Subprocedure Implementation

```
H NOMAIN OPTION(*NODEBUGIO:*SRCSTMT) BNDDIR('QC2LE')
H Copyright('(c) 2006 Robert Cozzi, Jr. All rights reserved.')

 /INCLUDE rpgtnt/QCPYSRC,rpgtnt
D UP              C                         'ABCDEFGHIJKLMNOPQRSTUVWXYZ'
D low             C                         'abcdefghijklmnopqrstuvwxyz'

P SetClassPath    B                         Export
D SetClassPath    PI
D  newCP                          4096A     Const Varying

D pOldCP          S                 *       Inz(*NULL)
D oldCP           S              4096A      Varying
D cpath           S              4096A      Varying
D classpath       S                20A      Varying Inz('CLASSPATH')
D szSep           S                 2A      Varying
D find_symbol     C                         Const('%')
D sep_SYMBOL      C                         Const(':')
D nPos            S                10I 0

 /free
      Monitor;  // Get current classpath
        pOldCP = getenv(classpath);
        if (pOldCP <> *NULL);
          oldCP = %str(pOldCP);
        endif;
      on-error *ALL;
        oldCP = '';
      endmon;

      classpath = find_symbol + %TRIM(classpath) + find_symbol;
      nPos = %scan(classpath: %xlate(low:up:newCP));

      if (nPos > 0);  // Replace '%CLASSPATH%' with current path
        if (%len(oldCP) > 0);
          szSep = sep_SYMBOL;
        endif;
        cPath = %Replace(oldCP+szSep : newCP : nPos : %Len(classpath));
      endif;

      putenv('CLASSPATH=' + cpath);

      return;
 /end-free

P SetClassPath    E
```

Epilogue

One of the benefits of RPG IV today is that it is as powerful a language as is needed, mostly because of its ability to leverage its own opcodes as well as C and MI operations as seemingly native interfaces. In addition, the number of system APIs available to the RPG IV programmer is mind-boggling.

Certainly there are many more than 101 tips 'n' techniques with RPG IV, but the ones I selected for this book are some of the most beneficial and powerful that I have found. In addition, they are applicable to a wide range of situations. I have seen many techniques that apply to one or two situations, but to me, those are just normal programming styles and do not warrant inclusion in a book of this type.

It has been 20 years since I wrote the first pages of *The Modern RPG Language*. That book and its followup, *The Modern RPG IV Language*, have sold more than 65,000 copies worldwide.

My goal with those original books was to help RPG programmers succeed. My goal with this book is to help you accomplish more than you ever thought you could with RPG IV.

I've provided the solutions. What you do with this knowledge is up to you.

Appendix

Source Member RPGTnT in QCPYSRC

The examples used throughout this book often refer to Data Structure *Templates*, Subprocedure Prototypes, and APIs that are not always listed with the example. These items are included here in their entirety.

This source code used throughout this book is available in its entirety for small, one-time license fee. For more information visit our website at www.rpg iv.com.

1. QUSEC — The API Error Data Structure

```
************************************************************
**   QUSEC_T - The basic API Error Data Structure
**     Use when calling most APIs.
**     Specify as a template name via the LIKEDS keyword.
**     Usage should be with INZ as follows:
**   D apiError    DS                  LikeDS(QUsec_T) Inz
************************************************************
D QUSEC_T         DS                  QUALIFIED Based(NULL)
D  bytesProvided             10I 0
D  bytesProv                 10I 0 Overlay(bytesProvided)
D  dsLen                     10I 0 Overlay(bytesProvided)
D  bytesAvail                10I 0
D  cpfmsgID                   7A
D  reserved                   3I 0
D  exceptionData             64A
```

2. OBJD0100 — Return Structure for QUSROBJD API

```
************************************************************
**   OBJD0100_T - The QUSROBJD API Data Structure
**     Specify as a template name via the LIKEDS keyword.
**     Usage should be with INZ as follows:
**   D myObjD     DS                  LikeDS(objd0100_T)
**   D                                Inz
************************************************************
D OBJD0100_T      DS                  QUALIFIED Based(NULL)
D  bytesRtn                  10I 0
D  bytesAvail                10I 0
D  name                      10A
D  library                   10A
D  type                      10A
D  objtype                   10A    Overlay(type)
D  rtnLibrary                10A
D  rtnLib                    10A    Overlay(rtnLibrary)
D  ASP                       10I 0
D  domain                     2A
D  crtDate                   13A
D  chgDate                   13A
```

3. Data Structures Used by QWCCVTDT API

```
**   Use with 6-digit dates/century digit and milli-seconds
**   Note: Julian dates should be left-justified, blank-filled
D CvtDT16_T       DS                      Qualified BASED(NULL)
D  century                    1A
D  date                       6A
D  time                       6A
D  milliSeconds               3A

**   Use with 8-digit dates and milli-seconds
**   Note: Julian dates should be left-justified, blank-filled
D CvtDT17_T       DS                     Qualified BASED(NULL)
D  date                       8A
D  time                       6A
D  milliSeconds               3A

**   Use with 6-digit dates/century digit and micro-seconds
**   Note: Julian dates should be left-justified, blank-filled
D CvtDT19_T       DS                     Qualified BASED(NULL)
D  century                    1A
D  date                       6A
D  time                       6A
D  microSeconds               6A

**   Use with 8-digit dates and micro-seconds
**   Note: Julian dates should be left-justified, blank-filled
D CvtDT20_T       DS                     Qualified BASED(NULL)
D  date                       8A
D  time                       6A
D  microSeconds               6A

**   Use with DOS GetDateTime()
D DOSGetDateTime_T...
D                 DS                    Qualified BASED(NULL)
D  hours                      3I 0
D  minutes                    3I 0
D  seconds                    3I 0
D  hseconds                   5I 0
D  day                        3U 0
D  month                      3U 0
D  year                       5U 0
D  UTCOffset                  5I 0
D  dayOfWeek                  3U 0
```

4. iconv()-Related Conversion APIs and Data Structures

```
 **   iconv() conversion environment handle
D iconv_t         DS                      Qualified Based(NULL)
D  rtn_value                     10I 0
D  cd                            10I 0 Dim(12)

 ** QtqIconvOpen() from/to conversion structure
D QtqCode_T       DS                      Qualified Based(NULL)
D  CCSID                         10I 0
D  CvtAlt                        10I 0
D  SubstAlt                      10I 0
D  shiftState                    10I 0
D  inLengthOpt                   10I 0
D  errMixDataOpt                 10I 0
D  reserved                       8A

 **   ICONV_ERROR - The -1 value returned by iconv()
 **             when it fails.
D iconv_ERROR     C                       Const(X'FFFFFFFF')

 ** QtqIconvOpen() Open/Create iconv() environment
D QtqIConvOpen    PR                      extProc('QtqIconvOpen')
D                                         LikeDS(iconv_t)
D  toCCSID                               LikeDS(QtqCode_T)
D  fromCCSID                             LikeDS(QtqCode_T)

 ** iconv() Convert data using conversion environment handle
D iconv           PR             10U 0 extProc('iconv')
D  hConv                               LikeDS(iconv_t) Value
D  pInBuff                        *
D  nInLen                        10U 0
D  pOutBuff                       *
D  nOutLen                       10U 0

 **   iconv_close() Destroy conversion environment
D iconv_close     PR             10I 0 extProc('iconv_close')
D  hConv                               LikeDS(iconv_t) Value
```

5. CEE4RAGE and CEE4RAGE2 Prototypes

```
/IF DEFINED(*V5R3M0)
 **  64-bit - Register A/G Exit Proc (64-bit marker)
D reg_exit_proc   PR                      extProc('CEE4RAGE2')
/ELSE
 **  32-bit - Register A/G Exit Proc (32-bit marker)
D reg_exit_proc   PR                      extProc('CEE4RAGE')
/ENDIF
D  myExitProcPtr                  *    PROCPTR CONST
D  fc                            12A    OPTIONS(*OMIT:*VARSIZE)
```

6. Regular Expression Base Data-types

```
/IF NOT DEFINED(SIZE_T)
/DEFINE SIZE_T
D size_T          S              10U 0
/ENDIF

/IF NOT DEFINED(OFF_T)
/DEFINE OFF_T
D off_T           S              10I 0
/ENDIF

/IF NOT DEFINED(LC_COLVAL_T)
/DEFINE LC_COLVAL_T
D LC_COLVAL_T     S              10I 0
/ENDIF

/IF NOT DEFINED(MBSTATE_T)
/DEFINE MBSTATE_T

/if DEFINED(UTF32)
D mbState_T       S              10I 0
/else
D mbState_T       S               5I 0
/endif

/ENDIF
```

7. REGEX_T Data Structure Template

```
D regex_t         DS                           Qualified Align
D  re_nsub                                      Like(size_T)
D  re_comp                             *        Inz(*NULL)
D  re_cflags                        10I 0
D  re_erroff                                    Like(size_T)
D  re_len                                       Like(size_T)
D  re_ucoll                                     Like(LC_COLVAL_T) Dim(2)
D  re_lsub                             *        Inz(*NULL)
D  lsub_ar                                      Like(size_T) dim(16)
D  esub_ar                                      Like(size_T) dim(16)
D  reserved1                           *        Inz(*NULL)
D  re_esub                             *        Inz(*NULL)
D  re_specchar                         *        Inz(*NULL)
D  re_phdl                             *        Inz(*NULL)
D  comp_spc                          1A         Dim(112)
D  re_map                            1A         Dim(256)
D  re_shift                                     Like(mbState_T)
D  re_dbcs                           5I 0
```

8. REGMATCH_T Data Structure Template

```
D regMatch_t      DS                    Qualified
D  rm_so                                Like(off_T)
D  rm_ss                                Like(mbState_T)
D  rm_eo                                Like(off_T)
D  rm_es                                Like(mbState_T)
```

9. Regular Expression Named Constants

```
D REG_BASIC       C                     Const(X'00')
D REG_EXTENDED    C                     Const(X'01')
D REG_ICASE       C                     Const(X'02')
D REG_NEWLINE     C                     Const(X'04')
D REG_NOSUB       C                     Const(X'08')
D REG_ALT_NL      C                     Const(X'10')

D REG_NOTBOL      C                     Const(X'0100')
D REG_NOTEOL      C                     Const(X'0200')

D REG_NOMATCH     C                     Const(1)
D REG_BADPAT      C                     Const(2)
D REG_ECOLLATE    C                     Const(3)
D REG_ECTYPE      C                     Const(4)
D REG_EESCAPE     C                     Const(5)
D REG_ESUBREG     C                     Const(6)
D REG_EBRACK      C                     Const(7)
D REG_EPAREN      C                     Const(8)
D REG_EBRACE      C                     Const(9)
D REG_BADBR       C                     Const(10)
D REG_ERANGE      C                     Const(11)
D REG_ESPACE      C                     Const(12)
D REG_BADRPT      C                     Const(13)
D REG_ECHAR       C                     Const(14)
D REG_EBOL        C                     Const(15)
D REG_EEOL        C                     Const(16)
D REG_ECOMP       C                     Const(17)
D REG_EEXEC       C                     Const(18)
D REG_LAST        C                     Const(18)
```

10. Retrieve Environment Variable (RTVENVVAR)

```
H NOMAIN OPTION(*NODEBUGIO:*SRCSTMT)
H Copyright('(c) 2006 Robert Cozzi, Jr. All rights reserved.')

       //////////////////////////////////////////////////////////
       // Extension library for RPG IV.
       // From Bob Cozzi's "RPG TNT: 101 Tips 'n Tech"
       // (c) 2007 by Robert Cozzi, Jr.
       // All rights reserved.
       // ------------------------------------------------------
       // Permission to use for any programming purpose such as
       // commercial, free, or open-source is hereby granted.
       // Permission is denied to republish this source except
       // as indicated herein.
       //////////////////////////////////////////////////////////

    /INCLUDE rpgtnt/QCPYSRC,rpgtnt

    **  Retrieve Environment Variable Value text
    P RtvEnvVar       B              Export
    D RtvEnvVar       PI       10I 0 OPDESC
    D  varname            128A       Const Varying
    D  rtnValue          4096A       OPTIONS(*VARSIZE)

    D nType          S        10I 0
    D nCurLen        S        10I 0
    D nMaxLen        S        10I 0

    D nLen           S        10I 0
    D pValue         S           *

     /free
         ceegsi(2 : nType:nCurLen:nMaxLen:*OMIT);

         Monitor;  // Monitor for Null return value
           pValue = getenv(varName);
           if (pValue <> *NULL);
             nLen = %Len(%str(pValue));
             if (nCurLen > 0);
               %subst(rtnValue:1:nCurLen) = %str(pValue:
nCurLen);
             endif;
           endif;
         on-error *ALL;
           nLen = 0;
           %subst(rtnValue:1:nCurLen) = ' ';
         endmon;

         return nLen;
     /end-free

    P RtvEnvVar       E
```

Continued…

...continued

```
      **   Retrieve Environment Variable Value as integer (20i0)
     P RtvEnvInt      B                      Export
     D RtvEnvInt      PI              20I 0
     D  varname                       128A   Const Varying

     D nLen           S               10I 0
     D szValue        S               32A
     D nValue         S               20I 0
      /free
          if (varName <> *Blanks);
             nLen = RtvEnvVar(varName : szValue);
             if (nLen > 0 and szValue <> *Blanks);
                monitor;
                  nValue = %Int(%Trim(szValue));
                on-error *ALL;
                  nValue = 0;
                endmon;
             endif;
          endif;
          return nValue;
      /end-free
     P RtvEnvInt        E
      **   Retrieve Environment Variable Value as integer (20i0)
     P RtvEnvDec      B                      Export
     D RtvEnvDec      PI              31P10
     D  varname                       128A   Const Varying

     D nLen           S               10I 0
     D szValue        S               32A
     D nValue         S               31P10
      /free
          if (varName <> *Blanks);
             nLen = RtvEnvVar(varName : szValue);
             if (nLen > 0 and szValue <> *Blanks);
                monitor;
                  nValue = %Dec(%Trim(szValue):31:11);
                on-error *ALL;
                  nValue = 0;
                endmon;
             endif;
          endif;
          return nValue;
      /end-free
     P RtvEnvDec        E
```